Cultural Pluralism, Identity Politics, and the Law

The Amherst Series in Law, Jurisprudence, and Social Thought

Each work included in The Amherst Series in Law, Jurisprudence, and Social Thought explores a theme crucial to an understanding of law as it confronts the changing social and intellectual currents of the twenty-first century.

The Fate of Law, edited by Austin Sarat and Thomas R. Kearns

Law's Violence, edited by Austin Sarat and Thomas R. Kearns

Law in Everyday Life, edited by Austin Sarat and Thomas R. Kearns

The Rhetoric of Law, edited by Austin Sarat and Thomas R. Kearns

Identities, Politics, and Rights, edited by Austin Sarat and Thomas R. Kearns

Legal Rights: Historical and Philosophical Perspectives, edited by Austin Sarat and Thomas R. Kearns

Justice and Injustice in Law and Legal Theory, edited by Austin Sarat and Thomas R. Kearns

Law in the Domains of Culture, edited by Austin Sarat and Thomas R. Kearns

Cultural Pluralism, Identity Politics, and the Law, edited by Austin Sarat and Thomas R. Kearns

History, Memory, and the Law, edited by Austin Sarat and Thomas R. Kearns

Human Rights: Concepts, Contests, Contingencies, edited by Austin Sarat and Thomas R. Kearns

Cultural Pluralism, Identity Politics, and the Law

Edited by
AUSTIN SARAT
and
THOMAS R. KEARNS

Ann Arbor
THE UNIVERSITY OF MICHIGAN PRESS

First paperback edition 2001
Copyright © by the University of Michigan 1999
All rights reserved
Published in the United States of America by
The University of Michigan Press
Manufactured in the United States of America
⊗ Printed on acid-free paper

2004   2003   2002   2001   6   5   4   3

No part of this publication may be reproduced, stored in a retrieval system, or transmitted in any form or by any means, electronic, mechanical, or otherwise, without the written permission of the publisher.

A CIP catalog record for this book is available from the British Library.

Library of Congress Cataloging-in-Publication Data

Cultural pluralism, identity politics, and the law / edited by Austin Sarat and Thomas R. Kearns.
    p. cm. — (Amherst series in law, jurisprudence, and social thought)
   Includes bibliographical references and index.
   ISBN 0-472-10911-1 (cloth : alk. paper)
    1. Critical legal studies.   2. Sociological jurisprudence.
3. Multiculturalism.   4. Group identity.   5. Jurisprudence—United States.   I. Sarat, Austin.   II. Kearns, Thomas R.   III. Series.
K376.C85   1998
340'.115—dc21   98-42509
                                                          CIP

ISBN 0-472-08851-3 (pbk. : alk. paper)

Acknowledgments

Questions of how we live with difference and of the way law contributes to our responses to difference are among the most vexing questions that we face at the end of the twentieth century. This volume, the ninth in the Amherst Series in Law, Jurisprudence and Social Thought, brings together essays by five distinguished scholars from several different disciplines, each of which takes on those questions. They were first presented at Amherst as lectures under the auspices of the Charles Hamilton Houston Forum on Law and Social Justice. The forum honors Charles Hamilton Houston, one of Amherst College's most distinguished graduates. Houston had an outstanding academic career at Amherst and carried what he learned at the college into the world to struggle for social justice. He played a key role in devising the legal strategy that ultimately led to the decision in *Brown v. Board of Education*. As Richard Kluger put it, in the struggle for racial justice through law "Charles Houston became the critical figure who linked the passion of Frederick Douglass demanding black freedom and of William Du Bois demanding black equality to the undelivered promises of the Constitution of the United States." Houston's life as a lawyer and as a legal educator exemplifies a vision that reminds us that our law is more than a device for maintaining social order; it is and can be a tool for changing the society that it serves.

We thank the Amherst College Faculty Lecture Committee for its support. We are also grateful to our Amherst colleagues and students who participated in the Houston Forum during 1995–96 and to Lawrence Douglas, Martha Umphrey, and the majors in the Department of Law, Jurisprudence and Social Thought for their help in thinking about issues of cultural pluralism and identity politics and the law. We would also like to express our appreciation to Hendrik Hartog, Sarah Gordon, and Katherine Stone for their generous help in preparing Elizabeth Clark's essay for publication.

Contents

Responding to the Demands of Difference:
An Introduction   1
Austin Sarat and Thomas R. Kearns

Breaking the Mold of Citizenship:
The "Natural" Person as Citizen in
Nineteenth-Century America (A Fragment)   27
Elizabeth B. Clark

The Subject of True Feeling: Pain, Privacy, and Politics   49
Lauren Berlant

Why Culture Matters to Law:
The Difference Politics Makes   85
Dorothy E. Roberts

Civil Rights Rhetoric and White Identity Politics   111
George Lipsitz

Does Integration Have a Future?   139
Kenneth L. Karst

Contributors   169

Index   171

Responding to the Demands of Difference: An Introduction

Austin Sarat and Thomas R. Kearns

"The other" remains to be discovered.... [W]e want equality without its compelling us to accept identity; but also difference without its degenerating into superiority/inferiority.... [H]uman life is confined between ... two extremes, one where the I invades the world, and one where the world ultimately absorbs the I.... And just as the discovery of the other knows several degrees, from the other-as-object, identified with the surrounding world, to the other-as-subject, equal to the I but different from it ... we can indeed live our lives without ever achieving a full discovery of the other.
—Tzvetan Todorov,
The Conquest of America; The Question of the Other

As the twentieth century draws to a close, we are witnessing the growing assertiveness of racial, ethnic, and other social groups both in the United States and abroad.[1] These groups are demanding recognition of their distinctive histories and traditions as well as opportunities to develop and maintain the institutional infrastructure necessary to preserve them.[2] As Charles Taylor notes, "The development of the modern

---

1. See Michael Walzer, "The New Tribalism: Notes on a Difficult Problem," *Dissent* (1992): 164. See also Edgar Epps, ed., *Cultural Pluralism* (Berkeley: McCutchan Publishers, 1974); and Benjamin Barber, *Jihad vs. McWorld* (New York: Times Books, 1995).

2. Adeno Addis describes the efforts of groups to "find conceptual and institutional ways by which those who are defined to be different by the dominant culture, and consequently marked out to be marginal in the social and political life of the polity, will be able to actively participate in the formation and reformation of the social and political space they inhabit." See "Individualism, Communitarianism, and the Rights of Ethnic Minorities," *Notre Dame Law Review* 67 (1992): 618. See also Charles Lawrence, "Foreword: Race, Multiculturalism, and the Jurisprudence of Transformation," *Stanford Law Review* 47 (1995): 819.

notion of identity has given rise to a politics of difference."[3] Whereas once it seemed that the ideal of American citizenship was found in the promise of integration and in the hope that none of us would be singled out for, let alone judged by, our race or ethnicity,[4] today integration is often rejected, and new terms of inclusion are sought.[5] Critics allege that integration is a mask for cultural domination (if not a form of cultural genocide) and that it signals the triumph of dominant identities over the rich mosaic of social and cultural difference.[6] Integration is now often taken to mean assimilation, and that, in turn, means the denial of identity and history for disadvantaged or subordinated racial, gender, sexual, or ethnic groups.[7]

Advocates of cultural pluralism seek a kind of cultural autonomy for themselves; for the larger society they call for toleration. The cultural pluralism they seek refers to a "loosely connected set of attitudes and practices sharing . . . the notion that American society should be understood as a collection of diverse cultural groups rather than as a single, unified national body or as simply an aggregate of atomized

---

3. Charles Taylor, *Multiculturalism and "The Politics of Recognition"* (Princeton: Princeton University Press, 1992), 38. Taylor notes that "a number of strands in contemporary politics turn on the need, sometimes the demand, for recognition. The need, it can be argued, is one of the driving forces behind nationalist movements in politics. And the demand comes to the fore in a number of ways in today's politics, on behalf of minority or 'subaltern' groups, in some forms of feminism and what is today called the politics of 'multiculturalism'" (25).

4. See Nathan Glazer, "Individual Rights against Group Rights," in *The Rights of Minority Cultures*, ed. Will Kymlicka (New York: Oxford University Press, 1995), 137.

5. Michael Middleton, "*Brown v. Board:* Revisited," *Southern Illinois University Law Journal* 20 (1995): 19; Joshua Limerling, "Black Male Academies: Re-Examining the Strategy of Integration," *Buffalo Law Review* 42 (1995): 829; Alexandra Natapoff, "Madisonian Multiculturalism," *American University Law Review* 45 (1996): 751. Natapoff criticizes the Supreme Court for imposing "a color-blind mandate on an increasingly multicultural, racially diverse body politic" (761).

6. Alex Johnson, "Bid Whist, Tonk, and *United States v. Fordice*: Why Integration Fails African-Americans Again," *California Law Review* 81 (1993): 1401. Johnson says that "integrationism has failed to help African-Americans to achieve progress in this society" (1409).

7. For a description of the drive for assimilation in American culture, see Milton Gordon, *Assimilation in American Life: The Role of Race, Religion, and National Origins* (New York: Oxford University Press, 1964); see also William Newman, *American Pluralism: A Study of Minority Groups and Social Theory* (New York: Harper and Row, 1973); Philip Gleason, "American Identity and Americanization," in *Concepts of Ethnicity*, ed. William Petersen, Michael Novak, and Philip Gleason (Cambridge: Harvard University Press, 1980); and Robert Moran, "Commentary: The Implications of Being a Society of One," *University of San Francisco Law Review* 20 (1986): 503.

individuals. . . . [It] implies that government must recognize and respect if not nurture the diversity and integrity of racial and ethnic communities."[8] Policies providing such recognition and respect include bilingual education,[9] university programs in areas such as African-American, Asian-American, Hispanic, and Jewish Studies,[10] legal acceptance of so-called cultural defenses,[11] and exemptions for particular groups from the reach of otherwise valid positive law.[12] Instead of seeking to transcend our differences and locate the basis of citizenship in the most abstract and universalized common traits, we should, so the argument goes, seek a form of citizenship that recognizes difference but nonetheless claims equality. As Chantal Mouffe argues, "the respect of pluralism and differences must be at the core of a radical democratic conception of citizenship. Nevertheless it is also necessary to indicate that such a view . . . needs to acknowledge the limits of pluralism which are required by a democratic politics."[13] The good society, on this view, is one in which groups can be valued for their distinct cultures and ways of being. The good society values diversity as the basis of inclusion.[14] Shared citizenship is not based on a universally shared culture or common identity.[15] Cultural pluralism asks us to

---

8. See Gary Peller, "Cultural Imperialism, White Anxiety, and the Ideological Realignment of *Brown,*" in *Race, Law and Culture: Reflections on Brown v. Board of Education,* ed. Austin Sarat (New York: Oxford University Press, 1997), 193.

9. Christina Paulson, *Bi-lingual Education: Theories and Issues* (Rowley, Mass.: Newbury House, 1980).

10. Ramon Guttierrez, "Ethnic Studies: Its Evolution in American Colleges and Universities," in *Multiculturalism: A Critical Reader,* ed. David Theo Goldberg (Boston: Blackwell, 1994).

11. For a discussion of the legal response to cultural defenses, see Daina Chiu, "The Cultural Defense: Beyond Exclusion, Assimilation, and Guilty Liberalism," *California Law Review* 82 (1994): 1053. See also Alison Dundes Renteln, "A Justification of the Cultural Defense as Partial Excuse," *Southern California Review of Law and Women's Studies* 2 (1993): 437.

12. See Austin Sarat and Roger Berkowitz, "Disorderly Differences: Recognition, Accommodation, and American Law," *Yale Journal of Law and the Humanities* 6 (1994): 285. See also Martha Minow, "Partial Justice; Law and Minorities," in *The Fate of Law,* ed. Austin Sarat and Thomas R. Kearns (Ann Arbor: University of Michigan Press, 1991).

13. Chantal Mouffe, "Democratic Politics and the Question of Identity," in *The Identity in Question,* ed. John Rajchman (New York: Routledge, 1995) 39.

14. Harold Cruse, *Plural but Equal: A Critical Study of Blacks and Minorities and the American Plural Society* (New York: William Morrow, 1987).

15. For one effort to articulate the basis for a universally shared civic culture that recognizes and accommodates cultural differences while providing an allegedly neutral public sphere in which groups can communicate, see Jürgen Habermas, "Multiculturalism and the Liberal State," *Stanford Law Review* 47 (1995): 849.

acknowledge and embrace difference, "rather than assuming . . . that there was a neutral, acultural institutional reality, in public schools or other places."[16]

This recent advocacy of cultural pluralism and identity politics has been met by a wide variety of responses.[17] Some critics worry about essentialist tendencies in the way advocates of cultural pluralism and identity politics speak about culture and identity.[18] They worry that cultural pluralism and identity politics treat the terms of personhood and membership as historical givens or accidents of birth. Gary Peller notes that "mutual respect and cultural self determination . . . [depend] on there being some transcultural basis on which to identify . . . cultural boundaries. . . . The more formalist, essentialist, a historic, and traditionalist the definition of the other culture's mores, the more compelling the case for deference will be."[19] For Peller and others it is a mistake to see identity in this way or to make race, ethnicity, or gender an unproblematic basis for group solidarity or political action.[20] Identity and culture are performed or enacted in socially prescribed ways.[21] Relations among group members are not established by birth. Persons, in this view, can and should be more than one thing.[22] Identity should be loose fitting, fluid, instead of fixed. As Etienne Balibar and Immanuel Wallerstein argue, "There is no . . . identity that is not his-

---

16. Cruse, *Plural but Equal*, 411.

17. For one of the most interesting of those responses, see Sanford Levinson, "Some Reflections on Multiculturalism, 'Equal Concern and Respect,' and the Establishment Clause of the First Amendment," *University of Richmond Law Review* 27 (1993): 989.

18. See Robert Ackerman, *Heterogeneities: Race, Gender, Class, Nation and State* (Amherst: University of Massachusetts Press, 1996).

19. Peller, "Cultural Imperialism," 211.

20. It makes more sense, Joan Scott says, "to teach our students and tell ourselves that identities are historically conferred, that this conferral is ambiguous . . . that subjects are produced through multiple identifications, some of which become politically salient for a time in certain contexts, and that the project of history is not to reify identity but to understand its production as an ongoing process of differentiation . . . subject to redefinition, resistance and change." See "Multiculturalism and the Politics of Identity," in *The Question of Identity*, ed. John Rajchman (New York: Routledge, 1995), 11.

21. See Judith Butler, *Gender Trouble: Feminism and the Subversion of Identity* (New York: Routledge, 1990). See also Angela Harris, "Foreword: The Unbearable Lightness of Identity," *Berkeley Women's Law Journal* 11 (1996): 207.

22. Iris Young notes that within each of the groups asserting its own claims to recognition there are often strong internal differences that make it hard to speak meaningfully of the "group." See *Justice and the Politics of Difference* (Princeton: Princeton University Press, 1990), 162–63. See also Leslie Espinoza, "Multi-Identity: Community and Culture," *Virginia Journal of Social Policy and Law* 2 (1994): 23.

torical or, in other words, constructed within a field of social values, norms or behavior and collective symbols.... The real question is how the dominant reference points of individual identity change over time."[23]

Another response to cultural pluralism and identity politics highlights the emergence of a new globalism, in which connections are forged by crossing boundaries. Old identities give way in the face of a new level and intensity of culture contact.[24] This response welcomes the emergence of a cosmopolitan consciousness in which new technologies make possible new arrangements and new cultural configurations.[25] As Jeremy Waldron argues, "We live in a world formed by technology and trade; by economic, religious, and political imperialism and their offspring; by mass migration and the dispersion of cultural influences. In this context to immerse oneself in the traditional practices of, say, aboriginal culture might be fascinating to an anthropologist, but it involves an artificial dislocation from what actually is going on in the world."[26] Globalization, so these critics claim, makes national boundaries less significant and promotes cultural homogenization.[27] It brings peoples together and promises to forge a new, global community.

Still others respond to calls for cultural pluralism and identity politics by asserting the need for greater commonality at home, for cultural

---

23. Etienne Balibar and Immanuel Wallerstein, *Race, Nation, Class: Ambiguous Identities* (London: Verso, 1991), 21–22.

24. Benjamin Barber, "Global Democracy or Global Law: Which Comes First?" *Indiana Journal of Global Legal Studies* 1 (1993): 119. See also David Hunter, "Toward Global Citizenship in International Environmental Law," *Williamette Law Review* 28 (1992): 547.

25. On the idea of a cosmopolitan consciousness, see Martha Nussbaum, "Patriotism and Cosmopolitanism," *Boston Review* (October/November 1994): 3. See also Elizabeth Kiss, "Is Nationalism Compatible with Human Rights? Reflection on East-Central Europe," in *Identities, Politics and Rights,* ed. Austin Sarat and Thomas R. Kearns (Ann Arbor: University of Michigan Press, 1996).

26. Jeremy Waldron, "Minority Cultures and the Cosmopolitan Alternative," in *The Rights of Minority Cultures,* ed. Will Kymlicka (New York: Oxford University Press, 1995), 100.

27. Rosemary Coombe, "The Cultural Life of Things: Anthropological Approaches to Law and Society in Conditions of Globalization," *American University Journal of International Law and Policy* 10 (1995): 791. See also Rosemary Coombe, "Contingent Articulations: A Critical Cultural Studies of Law," in *Law in the Domains of Culture,* ed. Austin Sarat and Thomas R. Kearns (Ann Arbor: University of Michigan Press, 1998). As Coombe says, "The global restructuring of capitalism, and new media, information, and communications technologies further challenge the idea of discrete cultures.... [M]ass media communications enable people to participate in communities of others with whom they share neither geographic proximity nor a common history" (23).

and social assimilation, and for citizenship based on common purposes and common values.[28] For them cultural pluralism promises only balkanization, retreat into hostile enclaves of separatism, and ultimately disintegration of the fragile fabric of common citizenship.[29] They criticize policies, such as bilingual education, that preserve a hyphenated Americanism and instead advocate policies, such as making English the "official language" of the United States, that express as well as promote unity and assimilation.[30]

Amid the welter of claims and counterclaims concerning the virtues and vices of cultural pluralism and identity politics, these are indeed strange times, confused and confusing times, for all Americans. This confusion was reflected recently in a series of Supreme Court cases in which the Court articulated new standards in dealing with affirmative action and so-called racial gerrymandering.[31] In one of those cases Justice Antonin Scalia announced the following view of race. "In the eyes of government," Scalia said, "we are just one race here. It is American."[32] In another of those cases Justice Clarence Thomas, normally a lockstep ally of Scalia, said, "It never ceases to amaze me that the courts are so willing to assume that anything that is predominantly black must be inferior. . . . Because of their 'distinctive histories and traditions,' black schools can function as the center and symbol of black communities, and provide examples of independent black leadership, success, and achievement."[33] In this sentiment Thomas was echoing Malcolm X, who, in the early 1960s, declared:

---

28. See Arthur Schlesinger Jr., *The Disuniting of America* (New York: W.W. Norton, 1992).

29. Michael Lind, *The Next American Nation: The New Nationalism and the Fourth American Revolution* (New York: Free Press, 1995). See also J. Harvie Wilkinson, "The Law of Civil Rights and the Dangers of Separation in Multicultural America," *Stanford Law Review* 47 (1995): 993.

30. On 1 August 1996 the United States House of Representatives passed the English Empowerment Act of 1996. This bill would declare English the official language of the United States and require the federal government to conduct all of its official business in English. Newt Gingrich argued in favor of the bill by saying that "part of becoming American involves English. It is vital historically to assert and establish that English is the common language at the heart of our civilization." See "House Votes to Make English 'Official,'" *Boston Globe*, 2 August 1996, A10.

31. See *Adrand Constructors, Inc. v. Pena*, 115 S.Ct 2097 (1995). Also *Bush v. Lawson*, 1996 WL 315857; *Shaw v. Hunt*, 1996 WL 315870; *Miller v. Johnson*, 115 S.Ct. 2475 (1995).

32. *Adrand*, at 2119 (Scalia, concurring).

33. *Missouri v. Jenkins*, 115 S. Ct. (1995), at 2061.

> If we can get an all-Black school that we can control, staff it ourselves with the type of teachers that have our good at heart ... then we don't feel that an all-Black school is necessarily a segregated school. It's only segregated when it is controlled by someone from the outside.... So what the integrationists ... are saying when they say that whites and Blacks must go to school together is that the whites are so much superior that their presence in a Black classroom just balances it out.[34]

It is, in one sense, astounding that at the end of the twentieth century two justices of the Supreme Court could speak about identity issues in these terms, one seemingly denying the rich diversity of our cultures and histories in the name of an allegedly unmarked Americanism, the other, the Court's only African-American justice, seemingly rejecting the integrationist ideals that once marked the struggle for black civil rights.[35] In another sense, however, it is not astounding at all. Scalia and Thomas simply express two poles in the continuing debate about cultural pluralism, identity politics, and about law's role in relation to both. While Thomas emphasizes the distinctiveness of the black experience and asks law to recognize and respect it, Scalia demands that, when we engage in the acts of citizenship, we do so not as Jews or blacks or gays but as "Americans." While Thomas values the cultivation of racial identity in and through a community's own institutions, Scalia believes that it is only when we leave our diverse identities behind that a just society can be achieved. While Thomas accepts cultural separation so long as it is genuinely voluntary and not the coerced result of majoritarian prejudices, Scalia seeks unity in an abstract and universal Americanism.

The voices of Scalia and Thomas simply remind us that to be an American is today, as it has always been, to live an ambivalent relationship to the claims of identity and difference, of assimilation and

---

34. Malcolm X, *By Any Means Necessary: Speeches, Interviews and a Letter*, ed. G. Breitman (New York: Pathfinder Press, 1970), 16–17.

35. Thomas, of course, is a proponent of neither cultural pluralism nor identity politics. For him, like Scalia, the state must be "color-blind" in its treatment of persons. Yet, unlike Scalia, Thomas seems to have developed a nationalist flavor to his understanding of how the black community might develop itself within the frame of the color-blindness principle. See Scott Gerber, "Justice Clarence Thomas: First Term, First Impressions," *Howard Law Journal* 35 (1992): 115; and Chelsey Parkman, "*Missouri v. Jenkins:* The Beginning of the End for Desegregation," *Loyola University of Chicago Law Journal* 27 (1996): 715.

cultural pluralism.[36] That ambivalence is conveyed by the metaphor of the melting pot, which acknowledges and celebrates our differences but insists on the painful process of melting down those differences and molding a new and unique society.[37] *E pluribus unum:* Out of many one.[38] Yet cultural pluralism and identity politics are integral parts of something called American culture; America has been and remains a hybrid nation. Individual and cultural difference, as well as the conflicts and disputes they generate, has been a part of the cultural life of Americans since the nation's founding. As Alexis de Tocqueville observed at the start of the nineteenth century:

> The human beings who are scattered over this space do not form, as in Europe, so many branches of the same stock. Three races, naturally distinct, and, I might almost say, hostile to each other are discoverable amongst them at the first glance. Almost insurmountable barriers had been raised between them by education and law, as well as by their origin and outward characteristics; but fortune has brought them together on the same soil, where, although they are mixed, they do not amalgamate.[39]

---

36. The argument that is developed in the following pages is laid out in greater detail in Sarat and Berkowitz, "Disorderly Differences."

37. See Milton Gordon, "Models of Pluralism: The New American Dilemma," *Annals* 454 (1981): 178. See also Robert Post, "Cultural Heterogeneity and the Law: Pornography, Blasphemy and the First Amendment," *California Law Review* 76 (1988): 297.

38. While we sympathize with those who have recently tried to challenge the melting pot metaphor as assimilationist and racist and sought to replace it with alternatives like the American mosaic or the American Kaleidoscope (see Lawrence H. Fuchs, *The American Kaleidoscope: Race, Ethnicity, and the Civic Culture,* cited in Andrew Delbanco, "Pluralism and Its Discontents," *Transition* 55 [1992]: 83), the melting pot remains a powerful metaphor for many Americans' conceptions about difference and order. Opponents of multiculturalism and ethnic plurality, for example, often frame the debate in these terms (see, e.g., Schlesinger, *Disuniting of America*).

39. Alexis de Tocqueville, *Democracy in America,* trans. Henry Reeve (Boston: John Allyn, 1876), 425. While continuing appeals to difference and pluralism suggest that the now numerous American races and ethnicities have not fully amalgamated, they are no longer naturally distinct. Both genetically and culturally, America's many racial groups have interacted with and melded into one another to the point where it is often difficult if not impossible to distinguish black from white, Caribbean from North American, Muslim from Jew, etc. (see, e.g., Adrian Piper, "Passing for White, Passing for Black," *Transition* 58 [1993]: 4). Piper acknowledges that, both genetically and culturally, the differences between blacks and whites are diminishing; at the same time, however, she argues that our collective unwillingness to give up our stable racial identities—our refusal to "reinternalize the external scapegoat"—is the "last outpost of racism" (20–21). See also F. James Davis, *Who Is Black? One Nation's Definition* (University Park: Pennsylvania State University Press, 1991).

Throughout this century the United States has been renewed by waves of immigration. In each period the question of how to be American has been most salient, as new groups have energized our political and cultural life but have also posed new challenges to the capacity of the polity to live up to its loftiest ideals.

To whatever extent the now many races and ethnicities that compose the United States have or have not amalgamated, the perception and fear that the United States would be a nation of many peoples who would not "amalgamate" has prompted a strong desire for sameness and community in people such as Justice Scalia. This desire for unity in the face of cultural difference creates what Michael Kammen calls "a dialectic of pluralism and conformity."[40] That dialectic, Kammen argues, lies "at the core of American life."[41] While embracing freedom and diversity, Americans also value connection; we strive to remain individuals, but we also wish to be "a people."

For a nation with such a rich (if inconsistent) historical, literary, and artistic tradition of celebrating difference, Americans speak about cultural pluralism and identity politics in a cramped vocabulary. We have had, until the most recent emergence of cultural pluralism and identity politics, few ways to see and speak of difference, except to mark its threats to order or to wish for its end. This observation is not obvious; on the contrary, one could argue that liberal tolerance provides a powerful and proven vocabulary for speaking about difference. Many Americans pride themselves on being tolerant, even of those who themselves are intolerant.

Ideally, tolerance means that differences are not merely accepted but, rather, are sought out and celebrated. Tolerance, however, as it is understood and practiced, is a minimal vocabulary of difference.[42] Though it appears relativistic, tolerance is, in fact, hierarchical. Toler-

---

We may yearn for stable categories to label certain individuals and certain activities as white and others as black, some as American, others as foreign, but those categories are wholly inadequate to describe the present reality. Modern society is already a mixed and hybrid society in which racial and ethnic categories themselves are in question. See Henry Louis Gates Jr., *Loose Canons: Notes on the Culture Wars* (New York: Oxford University Press, 1992), xvi; and "Pluralism and Its Discontents," *Contention* 2 (1992): 69, 74–75.

40. See Michael Kammen, *People of Paradox: An Inquiry Concerning the Origins of American Civilization* (New York: Knopf, 1972), 128.

41. Ibid.

42. We agree with Kirstie McClure that it is high time for a critical look at the practice of tolerance as a vocabulary for recognizing and accommodating difference. See "The Limits of Toleration," *Political Theory* 18 (1990): 362. Yet we do not seek to abandon tolerance simply because it often has been and is used in ways inconsistent with the fullest

ance is "permission granted by authority," an "allowance, with or without limitations, by the ruling power," and the allowing of "that which is not actually approved; forbearance; sufferance."[43] Tolerance presupposes a hierarchical relationship between someone who requests tolerance and an authority that tolerates only if and when it wishes. It is this complicity between tolerance and power that has led some to question its desirability as a vocabulary for organizing our response to cultural pluralism and identity politics.[44]

Kammen's dialectic of pluralism and conformity as well as the inadequacy of tolerance is reflected, moreover, in the contemporary dialogue about the implications of difference for law.[45] That dialogue grows more, not less, difficult as new groups enter our national life and as we confront, in new ways, the insidious effects of treatment that unjustifiably focuses on and highlights difference. Everywhere it seems that, the more difference is recognized, the more vexing the effort to accommodate difference in our institutional lives and practices becomes.[46] As Kenneth Karst observes, "In all times and places, cultural differences have bred suspicion and fear. . . . [Thus] behind the bland terms 'intercultural relations' lies the menace of violence."[47] Cultural pluralism is frequently seen as the fearsome presence within, rather than the enlivening wellspring of, democratic politics.

---

meaning of respect and accommodation of others. It may very well be that tolerance *is*, according to its ideal usage, respect for and accommodation of difference and, simultaneously, *is* a gross reformism in the service of power. While these appear to be contradictory definitions, they need not be; in this we follow the suggestion of Hannah Pitkin. Pitkin argues that a large class of words, such as *justice*, can often mean two very different things, both of which are true. The two meanings correspond not to different words but, rather, to a distinction between form and substance depending upon the context in which the word is used. See Hannah Fenichel Pitkin, *Wittgenstein and Justice* (Berkeley: University of California Press, 1973), 186–92. See also Herbert Marcuse, *One-Dimensional Man* (Boston: Beacon, 1964), 214–15.

43. *Oxford English Dictionary*, cited in McClure, "Limits of Toleration," 362.

44. Herbert Marcuse, "A Critique of Pure Tolerance," in *A Critique of Pure Tolerance*, ed. Robert Paul Wolff (Boston: Beacon Press, 1965).

45. See Barbara Johnson, *A World of Difference* (Baltimore: Johns Hopkins University Press, 1987). See also William Connolly, *Identity/Difference: Democratic Negotiations of Political Paradox* (Ithaca: Cornell University Press, 1991).

46. See Martha Minow, *Making All the Difference: Inclusion, Exclusion, and American Law* (Ithaca: Cornell University Press, 1990). See also Alice Jardine, "Prelude: The Future of Difference," in *The Future of Difference*, ed. Hester Eisenstein and Alice Jardine (Boston: G. K. Hall, 1980).

47. Kenneth Karst, "Paths to Belonging: The Constitution and Cultural Identity," *North Carolina Law Review* 64 (1986): 305, 310–11.

Calls for cultural pluralism and identity politics would seem at first glance to pose special challenges to and for law.[48] The first of those challenges is at the level of legal policy and legal doctrine. How can and should law respond to demands for cultural recognition and exemption from particular regulations that would denigrate or deny an important cultural practice? There are at least two places to look for answers. The first is to the way law has expressed and understood the antidiscrimination principle.[49] In the complicated politics of affirmative action there are few moments when diversity for diversity sake, the protection of difference, has been the overriding goal.[50] Generally, color blindness, gender blindness, blindness to differences of sexual preference—these have been the beacons of our law.[51] Law has been unable or unwilling to foster actively a society in which cultural pluralism and identity politics could flourish.

Another place to look to see law's response to demands for recognition are to instances in which particular groups have sought exemptions from the reach of otherwise valid state regulations in order to preserve some element of their history or culture. While the story is complex, the general pattern has been a pattern of refusal. As Aviam Soifer puts it, "It makes sense to think that most judges are inclined to squelch the norms generated by groups other than the state.... Unsurprisingly, they want to control or eliminate alternative narratives and competing notions of morality."[52] The demands of cultural preservation or cultural expression have to give way to the uniform obligations of citizens before the law. And in the few instances in which difference seems to have been recognized and accommodated it is only because law refused to see the very difference it was accommodating.

---

48. See Suzanna Sherry, "The Sleep of Reason," *Georgetown Law Jurnal* 84 (1996): 453.

49. See Paul Gewirtz, "The Triumph and Transformation of Anti-Discrimination Law," in *Race, Law and Culture: Reflections on Brown v. Board of Education*, ed. Austin Sarat (New York: Oxford University Press, 1997).

50. One important example is found in the majority opinion in *Metro Broadcasting, Inc. v. FCC*, 110 S. Ct. 2997 (1990); see also Patricia Williams, "Metro Broadcasting, Inc. v. FCC: Regrouping in Singular Times," *Harvard Law Review* 104 (1990): 525.

51. Andrew Kull, *The Color-Blind Constitution* (Cambridge: Harvard University Press, 1992).

52. Aviam Soifer, *Law and the Company We Keep* (Cambridge: Harvard University Press, 1995), 100.

This is exemplified in the well-known case of *Wisconsin v. Yoder*.[53] In *Yoder*, members of the Old Order Amish challenged the Wisconsin compulsory school attendance law, which required them to send their children to a certified public or private school until they reached the age of sixteen, by claiming that compliance with the state statute would require them to violate the commands of their church and also "endanger their own salvation and that of the children."[54] In addition, they argued that their religion required "life in a church community and apart from the world and worldly influence."[55] *Yoder* is one of the relatively few cases in the American constitutional tradition in which requests for exemption from the reach of valid state laws were granted and in which the claims of difference were apparently accommodated and recognized.[56] Yet, in Justice Warren Burger's majority opinion, difference is neither recognized nor accommodated; it is made to disappear. As Burger put it, "The Amish communities singularly parallel and reflect many of the virtues of Jefferson's ideal of the 'sturdy yeoman' who would form the basis of what he considered as the ideal of democratic society."[57] Here the member/stranger distinction, into which all claims of cultural pluralism and identity politics can be collapsed, itself dissolves into identity. Once commonality is established recognition can be accorded.

But gestures of accommodation, like Burger's in *Yoder*, infrequent as they are, are nonetheless violent in their response to cultural pluralism and identity politics. They deny difference even as they seem to embrace it. The challenge of recognizing and living with and in a plural culture is displaced through a process of identification. As William

---

53. 406 U.S. 205 (1971).
54. Ibid., 209.
55. Ibid., 210. See Timothy Hall, "Religion and Civic Virtue," *Tulane Law Review* 67 (1992): 87.
56. Others include *People v. Woody*, 40 Cal. R. 69 (1964) (exemption for use of peyote in an Indian religious ritual); *Frank v. Alaska*, 604 P2d 1068 (1979) (exemption from a hunting regulation for an Indian tribe); *Sherbert v. Verner*, 374 U.S. 398 (1962) (upholding claim for unemployment compensation by Seventh Day Adventists who refused to work on the Sabbath); *Thomas v. Indiana Review Board*, 450 U.S. 707 (1980) (upholds claim to unemployment benefits by a Jehovah's Witness). See "Religious Exemptions under the Free Exercise Clause: A Model of Competing Authorities," *Yale Law Journal* 90 (1980): 350; Philip Hamburger, "A Constitutional Right to Religious Exemption: An Historical Perspective," *George Washington University Law Review* 60 (1992): 915.
57. 406 U.S. 225–26.

Connolly argues, this response "erases the threat that difference presents."[58]

Violent accommodation by denial of difference may be built into the very structure of the law, which, in its commitment to equal treatment, promises to be indifferent to personal identity or group membership. This indifference is symbolized in the icon of legal justice—namely, the statue of Justicia, the blindfolded bearer of sword and balance.[59] Justicia is blindfolded to prevent her decision from being inappropriately influenced or determined by forces of fear, bias, or favoritism. Moreover, she is blindfolded—not blind—suggesting a self-willed refusal of vision. Justice, it seems, is a denial of sight though not of seeing, a regulation of information though not of knowing, a restriction on what is permissibly attended to though not a deficit of attention.

Law promises to treat all persons equally, to honor us by ignoring what marks us as different. Law, in theory, knows no culture and recognizes no identity. Yet these claims and the meaning of equal protection that they support have come under serious challenges in the work of feminists and Critical Race theorists.[60] Both suggest that law's claimed neutrality and willed blindness masks a posture that is, in fact, gendered and raced.[61] Law proclaims its neutrality, all the while protecting the privileged position of white males;[62] law, even when it proclaims nondiscrimination as its principle, holds out an invitation to a society in which the taken-for-granted position against which discrimination is defined has a gender and a race.

As Catherine MacKinnon explains, the traditional understanding of equal protection is based on sameness-difference.[63] The issue presented when equal protection claims are made is whether one person or

---

58. Connolly, *Identity/Difference*, 43.
59. See Dennis E. Curtis and Judith Resnik, "Images of Justice," *Yale Law Journal* 96 (1987): 1727.
60. Richard Delgrado, *Critical Race Theory: The Cutting Edge* (Phildelphia: Temple University Press, 1995).
61. Ibid.
62. See Ian Haney Lopez, "The Social Construction of Race: Some Observations on Illusion, Fabrication, and Choice," *Harvard Civil Rights–Civil Liberties Law Review* 29 (1994): 1.
63. Catherine MacKinnon, *Feminism Unmodified: Discourses on Life and Law* (Cambridge: Harvard University Press, 1987).

situation is different from another. The difference principle thus requires a point of comparison against which differences can be measured. In equal protection doctrine, MacKinnon argues, that standard is neither neutral nor universal. As she says: "There is a politics to this. Concealed is the substantive way in which man has become the measure of all things. Under the sameness standard, women are measured according to our correspondence with man, our equality judged by our proximity to his measure. Under the difference standard, we are measured according to our lack of correspondence with him. . . . Gender neutrality is thus simply the male standard."[64] For MacKinnon and others law has then always had an implicitly, if not explicitly, hostile response to cultural pluralism and identity politics, demanding sameness as the condition of inclusion.

Advocates of cultural pluralism and identity politics seek to expose the cultural bias hidden in law not to search for a "truly" objective or neutral position from which to make legal decisions but, rather, to hold law accountable. If law already is responsive to culture, then the hope would be to open it up to new views, new values, new ways of being in the world. Law, understood in this way, might play a critical role in a dialogue about culture, identity, and the meaning of citizenship in a plural society. Law might be more than simply a structure of restraint, repressing the expression of difference. Law might become a "true foundation of the social order. . . . The problems of order and freedom would be cast in a different light if we could think of these norms of conduct as ends whose fulfillment would bring our worthiest capacities to their richest development rather than as constraints imposed by an external will."[65]

But it is not enough to criticize law for its resistance to cultural pluralism and identity politics and to urge recognition and accommodation. Recognition and accommodation do not, in and of themselves, guarantee justice or even progressive social change. Accommodating the desire to preserve a cultural heritage should not be a substitute for holding it accountable for its own inequities and exclusions.[66] One

---

64. Ibid., 34.
65. Roberto Unger, *Knowledge and Politics* (New York: Free Press, 1975), 76–77.
66. "Without respect for internal minorities, a liberal society risks becoming a mosaic of tyrannies. . . . The task of making respect for minority rights real is thus one that falls not just to the majority but also to the minority groups themselves." See Leslie Green, "Internal Minorities and Their Rights," in *The Rights of Minority Cultures*, ed. Will Kymlicka (New York: Oxford University Press, 1995), 270. See also Hazel Carby, "The Multicultural Wars," *Radical History Review* 54 (1992): 7.

should no more romanticize the authentic expressions of culture and identity than one should idealize their denials.

Cultural Pluralism, Identity Politics, and the Law asks us to examine carefully the relation of cultural struggle and material transformation and law's role in both. A legal embrace of cultural pluralism would be no substitute for coping with the pervasive realities of material inequity and injustice in this society. Thus, law may be criticized for its infrequent moments of incorporation as well as for its far more frequent, though subtle, practices of denial. As the essays in this book make clear, one's position on law's proper relationship to cultural pluralism and identity politics should be, in this sense, rigorously indeterminate.

Whatever one's view of the possibility or desirability of building a new legality more openly hospitable to cultural pluralism and identity politics, one can step back and ask what are the terms of inclusion that both now and in the past have established the basis for claims of citizenship? What arguments are available to persuade existing majorities to extend the rights and responsibilities of citizenship to new groups? What role, if any, has law played in structuring the terms on which recognition, accommodation, and inclusion are accorded to persons and groups in the United States? One can also ask: How much of the taken-for-granted in law and legal theory is defined by an ideal of integration and assimilation? Are there domains of law in which questions of culture and identity take on particular salience and others in which they cannot easily be accommodated? What happens to law when the subject/claimant is constituted by membership in a distinct cultural group or by a distinct identity? What challenges do cultural pluralism and identity politics pose for notions of procedural fairness and/or legal justice? Do cultural pluralism and identity politics offer a way for legal institutions to incorporate and, at the same time, co-opt voices of protest and, in so doing, deflect energy from the struggle for a more just and equitable society?

It is to these questions that *Cultural Pluralism, Identity Politics, and the Law* addresses itself. The essays collected here are written by scholars with distinctive disciplinary expertise and distinctive theoretical inclinations. Yet, taken together, they challenge orthodox understandings of the nature of identity politics, Kammen's dialectic of pluralism and conformity, and contemporary debates about separatism and assimilation. They ask us to think seriously about the ways law has been, and is, implicated in those debates, and they reject the false choices that have so far dominated discussion. *Cultural Pluralism, Identity Politics, and the Law* opens up new and, hopefully, more fruitful avenues for future thought about these compelling yet vexing subjects.

Cultural Pluralism, Identity Politics, and the Law begins by taking us back over a hundred years to consider the political struggle to extend citizenship to African Americans and to women during the nineteenth century. Elizabeth Clark's essay "Breaking the Mold of Citizenship: the 'Natural' Person as Citizen in Nineteenth-Century America" notes that those struggles were, in fact, about "identity politics" but that the identity issues in question were individual rather than group based. "The assertion," Clark notes, "that law and society must change to accommodate freed slaves and women depended largely on arguments about the person rather than about the group." Group rights were anathema to some reformers of the nineteenth century because they seemed to promise nothing more than a reprise of the old "corporatist politics" that had been used to repress women and blacks. Yet the assertion of individual identity as the basis for new claims of recognition faced the problem that citizenship had traditionally been a unitary category in which group characteristics—such as whiteness and/or maleness—were simply taken for granted. Thus, the strategy of reformers was to individualize the notion of citizenship itself.

The individuation strategy required breaking through the status relationships that traditionally provided the context for legal citizenship and for establishing new terms of inclusion. It had reformers arguing for political recognition of the disenfranchised, who, as Clark says, "in addition to being short of whiteness and maleness had little status, property, or education," by claiming that members of these groups were nonetheless "natural persons." As natural persons, they shared *universal* human attributes with those whom the law already recognized and protected; "they felt pain and pleasure and had immortal souls."

Clark's essay reminds us that one kind of identity politics is based upon a politics of identification rather than of differentiation. Women and blacks sought to mobilize legal reform by highlighting points of similarity between themselves and others at the level of sentiments and feelings. They made the personal political and, in so doing, both demanded legal recognition of the injustices to which they as persons were subject and tried to prompt legal recognition of shared human attributes.

By emphasizing the shared attributes of the natural person, reformers attacked both the customary rule of status relationships and the formal legal disabilities attached to denials of citizenship. The law, they claimed, should respect the individuality of all persons, an individuality deeply rooted in personal experiences of pain and pleasure. They turned to law with the optimistic hope that it would forge equality from difference. Deeply personal experiences provided a common point of reference for law in efforts that they hoped it would make to transcend the apparently differentiating attributes of gender and race. Reformers believed that markers of gender and race had to be "erased in the interest of compassionate identification" rather than celebrated as "culture-constituting" attributes.

Clark shows how nineteenth-century reformers drew upon philosophical and literary traditions that stressed the depth and diversity of human experience while praising our shared capacities for imagination, intuition, and empathy. By deploying diversity and shared capacity, they could argue both for the "immutability and universality of individual rights" and that rights were "as individual and open-ended as the vista for each body and soul."

Reformers hoped to demonstrate how no uniform structure of law could adequately "take account of individual difference." Romantic notions of the depth and diversity of individual experience brought to the fore private experiences such as pain as a way of destabilizing "ingrained oppressive patterns of law and custom." Such notions are themselves antecedents of the multiple challenges to law that are today made in the name of individuation and identity.

Lauren Berlant's essay "The Subject of True Feeling: Pain, Privacy, and Politics" shows how all sides of the contemporary political spectrum invoke subjective experiences of the kind that Clark finds in the antebellum struggles of abolitionists and suffragettes. Sentiment and suffering provide the terms on which appeals now are made for legal protection and legal change. In addition, Berlant notes that this "feeling culture" has also become a staple of current identity politics. Much identity politics, she argues, is based on a strategy in which "the wronged take up voice and agency to produce transformative testimony," the power of which depends on "an analogous conviction about the *self-evidence* and therefore the *objectivity* of painful feeling."

Sentimentality and suffering, as two ways of making claims for legal recognition and redress, seem to specify and highlight cultural and individual differences—not all of us suffer equally or in the same way—while at the same time effacing those very differences. What counts is the assumption that cultural pluralism and identity-based differences are epiphenomenal, while feelings are the evidence of an underlying shared humanity. Thus, the politics of sentiment and suffering is one way of overcoming the allegedly fragmenting, balkanizing impact of cultural pluralism and identity politics, a politics that claims a universal subjectivity beyond cultural difference, individuated identity, and history itself. As Berlant puts it, "What happens to questions of managing alterity or difference in collective life when feeling *bad* becomes evidence for a structural condition of injustice?"

Berlant's essay suggests that the politics of the late twentieth century in America have been marked by a "desperate search to protect the United States from what seemed to be an imminently powerful alliance of parties on the bottom of so many traditional hierarchies—the poor, people of color, women, gays and lesbians." Put in its place is a politics dedicated to the identification, protection, and liberation of "the American innocent." The most important icon of this politics of innocence is the fetus—imagined as a universal, unmarked, rights-bearing subject whose interests are set against the identity politics of class, race, and gender. The politics of innocence works through revelations of trauma, incitements to rescue, and the notion, very reminiscent of Clark's story of the nineteenth century, that "the feeling self is the true self." It reveals itself today in an effort to "juridically and culturally administer society as a space ideally void of struggle and ambivalence," a space beyond cultural pluralism and identity politics.

The turn to sentimentality and suffering, Berlant argues, is particularly visible in legal discourse, especially in decisions dealing with sexual privacy and abortion. Paradoxically, it is also apparent in the responses of some proponents of cultural pluralism and identity politics who criticize those decisions. Law, as well as many critics of law, is complicit in the effacement of cultural and identity difference and the political struggles and ambivalence that are necessarily attached to them. Thus, the privacy imagined in cases such as *Griswold v. Connecticut* is a space beyond turmoil, in which "freedom and desire meet up in their full suprapolitical expression." That privacy ultimately gives way, however, under the force of criticisms by scholars such as MacKinnon and schools such as Critical Race Theory. Its sentimental story is replaced, in *Planned Parenthood v. Casey*, by a narrative of "*women's pain in heterosexual culture*" as the basis for maintaining abortion rights.

How far have we come when sentimentality is replaced by suffering? Both, Berlant contends, deny difference in a comforting, if not very comfortable, assertion of a more basic unity. Both encourage a turn to law; both imagine "'relief,' somehow, through juridicalized national remedies." Law respectfully responds to such imaginings, since juridicalizng remedies is one acknowledgment of law's hegemonic status.

Berlant warns that the politics of pain has the tendency to efface politics itself because the move from sentimentality to suffering directs our attention away from structural violence and toward individual remedy.[67] She suggests that the politics of pain undermines cultural pluralism and identity politics, since the different stories of pain wielded in the domain of identity politics begin "to compete furiously with one another, for fear that the available soupçon of empathy . . . . the privileged might distribute would go to the other Othered population." Berlant ends her essay by calling for a kind of politics that feeling cannot provide.

A similar interest in, and idea of, politics also animates Dorothy Roberts's response to claims for cultural recognition and cultural pluralism that currently are being made in and around the legal arena. Roberts begins her essay "Why Culture Matters to Law: The Difference Politics Makes" by acknowledging the many ways in which culture is always already inside law. For her, then, the question is not whether culture matters to law, not whether law notices and responds to cultural difference, but, rather, how it matters and why it matters as it does. As she puts it, echoing the arguments of Critical Race theorists: "It is hard to notice the law's bias because the dominant perspective has seeped into the pre-existing language that shapes our jurisprudence. . . . Thus, law, although infused with culture, appears to be without culture." One manifestation of a group's status and power, Roberts claims, is its ability to have its cultural perspective not labeled as a perspective

---

67. As Chandra Mohanty notes, "There has been an erosion of the politics of collectivity through the reformulation of race and difference in individualistic terms. The 1960s and 70s slogan 'the personal is political' has been recrafted in the 1980s as 'the political is personal.' In other words, all politics is collapsed into the personal, and questions of individual behaviors, attitudes, and life-styles stand in for political analysis of the social. Individual political struggles are seen as the only relevant and legitimate form of political struggle." See "On Race and Voice: Challenges for Liberal Education in the 1990s," *Cultural Critique* 14 (Winter 1989–90): 204.

at all but just accepted as the way things happen to be. The attribution of culture and identity to a group is then a mark of its marginality or disadvantage.

Roberts is cautious about the current embrace of cultural pluralism and identity politics by certain segments of the white community in the United States. Whites celebrate America's cultural diversity, Roberts argues, "so long as it does not entail any redistribution of wealth and power." It is precisely a pluralism without power that groups may end up with when they turn to law for protection and preservation of their heritage and their way of life. Cultural preservation, Roberts writes, is no guarantee of justice either among members of the group whose culture is preserved or between that group and others in society. She makes this point through an examination of one instance in which law has given into this instinct for cultural pluralism, the Indian Child Welfare Act, as well as other generally less successful instances—the assertion of so-called cultural defenses in criminal cases. Law, in her view, admits or acknowledges the relevance of culture, as we saw in the example of *Yoder*, only when the conduct in question "does not depart too drastically from the dominant cultural norm."

Calls for cultural recognition or preservation are in and of themselves not politically progressive. For culture to matter to law in ways that do not contribute to the maintenance of a status quo of cultural domination and cultural denial, substantial political change, resulting in the empowerment of cultural minorities, would have to take place first. Yet Roberts notes that the political situation in relation to cultural pluralism and identity politics is far from straightforward, since both may themselves be prerequisites for that change. As she puts it, the "best insight for eradicating systemic injustices and defining the contours of a just society will flow from the cultures that have suffered most." One must work to develop cultural institutions that themselves are free from inequity and exclusion so that one can draw on those institutions in the political struggle for a more just society.

Law should recognize, support, and incorporate cultural pluralism and identity politics only to the extent that they are demonstrably linked to a political project to end subordination. Like Berlant, Roberts worries that law will embrace empathy as a much less costly substitute for political and social transformation. Empathy, Roberts warns, "is not powerful enough to overcome the allure of white social privilege . . . [or to change] the inferior position of minority cultural groups." If there is to be a cultural pluralism and identity politics worth having, it will require careful attention to material and structural conditions that all too often a culturalist position seems to neglect. Citizenship, Roberts concludes, "in a *multicultural* America that 'preserves traditions, observances . . . creeds, customs, and cuisines' while maintaining its profound disparities in wealth and privilege is no less repugnant."

The warning that cultural pluralism and identity politics may be embraced in legal policy and reform as a way of accommodating difference while, at the same time, maintaining privilege provides the backdrop for George Lipsitz's examination of contemporary criticism of affirmative action as an expression of "race-conscious 'separatism' and self-interested 'pork barrel' politics." Like all of the authors in this book, in "Civil Rights Rhetoric and White Identity Politics" Lipsitz attends to the relationship between culture and the material conditions out of which a culturalist politics emerges. In addition, he describes what might be called a double gesture in law's response to demands for inclusion. One side of this double gesture is the enactment of various reforms seemingly designed to end discrimination and promote the inclusion and advancement of black citizens. The other side is a pattern of exemption, under-enforcement, or administrative interpretation that has systematically protected white privilege, what Lipsitz quite evocatively calls "the possessive investment in whiteness." Law's gestures of inclusion are inconceivable without its accompanying gestures of protection for those with most at risk when antidiscrimination principles are taken seriously.

Lipsitz examines three areas in which principles of nondiscrimination have apparently been triumphant in U.S. law—fair housing, school discrimination, and fair hiring. In each area he asks whether blacks have abandoned the quest for nondiscrimination in favor of a "short-sighted 'identity politics.'" He begins with the National Housing Act of 1934, which, he argues, "made home ownership a possibility for millions of U.S. families by mobilizing the resources of the federal government to guarantee home loans." The Home Owners Loan Corporation, which administered the act, engaged in systematic racial discrimination, Lipsitz argues, by giving highest priority for loans to people who bought homes in areas that were all white and all Christian. Residents of low-income, minority neighborhoods, on the other hand, found it very hard to obtain NHA loans. Similar skewing of opportunities for decent housing along racial lines were undertaken by the Federal

Housing Administration and in the development of federally financed public housing. And, when law did act to end racially restrictive covenants in housing, it did so only to the extent of prohibiting state enforcement of those covenants. It did not make it illegal for property owners to adhere to such covenants voluntarily. As Lipsitz puts it, "Every judicial, legislative, and executive victory in the fight against housing discrimination fell victim to subterfuge and subversion by defenders of discrimination." The result is that housing in the United States has become hypersegregated, not as a result of a willed desire for racial separation on the part of African Americans but, rather, as a result of a set of political strategies and choices made by whites.[68]

A similar story, Lipsitz contends, can be told with respect to school desegregation. Today, more than forty years after *Brown*, America's schools—especially those in our inner cities—remain highly segregated on the basis of race. Here again, separation is not the triumphant result of black nationalist politics. It is, instead, a testimony to the failure of school desegregation efforts to address the ways in which discrimination in housing, employment, and access to public services "enabled whites to resegregate the schools by moving to suburban districts." *Brown* seemed to promise a movement to end the separation of the races in schools, but it was defeated by white resistance not of the in-your-face Southern kind but of the genteel, without words, withdrawal of whites from schools in which black students came to be concentrated. The advantages of de jure discrimination have thus been preserved long after law embraced race neutrality as the principle governing assignment of students within school districts. The possessive investment of whites in race privilege is much more responsible for separatism than the occasional efforts of blacks and other minorities to secure outposts of cultural recognition and preservation in colleges and universities and in the curricula of some of our public schools.

The possessive investment in whiteness has also prevailed in the regime of fair hiring laws. Here too, even where law assumed a posture supportive of racial justice, it also embraced provisions that "undermined its stated goals." The most important of these is found in the protection accorded existing seniority systems by Title VII of the 1964 Civil Rights Act and in the special sensitivity that the courts have dis-

---

68. See also Ankur Goel, "Maintaining Integration against Minority Interests: The Anti-Subjugation Theory for Equality in Housing," *Urban Law* 22 (1990): 369.

played to potential civil rights violations against whites in hiring and employment practices. So strong are these protections for white privilege that, for equal protection purposes, whites have become the "protected 'discrete and insular minority.'"

Lipsitz concludes by arguing that the civil rights struggles of the last half of the twentieth century were not designed to secure state neutrality in relation to race. They were designed, instead, to secure concrete gains in housing, education, and political power, rather than in the area of culture or identity politics. When recognition of culture and identity emerge as goals of political action, they emerge as subsidiary goals, or as expressions of frustration at the failure of this society to produce racial justice.

Law is, in Lipsitz's view, complicit in that failure. It is a powerful tool that has been used to maintain an ideological legitimation of white privilege thus helping to ensure its perpetuation. Law has helped whites disavow racism while engaging in the ongoing reproduction of its material practices. The possessive interest in whiteness is responsible for the separation that is now hypocritically decried by the very whites who live in segregated suburbs, send their children to largely white private schools, and work in environments in which black tokenism more than black power is the order of the day.

Cultural Pluralism, Identity Politics, and the Law concludes with Kenneth Karst's essay "Does Integration Have a Future?" Karst asks this question against the background of new assertiveness on behalf of cultural pluralism and identity politics of the kind sketched at the start of the present essay. He insists that it can be answered only if we take a broad, historical perspective. Such a perspective suggests that we should reject the "polarity itself, the false assumption that the United States is faced with an either/or choice" of cultural pluralism or assimilation, of segregation or integration. Karst contends that our history has been, and remains, "characterized by a dynamic process involving both cultural pluralism and assimilation, both separation and integration."

Even he acknowledges, however, that today integration is in trouble. Law has refused to take those steps that would be necessary to move beyond the formality of the antidiscrimination principle to the reality of cultural, social, and racial integration. Moreover, "some members of racial and ethnic minorities have turned inward, embracing separatist views of community and politics." Yet Karst asks us again to look to history. When we do so, he says, we will see that neither integration nor separation can be complete, that no critique of integration nor embrace of it really threatens the *essential* place of both in the American story.

Karst argues that the lines that today divide our society into apparently disparate social groups are multiple and cross-cutting. No one is just one thing. Identities become increasingly hard to pin down as people come to see themselves as multiracial, multiethnic, multicultural. At the same time, a recognizable American culture "is visible all around us." This national culture is, Karst contends, a continuously reproducing amalgam, a process of mutual acculturation among various cultural traditions.

The dynamic of separation and assimilation, what Kammen called "pluralism and conformity," is driven on the side of assimilation by the pull of economic opportunity. Groups move into the "cultural mainstream" in order to move into the economic mainstream, and the latter movement, where it is successful, further accelerates the former. The response to this dynamic process among members of groups left behind, or sometimes in the generation whose parents made the integrationist move, is a "defensive solidarity." It is this response that sets off fears that the progress of integration will be undone, that cultural pluralism will undo national culture. Yet all of this, Karst contends, is part of the continuing dynamic of coming together and pulling apart that has always typified American life. Our nationhood depends on the well-being of the national identities to which it is often hyphenated. It is strengthened, not threatened, by them. And they, in turn, are transformed by the inevitable cultural contact, conflict, and cooperation that marks American life.

And what is the role of law in all of this? Unlike other authors in this volume, who look to law either to explain exclusion or as a focus for change, Karst is more modest in his assessment. While he agrees that law, all too often, has been a tool of exclusion, he notes two things that limit the role and response of law to cultural pluralism and identity politics. First is its flexibility. It can be, and has been, used on the side of diversity and of assimilation, of cultural preservation and cultural assimilation. Second is its limited efficacy. If anything is true of law it is its regular failure to deliver its promises, on whatever side they are made. As a result, law should not be used to promote one side or suppress the other in the continuing dynamic of cultural pluralism and integration. At best law can play a limited role in advancing what Karst calls equal citizenship and in helping us to come to terms with and accommodate cultural pluralism, identity politics, and their opposites. In the end Karst, like Roberts and Lipsitz, points away from law toward the achievement of material conditions necessary to make equal citizenship into a political reality.

Whether at the level of individual identity or group solidarity, law has and will continue to play some role in responding to the demands of difference. The essays in *Cultural Pluralism, Identity Politics, and the Law* highlight false choices—between cultural pluralism and economic justice, between identity politics and a dynamic engagement in political struggle, between the worlds of sentiment and suffering and the hard-edged assessment of group needs and group advantage—that have often structured the argument about what law can and should do. In addition, they suggest that we should neither expect law to transform nor be radically transformed by its engagement in the current conflicts and confusion about culture and identity. The demands of difference will neither overwhelm nor undo the fabric of legality. And legality alone will not provide a satisfactory response to those demands.

Breaking the Mold of Citizenship: The "Natural" Person as Citizen in Nineteenth-Century America (A Fragment)

Elizabeth B. Clark

Mary Wollstonecraft once said, probably with a sigh, "I do earnestly wish to see the distinction of sex confounded in society, unless where love animates the behavior." Two centuries later, many groups in American political life are still caught in the same dilemma: hoping that a just society will take account of an essential characteristic—race and sex spring to mind—in ways that will benefit the group, while eschewing the potentially harmful characterizations that lie just on the flip side of the coin.

Group identities were already an important part of the political structure well before nineteenth-century reform movements brought into play the interests of people who were not traditional political

---

Elizabeth Battelle Clark, 1952–97, delivered an early version of this paper as a Mellon Lecture at Amherst College. She was already ill at the time that she drafted the speaking version, and she was and remained unsatisfied with what she had written. After finding that she did not have the strength to complete a revision, she turned the work over to her friends Katherine Stone and Dirk Hartog, with the request that we try to do something with it. With the help of Sarah Gordon, we have tried to produce an essay that reflects Betsy Clark's hopes. We have only lightly edited the work, drawing on paragraphs from two drafts. We have decided not to annotate the piece. No conclusion and only a sketch of an introduction exist, and we are unwilling to impose an interpretive frame on her words. But we have included a bibliography of Betsy Clark's writings, to guide the interested reader to the sources on which she drew and to the larger themes that she was working on in this piece and in all of her writings.

actors; their entrance into the formal political arena only brought the question of groups to public notice. The introduction of new groups to political power fragmented the structure of representative citizenship on which the American system, like other Western systems, was based. This essay looks broadly at the destruction and reconstruction of group identities in the period from abolitionism to the Nineteenth Amendment, with an eye to implications for our own time.

I would like to focus here on three ways in which nineteenth-century liberal reform movements worked to challenge the legal order and to fragment older, monolithic models of citizenship in order to provide a more inclusive model, and on some of the consequences of those campaigns.

First, reformers challenged the legitimacy of the uniformity of law, not on the basis of the fact that it discriminated against groups (although that was one outcome), but because they argued that no uniform structure could take account of individual difference. This argument was influenced both by romantic notions of the depth and diversity of individual experience and by strongly Protestant notions of the supremacy of individual conscience over traditional authorities.

Second, I will talk about the new characteristics that qualified the person as a rights-bearing individual, qualities rooted in a natural view of personhood that brought to the fore "private" experiences like bodily pain and family and sexual relationships that had formerly been completely excluded from the persona of the citizen.

Third, I will talk about ways in which the women's movement in particular sought to destabilize ingrained oppressive patterns of law and custom by bringing the private world of family and domestic relations into the public sphere, for purposes of creating a rights regime that would reflect women's experiences.

Finally, I will address the ways in which this reform rhetoric paved the way for multiple claims and challenges to the neutrality and uniformity of law and rights regimes today, and some of the strengths and weaknesses of the antecedents on which we rely. In the nineteenth century, the highly politicized and fluid arena of rights consciousness offered an open forum for the struggle over importing an individual's subjective claims into law. The forms of claims for rights of the person developed in that arena have shaped our history ever since.

How did law accommodate the conflicting claims of disparately situated persons or groups in the period before the political upheavals of the mid–nineteenth century? The problem posed by the uniformity of formal laws under traditional citizenship models was muted or papered over by what nineteenth-century legal doctrine still labeled as the "law of persons," or the body of blended formal and customary regulations that governed status relationships like marriage, slavery, and apprenticeship. The bulk of formal law, although expressed as universal commands, was actually designed to enable, or in some cases restrain, the dominant partners in those relationships. The first chapter of Blackstone's *Commentaries on the Laws of England*, "Of the Absolute Rights of Individuals," for example, defines the right of personal security as "a person's legal and uninterrupted enjoyment of his life, his limbs, his body, his health, and his reputation." But everyone knew that these guarantees were not given freely to all comers. Such security at law clearly did not exist for dependent wives and slaves under the discipline or cover of husbands and masters; instead, subordinate groups were largely governed by the private powers of their superiors, a discretionary authority supported by both law and custom.

Some formal law did apply directly to dependents, of course; wives, servants, slaves, and children were all subject to moral and criminal sanctions from magistrates. But protections and entitlements were scarce and only triggered by extreme cases; even married women's property was largely protected by equitable devices rather than law until mid-century. Investing quasi-official figures with vast disciplinary powers over their subordinates, and to a great extent removing those subordinates from the direct application of the laws, created a large pocket of discretion in the governing order. The legal regime thus finessed the problem of writing uniform laws for individuals with disparate identities and stations by excluding large groups of dependents from its direct jurisdiction for many purposes.

Formal or positive law, then, addressed its benefits largely to the politically enfranchised, a group that was well defined by a set of salient common characteristics. Although no master document of the eighteenth century spelled out the components of citizenship in full formal detail, citizens had traditionally been male, white, heads of households, and property owners and were assumed to have some level of education. The category of "citizen" for most purposes, then, functioned as a unitary category; its most important constituent characteristics were by definition common to all holders of the title and did not need to be spelled out. Citizenship was in turn embedded in the status system. While the role of the citizen was formally uninflected by direct power over others, citizenship in fact carried with it status, control, responsibility, and obligations by virtue of the fact that the citizen was usually a husband, father, employer, or master as well. In fact, for both the dominant and subordinate classes, the richer and more textured identity was described, not through a political label, but through the subpolitical status relationships of husband–wife, parent–child, master–servant, or master–slave that encompassed such a large part of the population.

Even older notions of citizenship, then, carried one group of personal markers or identities with it, designations based on race, sex, and class. This did not make it easier in the long run, however, to expand the laundry list of personal attributes befitting a citizen. For one thing, to the extent that personal identities or characteristics determined power in the older model of citizenship, their acceptance was tacit. It was the mute social hierarchies of status systems like slavery and the family that did the work of supporting the power inhering in those identities, not the formal claims of liberal citizenship as committed to paper by the Founders.

The status structures that supported traditional citizenship were not to survive the nineteenth century intact; no system was more clearly marked for destruction by social reformers. Eighteenth-century reform was characterized by political philosophies and institutions that would limit the autocratic power of the state. Nineteenth-century reform, at least in America, made its mark by extending that same criticism of irresponsible power to the quasi-private status relationships in an attempt to bring them down. Both abolitionists and women's rights activists elaborated Jefferson's eloquent point that no man was by nature booted and spurred to ride another, firmly rejecting the idea that law or custom could invest any human being with authority over any other; and in fact, by the late nineteenth century, the sphere of private powers that constituted the world of status relationships had measurably shrunk. With them went the system of private governance that had kept order in a world where the state commanded only rudimentary force, having little police power and no regulatory agencies. As patriarchal structures deteriorated—slavery becoming illegal, family rule softened by a new egalitarian and humanitarian ethos—the quasi-official layer of intermediate authority that had stood between dependent classes and direct state power gave way as well.

The decline of status relationships and the enfranchisement of new groups undermined the context for an exclusive and unitary citizenship. In the antebellum years, though, finding a rationale for expanding citizenship status to include former subordinates was not easy for proponents of reform, in large part because the traditional unarticulated template of citizenship and its association with privileged identities were so strong. The disfranchised were short on whiteness and maleness; and slaves in particular had little status, property, or education to commend them. Again, abolitionists in particular had little reason to love arguments from group characteristics, or expect their success, and publicly rejected them at every turn. The tack they did take, however, opened a channel through which future claimants—women in particular—might begin to fashion arguments for group rights.

Articulating claims to privilege or legal recourse based on essential characteristics was a novel and dicey approach. It was an approach, however, that antebellum reformers had to take. Precisely to avoid the problem of their lack of traditional qualifications, abolitionists began to argue for political privileges or protection for African Americans as "natural" persons, because they felt pain and pleasure and had immortal souls, rather than because they possessed status or attributes that set them off from the rest of humanity. In reform discourse, and subsequently in political discourse, universal concepts of dignity, autonomy, and personhood began to replace elite categories of honor and status as the foundation for political participation. Reformers rushed to claim the mantle of citizenship for the legal benefits it would bring the disfranchised. At the same time they put forward theories of the "rights" of natural persons under which the most common human ordinances and activities—marriage, work, the needs of the body and soul—became dignified as worthy of political attention, and as the source of the "rights" that would protect those natural functions. In this way, the state was forced to take account of "private" experiences such as physical pain or family and sexual relationships that previously had been excluded from the persona of the citizen.

Thus, although the category of "citizen" formally survived as simply an expanded version of its former self, the standing and function of the citizen changed dramatically. No longer defined by the inherent cohesion of exclusivity or common attributes, and no longer automatically carrying with it the delegation of power over other individuals, citizenship claims came to depend on the qualities of the natural person in a way that provided a point of entry for personal characteristics into the political sphere.

Just as it was the common characteristics of humanity—the possession of a body and soul—that gave political entitlement in this argument, those same characteristics also gave rise to rights and protections. Subordinating the citizen to the person, abolitionists insisted that, important as the civic rights fought for by the Founders and enumerated in the Constitution were, the rights-bearing individual needed protection, not just in the public square, but in more private pursuits as well.

Antebellum reformers, not content with half measures, mounted a two-pronged attack on traditional sources of law and custom, savaging both the customary rule of status relationships and the formal rule of positive law. But while strategy might have dictated a turn to law to contain the dominion of petty domestic tyrants newly dispossessed, the group of radical Unitarians, Garrisonian abolitionists, and liberal women's activists I am concerned with here attacked positive law with just as much ferocity as they opposed private power. Down the road, reformers would have to grapple with the expanded powers of the post-Reconstruction government, and with the paradox that equality at home often meant "calling in the giant" of the state. But the antebellum movements that helped give rise to a flourishing new rhetoric of individual rights were unrelenting in their critique of the unitary categories of personhood that uniform regulations necessarily supposed, seeing them as gross impositions on the individuality of the person.

The tender regard that reformers showed for the individuality of the person went hand in hand with a new heuristic style that emphasized more personal or subjective forms of authority. Both the sources for and applications of the new respect for personal experiences and ideas as morally authoritative were legion in antebellum America. One source was German romanticism, which, in reaction against Enlightenment rationalism's assumptions of the uniformity of persons and the corresponding universality of laws, stressed subjectivity, originality, and diversity, as well as the roles of intuition and experience in revealing the right and the true. Certainly Kant's efforts to relocate morality in the individual were attractive to radical Unitarians and Transcendentalists, insofar as they understood him. But for most, whose tastes ran more to the British romantics, Coleridge in particular helped to popularize German romantic philosophy secondhand. In addition, the Scottish Common Sense scholars, whose teachings were pervasive in American institutions and influenced evangelicals and liberals alike, reintroduced certain forms of intuitionism into American moral philosophy, particularly the belief that each individual possessed a potentially complete innate moral sense, whose evidence was more trustworthy than authoritative sermons or didactic treatises. As Ronald Walters suggests, by the 1830s "there existed in America and in Europe a greater suspicion of intellect and a higher faith in emotions; the moral sense, as a result, gained stature from being identified with sentiment and feeling."

On the literary front, two popular nineteenth-century movements, romanticism and sentimentalism, both broke with classical and Enlightenment epistemological modes, abandoning models of uniformity for ones that stressed the depth and diversity of human experience, and emphasizing imagination, intuition, and empathy over reason and knowledge. Transcendentalism, too, was a homegrown intuitionist philosophy inspired by romanticism that manifested itself through its widely read literary productions. An outgrowth rather than the antithesis of Unitarianism, the Transcendental movement shared some members and strong intellectual sympathies with antinomian abolitionists. Emerson staked out his ground against the mainstream Unitarian religion of reason in his infamous "Divinity School Address" delivered at Harvard in 1837, declaring that truth "is an intuition. It cannot be received at second hand." The answer to moral dilemmas, he suggested, cannot be found in bibles, constitutions, laws, or churches: "The Devil nestles comfortably into them all. There is no help but in the head and heart and hamstrings of a man." Abandoning the possibility of the comforts and safeguards of the external law internalized, Emerson cast the individual onto his own resources, with "no church for him but his believing prayer; no Constitution but his dealing well and justly with his neighbors." This same confidence in humans' innate and God-given moral nature as a reliable guide to right and wrong proved a strong point of agreement for a wide variety of antebellum reformers.

In the political arena, the intuitive moral faculty was known by its other name, conscience. The appeal to conscience as a superior form of truth seeking had a venerable history going back to the Protestant Reformation's elevation of private judgment, or the "Christian Liberty" of uncoerced belief. Lockean liberalism, grounded as much or more in the individual's material interests and experiences rather than in the inner life of the spirit, defended the citizen's right to hold any set of beliefs, but downplayed the function of conscience as a way of knowing, a method of inquiry, or a dynamic component of communication between individuals engaged in a common moral quest. Sheldon Wolin has described Locke's distrust of conscience's role as an effort to limit it to "an internalized expression of external rules rather than the externalized expression of internal convictions." By 1830 the Lockean demotion of private judgment did not sit well with liberal reformers in matters spiritual or political: the innate ideas which Locke had so convincingly dismissed reappeared in religious reform thought. Post-Revolutionary movements concerned with reasserting the moral authority of innate knowledge and the inner life reestablished conscience as a subjective and highly individualized function. Although there was some disagreement about its limitations, conscience, associated as it had traditionally been with piety and a heart open to God's will, commanded respect from a broad spectrum of antebellum Protestants from liberals to moderate evangelicals. For reformers, individual conscience became the highest expression of individual morality, which itself became the highest expression of right. Thomas Wentworth Higginson told the story from the East, popular again today, of the elephant resting on a stack of tortoises. But when asked what the last one rested on, Higginson—constitutionally unable to utter the response "another tortoise"—answered that it rested on "conscience and Reason, and if these are not infallible, nothing else is."

Perhaps most important for the development of an individual rights philosophy in this period, in radical reform thought conscience was a dynamic process, rather than a possessed attribute or a set of beliefs. The conscience that fed on "formal precedents and rules, [t]he low expediency of the states, the hollow maxims of the schools" was a frozen, insipid affair. It was William Ellery Channing's work—tremendously influential for radical Unitarians, Transcendentalists, Garrisonian abolitionists, and women's rights advocates alike—that best laid out its parameters. Spiritual freedom required perpetual vigilance; it was "moral energy . . . put forth against the world, and thus liberating the intellect, conscience, and will. . . . That mind alone is free which . . . in obedience to [God's will], governs itself, reveres itself, exerts faithfully its best powers, and unfolds itself by well doing." The free mind resists "passive or hereditary faith," habit, and public opinion in favor of constant, vigorous moral scrutiny and interrogations of authority. Conscience in reform thought had a critical role in public life, as a check on power and authority. But, like rights themselves, it was an attribute of the natural person, not controlled by or a gift of the state. Each individual soul was endowed by God with a conscience, whatever his or her station. The high functionalism of liberal Protestantism dictated that no faculty or talent was given that was not meant to be used; the right to exercise conscience was "guarantied . . . by the same principle that ensures us the use of our hands and feet, our eyes and ears," and was as dynamic and individual as those capacities.

The antebellum emphasis on the conscience's intuitive and immediate grasp of truth, "as the flower turns to the sun," and on the process of examining the legislator within for moral guidance, described a relation between the Christian and the law that departed from classic notions of sovereignty. Obedience to law for the "good man" became, not automatic compliance with sovereign commands, but an interactive process between two lawgivers, the public and the private. James Freeman Clarke sought to downplay the danger of anarchy by suggesting that in most cases the private lawmaker—conscience—sanctioned righteous public rules. While the Christian conscience might nullify the law, Clarke asserted, few had consciences so morally developed: "good men obey the law mainly from conscience, bad men mainly from fear, and the majority of men from self-interest." But at every juncture the good man, the moral role model, engaged in a complex assessment of right and wrong. Human rights, the particular province of the Christian conscience, required an especially careful evaluation: "rights do not admit of very precise definition, for the spiritual cannot be weighed and measured like the material." The Unitarian reformer Theodore Parker described Christianity not as a system of doctrines but as a method of moral scrutiny. In the liberal Protestant scheme that so influenced the growth of reform thought, the individual's role as law-finder was paramount.

The opposite side of the coin of individual conscience was liberal reformers' intense antilegalism, their antipathy to what they called "external" law, whether it was religious or secular. The Bible was toppled from its preeminent place as the infallible source of God's word and, while still recognized as a sacred text, subjected to the indignities of interpretation and critical examination. Thomas Wentworth Higginson labeled the Old Testament merely an "arbitrary collection of the best early Hebrew literature." Far from an infallible word, he argued, the Scriptures offered multiple interpretive possibilities, chosen by each reader according to "his own temperament, education, and circumstances"—a faithful echo of the revered Dr. Channing. American reformers didn't need European critical theory to clue them in to the problem of scriptural indeterminacy; pro- and antislavery forces often waged war in scriptural terms, each side wielding shards of divine writ to good effect. Reformers across a wide spectrum argued that the Bible, like "all books . . . require[s] in the reader or hearer the constant exercise of reason." The provocative Henry Clark Wright argued ad absurdum that the Bible was no more authoritative a script than Mother Goose.

The rejection of legalism served as a leitmotif in reformers' struggle against the slave-tolerating civil state as well. Bronson Alcott declared, "Church and State are responsible to me; not I to them . . . They cease to deserve our veneration from the moment they violate our consciences. . . . Why would I employ a church to write my creed or a state to govern me? Why not write my own creed? Why not govern myself?" The rigid formalism of law characterized the loveless reign of orthodox theology, as well as the corrupt rule of the slave-tolerating civil state. The letter of the law was literally killing; only its spirit gave life. Even antislavery conventions' own formal procedures came in for mockery: a group of adherents, adrift overnight in a small boat without provisions, passed resolutions asserting that they had had both rest and a repast, in parody of abolitionists' endless enthusiasm for platform measures. In fact, abolitionists assessed law's ability to effect change as on a par with that of the Indiana legislature, which in this century passed a bill setting the value of pi at an even three. Injustice and delusion did not change their spots because they were cloaked in statutory authority. As one abolitionist asked rhetorically, "When the French Assembly voted there was no God, was there, therefore, no God?"

In assessing the efficacy of human law, reformers drew on liberal Protestantism's new model of human life, both physical and spiritual, as naturally good and reflecting God's highest designs. The naturalist conventions of liberal religion in this period saw the entire physical world as harmoniously attuned to the same divine order and thus reflecting divine will more fully than older forms of authority such as revelation or miracles. Human law, then, should be judged by its conformity to the natural order of human life, rather than be seen as constituting that order. Critics often turned to the stock of human experience to illustrate law's impotence; they were fond of pointing out that any law that contravened human moral nature—a law sanctioning adultery or forbidding parental love, for example—was a dead letter regardless of its sovereign imprint. For better and worse, positive law was only good insofar as it conformed to the dictates of God and human nature. Rejecting any notion of law or rights as drawn from anterior sources, reformers instead used the patterns of human life as the measure of positive law.

Statutory law came in for particular criticism; it most fully represented the benighted attempt to capture the dynamic process of conscience-based moral inquiry in a frozen form, rather than appealing "from statute to justice . . . from the state to the soul . . . from dead words to living spirit." William Lloyd Garrison vowed never to consult "any other statute book than the bible," since government was too fallible and insensitive an instrument to be entrusted with the enactment of rules. Reformers criticized the gall of legislators who understood their job as constructing rather than discovering laws, "which they can no more do than they can manufacture the laws of gravitation and motion." The abolitionist William Goodell argued that, rather than searching for rulers, the people must realize that "the LAW is already made to their hands, (the law of their social nature as well as of their physical constitutions) that all they have to do is learn to obey and apply it."

Reformers sought to hold the state as well as positive law to a standard of accountability modeled on the moral individual. They insisted that groups "moving in a body and called the state" be held morally accountable under exactly the same rules as the individual: each individual "carries with him into the service of the community, the same binding law of morality and religion which ought to control his conduct in private life." No combination of individuals could get together to change the moral character of an act, nor escape moral accountability by acting at the behest of a group. Garrison made a sweeping dismissal of all forms of human lawmaking power in 1854, when at a Fourth of July celebration he burned in rapid succession a copy of the Fugitive Slave Law, a judicial decision, and the Constitution, to the wild cheers of his audience.

For its opponents, higher-law methods of consulting conscience or intuitive moral reasoning represented the antithesis of political truths "publicly arrived at and publicly demonstrable." When higher law challenged positive law on its own turf, notably in the fugitive slave cases, it was a flop. But the intuitive model of truth-seeking using human nature as a guide to divine laws was of paramount importance in another area: it provided reformers with a new method for discerning the "rights" of the individual and substantively shifted the focus from the rights of citizens in their public lives to the rights of persons in both their physical and spiritual lives. So closely was the abolitionist notion of rights tied to embodied personhood that arguments analogizing natural rights to bodily attributes were introduced as the most compelling. The right to liberty, William Hosmer argued, was no more within the control of government than the rights to see, to eat, or to walk; such "conditions of being" fall solely under God's jurisdiction. Conscience, the arbiter of rights, was a faculty so elemental it was as "man's . . . eyes, or his hands, or his feet—that is, a part of himself—made by the Creator." Relying on their Northern audiences' own conviction of self-ownership, abolitionists stressed that natural rights belong to the slave as "inalienably as the blood in his veins, or the breath in his lungs" (although in fact both were in doubt); to be deprived of rights would be the equivalent of "dismemberment." Humans' rights were made "unmistakably plain" by scrutinizing their natural constitutions; to mistake the needs and capacities that gave rise to rights would be about as likely as attempting "to walk on the hands instead of the feet, or to hear with the eyes instead of the ears."

The paradox here of course was that, on the one hand, Channing, Parker, and others argued vehemently for the immutability and universality of individual rights in order to establish their independence of the state, declaring that the notion that rights were "uncertain, mutable, and conceded by society, shows a lamentable ignorance of human nature." On the other hand, rights as they envisioned them were in fact as individual and open-ended as the vista for each body and soul. The Christian notion of rights carried with it a notion of universal entitlement, that "each child as a birthright has a code of laws engraven on its nature." But because God's design was most fully revealed not in the written word but in the natural world, the laws "written on body and soul" were also as distinctive as each body and each soul. Christian universalism was crossed with romantic individualism to create an unstable hybrid formulation. Recognizing both the body's and the soul's claims to individuality, Gerrit Smith had proclaimed, "Fifty or a hundred people in Peterboro or Cazenovia, however much alike in their views and spirit, should no more be required to adopt a common religious creed than to shorten or stretch out their bodies to a common length." Rights, William Goodell similarly claimed,

> must grow out of [man's] essential nature, capacities, relations, duties, and destiny. To the idea of these must the idea of his rights be conformed, and by these must those rights be defined. To understand what man is, what his Creator requires him to be and to do, and what he is destined to become, is to understand man's essential and inherent rights, and the tenure by which they are held.

Subordinating the citizen to the person, abolitionists insisted that, important as the civic rights fought for by the Founders and enumerated in the Constitution were, the rights-bearing individual needed protection, not just in the public square, but in more private pursuits as well. In the early years, abolitionists disagreed over whether emancipated slaves should be granted political rights, in particular the right to vote. Many also rejected or downplayed the notion of social rights lest it raise the controversial specter of intermarriage or social mingling, potentially detrimental to the cause. Much less contentious was the notion that all slaves should be protected by such civil rights as would allow them the equal protection of the laws of property, contract, and crime.

But the entitlement that abolitionists claimed passionately for slaves, and the one developed most fully in Garrisonian abolitionism, was to human or natural rights, the rights of slaves as "intelligent creatures of God, formed with susceptibilities of happiness and entitled to its pursuit." The natural person's laundry list of rights was expansive and open-ended; one particularly full definition comes from William Goodell's *The Democracy of Christianity*, which enumerates

> the right to be what his Creator made him, to do what he requires of him, to become what he designs him to become; the right to exercise freely and to expand fully his own faculties, unrestrained, except by the law of rectitude and the corresponding rights of those by whom he is surrounded; the right to obey God rather than

man; the right to do right, and to refuse wrong; the consequent right to investigate, to know, to utter, to argue freely, according to the dictates of conscience . . . the right to worship God in accordance with his own convictions; the right to provide for his own wants, and the wants of those naturally dependent upon him; the right to himself, to his own muscles, intellect, affections, and volitions; the right to the avails of products of his own industry, and to the free sale and interchange of them; the right to his equal share of the elements of nature, the earth, the air, and the ocean; to a dwelling place and a habitation on the earth which God has made and given to the children of men. In a word, the right to life, to liberty, to the pursuit of happiness, the pursuit of moral excellency, or immortal blessedness.

This strain of natural rights discourse represents a substantial departure from the standard menu of constitutional rights put in place by the revolutionary settlement. Going well beyond the vague formulations of "life, liberty, and happiness," abolitionists focused in a way earlier theorists had not on the physical wants and needs of the body on its daily rounds, whose deprivations slavery made so obvious. Rights claims that came under this heading included those to self-ownership; freedom of movement; freedom from physical abuse; the right to marry and establish domestic relations; to refuse nonconsensual sexual relations; to work and keep one's earnings; and to engage in social relations with others in their community. Giving new content to old forms, abolitionists claimed that these attributes gave rise to rights that were "natural," not in the sense of being anterior or uniform, but in the sense of being subjective and personal, deriving from the needs, habits, and intimate relations of the person.

In the early federal period, natural rights arguments, the common coin of revolutionary rhetoric, had been subordinated to the project of re-creating a system of institutions, including a positivist jurisprudence that would bind the whole. But natural law regained its rule in the philosophies of antebellum abolitionism and women's rights movements. And like their revolutionary ancestors, these reformers gave another half-twist to their theory. Under the English constitution, early rights declarations laid claim to concessions from those in power and served to frame a new relationship between the citizen and the state. Eighteenth-century American revolutionaries denied the state as the font of rights, but their rights claims largely sounded in the tradition of regulating the relationship between citizen and state in the public sphere. The antebellum reform tradition both denied that rights were from the state and also denied that they were about the state, or solely about the role of the citizen in his public capacity. Rather, this group of reformers cast rights in broader, aspirational terms; rights language expressed the terms on which individuals could best live out God's designs for human happiness. What was "natural," they claimed, was whatever contributed to the full realization of human potential.

At the same time, nature—spruced up into a nice civil order by the Founders—regained a worldly quality rooted in the intellectual, spiritual, and physical functions of everyday life. The pursuit of happiness, always a somewhat vague component in the revolutionary era, took on new specificity in claims to food, clothing, jobs, education, family relations, bodily integrity, and the rights to satisfy those claims. As Elisha Hurlbut wrote in his influential *Essays on Human Rights and their Political Guaranties*, "Wherever Nature has ordained desire, she has spread before it the means of gratification.—From this we infer the right to its indulgence—and hence, also, the rights of man." Many echoed Hurlbut, arguing fervently that natural rights "emanated from the nature and wants and emotions of mankind." Natural rights, they agreed, could not be pulled down from the sky, but could only be discerned by observing closely the mundane welter of human life. Reformers expanded on the belief that God gave no need or desire that he did not mean to be fulfilled, and no capacity that was not to be used. They made functionalist rights claims reflecting this belief in the congruence between capacity and right: "the wing of the bird indicates its right to fly; and the fin of the fish the right to swim. So in human beings, the existence of a power presupposes the right to its use."

These and similar arguments circulated through large, interconnected reform circles and were repeated in writings, lectures, and literature for public consumption; they did yeoman's service for abolitionists and women's rights advocates alike. (One man testified to the interchangeable nature of philosophies across a wide spectrum of reform movements when he refused a health nut's offer of a piece of Graham bread, saying that he had noted that when you began with Graham bread, you ended with infidelity.) In a broad sense, the natural person's claims paved the way for bringing the attributes of the private person into political discourse for the first time as a basis of entitlement;

in fact, the particular deprivations and abuses of slavery made it impossible to avoid that move. Clearly, deriving rights from a common human nature was good strategy; the need to establish a new foundation for political participation required the elevation of elemental human traits like the possession of a body, mind, and soul and the appetites that went with them into an argument for political privilege. There was no other basis on which to establish a political platform wide enough to accommodate those seeking access.

Such rights claims should be confused neither with a full-blown or authentic individualism nor with a strong group rights theory. In the years before the Civil War, abolitionist claims, as well as a large part of women's public demands, were based in strong universalist arguments about the common needs and talents of individuals in the brotherhood of man, and looked to broad entitlements based on patterns of social behavior generalized across racial groups and genders. In fact the argument for physical, intellectual, and spiritual sameness was critical to the enterprise of admitting slaves to political power; arguments from difference were shunned. Legal claims in particular gained power from asserting the likeness of the dispossessed to those with entitlements; rights by analogy, the most comfortable mode of legal reasoning, work best when the claim "I am like that rights-bearing person" is met with an answering embrace from the rights-bearing public. Here again the physical nature of humankind played a newly prominent role in the assertion of rights, as abolitionists and slave narrators relied heavily on graphic accounts of the pain experienced by slaves during punishment, not only to incite the compassion of the audience but also to make the point that slaves' experience of abuse was identical to what the reader would experience under similar circumstances. The portrayal of the slaves' pain proved the likeness of the human body across racial lines; as an abolitionist Miss Smith wrote of seeing a slave beaten by a mob, "I am ready to testify that it was *orthodox blood*. I should not have known it from my own." This same political agenda also precluded asserting strong racial group identity claims; in the public political discourse, race was a physical feature to be erased in the interest of compassionate identification, rather than a culture-constituting attribute.

As both abolitionism and women's rights matured, it became apparent that each had somewhat different mandates and constraints in their quest to redefine citizenship and the rights-bearing person. The ideology of the early women's movement was very heavily influenced by the radical Quakers and more particularly the Unitarians who, by contrast with a more corporate Catholicism, stressed the private nature of religious experience and the supremacy of the individual conscience. It was this sensibility, expressed in Gerrit Smith's caveat that Christian creeds could not be any more uniform than bodies, that gave rise to the rejection of the monolithic and unvaried character of regulation by positive law. It remained for the most liberal wing of the postwar nineteenth-century women's movement to continue on a two-track path that diverged from abolitionism's strategy; by detailing the patterns of life experience of women as a group as distinct from men as a basis for the rights of the natural person, in this case the natural woman; and at the same time by claiming for women a sphere of bodily autonomy that allowed for individual experience like the personal spiritual experience of liberal Protestantism.

First, the attempts of women's rights advocates to diagnose their wrongs by describing ill treatment meted out to women as a group differed from antislavery workers' similar attempts in an important way: unlike slaves, women confidently expected that, even after the reforms they were seeking to rectify their situation were enacted, they would not lose their former identity and blend into the whole, but would continue in society as a definable group with characteristics that for some purposes set them permanently apart from male citizens. Rejecting an equality that was ignorant of gender, role, or duty, women argued for the rights that would enable them to act their parts as wives and mothers. Keeping their gendered domain in mind, they echoed reform concerns about the gross instrument of uniform positive law, calling it "wholly masculine: it is created by our type or class of man nature. The framers of all legal compacts are thus restricted to the . . . thoughts, feelings, biases of men. . . . we can be represented only by our peers." Arguments of this sort made claims, not just for reform of particular laws, but that law recognize and accommodate as citizens a group defined by shared permanent attributes and interests not common to all citizens, not as a temporary measure until the discrepancy was corrected but as a new model of legal response to a permanent subgrouping. They stressed that law must vary its touch on different persons and groups to allow the full self-realization of all citizens; as the *Lily* proclaimed, "let man cease to . . . compel [woman] by his cruel and unnatural statutes to act in violation of her will and conscience."

This was not the only mode of portraying women's entitlement;

throughout the nineteenth century, equality and difference arguments went side by side in women's rights rhetoric. For the most part, though, those arguments were not randomly mixed; it is possible to discern two separate women's rights discourses coming out of the antebellum period. The first, usually associated with claims to traditional civic rights like the vote and property ownership, tracked both Revolutionary rhetoric and abolitionist discourse in stressing the commonality of human nature and the equality of inalienable rights, making its case with businesslike appeals to republican sentiments on the basis of "the great doctrine of equality as set forth in the Declaration of Independence." Like abolition, this argument made no effort to delineate women as a separate group with distinct common characteristics; sensibly enough, since the goal here was inclusion in an established rights paradigm.

But in addition, largely under the influence of Elizabeth Cady Stanton, woman suffrage's more radical members began to speak of domestic wrongs—wife abuse, unavailability of divorce, and loss of custody rights in particular—as situations that should give rise to rights; without them, women's physical and moral sensibilities were outraged without redress. In describing the model family, noncoercion rather than equality was the watchword. Instead of relying on the public political language of equality when outlining particular wrongs women suffered in the context of domestic relationships, reformers relied more heavily on language of personal fulfillment and the natural model of family life; on women's natural rights, similar to those claimed for slaves, to be happy wives and mothers. Again, while criticism of slavery was designed to bring the institution down, nineteenth-century criticism of the stringent anti-woman bias of family law was designed to reform the family, but not to destroy either monogamous, heterosexual marriage or the parent–child relationship. Women envisioned an ongoing rights regime—the maternal preference in custody cases is the best example—that would recognize and foster their best natures, again as a permanent subgroup of the citizenry as a whole.

Women's diagnoses of their wrongs were conveyed in archetypal tales of husbands' abuse, coercion, and desertion that made clear that the injustice worked by men's social and legal privilege touched every class of women. At the very least, early feminism made a compelling case for a group wrong of a sort that could not be dealt with by temporary expedients, but only by restructuring the law to accommodate its citizens' distinct gender identities. It also significantly furthered the natural rights agenda by advancing the interests of the private person/woman in marriage, sexual relations, reproduction, and parenting as appropriate claims in the public sphere. This agenda both forced various agents of state power to take cognizance of the differential needs of citizens and helped over the course of subsequent decades to expand the definition of the liberal citizen as one who was constituted by substantial rights in the private sphere, as well as by the traditional ability to exercise civic rights like property ownership and the political franchise. While these claims of the "private" individual did not make their way into constitutional jurisprudence until the later twentieth century, they were recognized to some degree by state and local courts and legislatures. By the Gilded Age, divorce was easier, married women were more secure in their property, the maternal preference in custody cases was well on its way to becoming the norm, and domestic abuse had at least been made a contested issue. In part, though there were certainly other driving forces, these developments had come about in response to the effective delineation of women's wrongs, specifically the wrongs of the woman in her private domestic role.

Whether the earliest of the founding mothers made effective claims to group rights, as opposed to group wrongs, is a more difficult question. Activist women often denied that they were seeking any kind of class or group right, arguing that it was exactly the treatment of people in groups or classes that had created the feudal politics of status relationships. At the level of theory, the Stantonites denied that women could or should be helped as a group. As good liberals should, they denied that protectionist measures could do anything but create dependence.

Rather, like abolitionists in the immediate aftermath of the war, they put their faith in their formal freedom, asking "When we talk of woman's rights, is not the right to her person, to her happiness, to her life, the first on the list?" The freed woman, like the freed slave, should be able to compete and flourish without seeking favor from the government.

Stanton elaborated on individual women's freedom and bodily autonomy by analogizing the domestic sphere to the market and arguing for women's "right" to be left alone to make their own decisions about marriage, divorce, and sexual behavior. Liberal feminists, relying on religious and abolitionist antecedents, argued for the elevation of a new decision maker, the individual, in questions involving intimate relationships; only the individual could make the subjective judgment whether to pursue an intimate association or to cut ties because the relationship proved offensive or coercive. In some respects this was a retrenchment from the early aspirational rights language of abolitionism, which sought to identify as rights positive needs including basic staples like clothing, shelter, and education—rights that, had they been recognized, would have required affirmative remedies from government. Rather, liberal women's rights language in its classic theoretical form sought to limit government's intrusion into the lives of citizens, a familiar form of rights claim, although here it applied to new domestic situations.

But indulging in this argument, whatever its political appeal, prevented liberal feminists from recognizing that their own rhetoric and political designs were often inconsistent with the simple libertarian notion "my body, my right." Even in the early years of the movement, some of the relief measures women sought in fact involved not limiting the power of the state but "calling in the giant" to redress wrongs imposed by other citizens—in this case largely husbands. Seeking relief in cases of custody disputes and wife abuse, for example, could not be characterized as a limitation on state power, but only as empowering the state to play the decision maker in what had formerly been privately decided matters.

In fact, whatever the strength of this limited form of rights claim in the 1870s, by the 1880s and 1890s the individualist formulation had lost much of its appeal; the liberal wing of the women's movement languished accordingly, while the evangelical suffrage and temperance organization, the Woman's Christian Temperance Union, gained ten times as many adherents as the National Women's Suffrage Association. From a different generation and a different persuasion, the WCTU eschewed the notions of privacy and individual autonomy that liberal feminists had taken from Protestant abolitionism, stressing a more communitarian approach. But they did continue to bring domestic matters into the political arena, in most respects much more successfully than liberal women had. Nor were they afraid to address the problems of women and families as problems of groups. Using a strong normative model of the family derived from middle-class evangelical Protestant culture, they pushed for a progressive array of relief programs, including nutritional programs, the eight-hour workday, and the living wage, at the same time as they pursued a theocratic agenda that sought to censor a variety of recreational habits, including reading "bad" literature and drinking, while seeking to install public prayer and Bible reading in the schools. (Little tattlers and liars)

In all of their endeavors, this group was among the earliest of the women's groups to seek relief, not through individual rights rhetoric (although they did not discard it entirely), but through group claims that returned more to the "need" language of early abolitionism. In addition, through their work in nascent public health and educational posts, they were instrumental in helping to establish the social framework of voluntarism that became the bedrock of the bureaucratic welfare state. Like a good mother, the "maternal state," as WCTU president Frances Willard called it, recognized the intimate needs of its citizens. But, circumventing the individually tailored remedies of rights litigation, they relied more on corporate forms of relief, more on protections than rights. In their politics they captured the concern for the needs of the natural person that had eluded the liberal feminists in their postwar stress on autonomy; but at the price of forsaking a healthy skepticism about the capacity of a uniform or universal form of regulation to administer the needs of individual citizens.

By the end of the nineteenth century, as I pointed out in the beginning, it was clear that citizenship was no longer equated with the private power of status relationships (and this despite the fact that women's franchise was not yet secured). But what of the abolitionists' attempts to integrate the notion of the citizen with the natural person, or to create a state that was truly responsive to the needs of citizens whose identities were now disparate, and whose needs were highly individual? In the nineteenth century, at least, the women's movement was the site of some of the most heated debate on this subject; but, by the end, the story is of two opponents, each of whom had given away one-half of the store. In theory (and with some exaggeration), liberal feminists posited an autonomous individual, whose new rights in the private sphere would consist in a skimpy government turning a blind eye to women's choices in the domestic setting. Evangelical feminists, on the other hand, made the personal into the political, but at the expense of respect for individual needs.

Selected Bibliography of Relevant Works by Elizabeth Battelle Clark

"Religion, Rights, and Difference in the Early Woman's Rights Movement," *Wisconsin Women's Law Journal* 3 (1987): 29–58.

"Self-Ownership and the Political Theory of Elizabeth Cady Stanton," *Connecticut Law Review* 21, no. 4 (summer 1989): 905–43.

"Matrimonial Bonds: Slavery and Divorce in Nineteenth-Century America," *Law and History Review* 8:1 (spring 1990): 25–54.

"The Sacred Rights of the Weak: Pain, Sympathy, and the Culture of Individual Rights in Antebellum America," *Journal of American History* 82:3 (September 1995): 463–93.

"The Politics of God and the Woman's Vote: Religion in the American Suffrage Movement, 1848–1895" (Ph.D. dissertation, History, Princeton University, 1989).

The Subject of True Feeling: Pain, Privacy, and Politics

Lauren Berlant

Liberty finds no refuge in a jurisprudence of doubt[1]

Pain

Ravaged wages and ravaged bodies saturate the global marketplace in which the United States seeks desperately to compete "competitively," as the euphemism goes, signifying a race that will be won by the nations whose labor conditions are most optimal for profit.[2] In the United States the media of the political public sphere regularly register new scandals of the proliferating sweatshop networks "at home" and "abroad," which has to be a good thing, because it produces *feeling* and with it something at least akin to *consciousness* that can lead to *action*.[3]

---

1. *Planned Parenthood of Southeastern Pennsylvania v. Casey* 112 S.Ct. 2791 (1992), at 2803.

2. See, for example, George DeMartino and Stephen Cullenberg, "Beyond the Competitiveness Debate: An Internationalist Agenda," *Social Text* 41 (1994): 11–39.

3. Take the case of the talk show host Kathie Lee Gifford, whose clothing line at the U.S. low-price megastore Wal-Mart generated for her ten million dollars of profit in its first year. During May and June 1996 Gifford was exposed by Charles Kernaghan, of the National Labor Education Fund in Support of Worker and Human Rights in Central America, for allowing her clothes to be made by tragically underpaid and mistreated young Honduran children, mostly girls. A Lexis/Nexus search under the keywords *Kathie Lee Gifford/Child Labor* nets close to two hundred stories, from all over the world, reporting on this event. A few main plots emerge from these stories: it is cast as a revenge story against privilege from the ranks of the less well-off, which strips from Gifford the protection of her perky, populist, and intimate persona to reveal the entrepreneurial profiteer beneath; it implicates an entire culture of celebrity-centered consumerism (Jaclyn

Yet, even as the image of the traumatized worker proliferates, even as evidence of exploitation is found under every rock or commodity, it competes with a normative/utopian image of the U.S. citizen who remains unmarked, framed, and protected by the private trajectory of his life project, which is sanctified at the juncture where the unconscious meets history: the American Dream.[4] In that story one's identity is not borne of suffering, mental, physical, or economic. If the U.S. worker is lucky enough to live at an economic moment that sustains the Dream, he gets to appear at his *least* national when he is working and at his most national at leisure, with his family or in semipublic worlds of other men producing surplus manliness (e.g., via sports). In the American dreamscape his identity is private property, a zone in which structural obstacles and cultural differences fade into an ether of prolonged, deferred, and individuating enjoyment that he has earned and that the nation has helped him to earn. Meanwhile, exploitation only appears as a scandalous nugget in the sieve of memory when it can be condensed into an exotic thing of momentary fascination, a squalor of the bottom too horrible to be read in its own actual banality.

The exposed traumas of workers in ongoing extreme conditions do not generally induce more than mourning on the part of the state and

---

Smith/K-Mart, The Gap, Spike Lee/Michael Jordan/Nike) that is organized around a "virtuous" role modelesque public figure or label that seems to certify healthy conscientious social membership for consumers; it becomes an exemplum of the banality of sweatshop labor in the United States and around the world; and a call to belated conscience. Through Gifford's apparent intimacy with her devoted audience a "public" outraged by child exploitation seemed instantly to emerge, which led in turn to a kind of state action, involving an intensified federal push for voluntary covenants against child labor and subminimum wages (measured by "local," not U.S., standards of remuneration). It also eventuated in the development of a new label, "No Sweat," to be put on any clothes produced by adequately paid workers—a sad substitute for the union labels of years past. This issue has quickly joined child abuse as an ongoing zone of fascination and (mainly) impotent concern in the political public sphere. See, for a relatively unjaded extended example, Sidney Schamberg, "Six Cents an Hour," *Life* (June 1996): 38–48. For a more general view of the political/media exploitation of the exploited child figure, see McKenzie Wark, "Fresh Maimed Babies: The Uses of Innocence," *Transition* 65 (Spring 1995): 36–47.

4. For more exposition on the ways political cultures that value abstract or universal personhood produce privileged bodies and identities that travel unmarked, unremarkable, and free of structural humiliation, see Lauren Berlant, "National Brands/National Bodies: *Imitation of Life*," in *The Phantom Public Sphere*, ed. Bruce Robbins (Minneapolis: University of Minnesota Press, 1993), 173–208; and *The Queen of America Goes to Washington City: Essays on Sex and Citizenship* (Durham: Duke University Press, 1997); Richard Dyer, "White," *The Matter of Images* (New York: Routledge, 1993), 141–63; and Peggy Phelan, *Unmarked: The Politics of Performance* (New York: Routledge, 1993).

the public culture to whose feeling-based opinions the state is said to respond. Mourning is what happens when a grounding object is lost, is dead, no longer living (to you). Mourning is an experience of irreducible boundedness: I am here, I am living, he is dead, I am mourning. It is a beautiful, not sublime, experience of emancipation: mourning supplies the subject the definitional perfection of a being no longer in flux. It takes place over a distance: even if the object who induces the feeling of loss and helplessness is neither dead nor at any great distance from where you are.[5] In other words, mourning can also be an act of aggression, of social deathmaking: it can perform the evacuation of significance from actually-existing subjects. Even when liberals do it, one might say, "others" are ghosted for a good cause.[6] The sorrow songs of scandal that sing of the exploitation that is always "elsewhere" (even a few blocks away) are in this sense aggressively songs of mourning. Play them backward, and the military march of capitalist triumphalism (*The Trans-Nationale*) can be heard. Its lyric, currently crooned by every organ of record in the United States, is about necessity. It exhorts citizens to understand that the "bottom line"[7] of national life is neither

---

5. The essay of Sigmund Freud's summarized here is "Mourning and Melancholia," in *General Psychological Theory*, intro. Philip Rieff (New York: Collier Books, 1963), 164–79.

6. The best work on the civilized barbarism of mourning has been done on AIDS discourse in U.S. culture: see Douglas Crimp, "Mourning and Militancy," in *Out There: Marginalization and Contemporary Cultures*, ed. Russell Ferguson, Martha Gever, Trinh T. Min-ha, and Cornell West (Cambridge: MIT Press, 1990), 233–45; and virtually every essay in Douglas Crimp, ed., *AIDS: Cultural Analysis/Cultural Activism* (Cambridge: MIT Press, 1988). Crimp is especially astute on the necessary articulation of sentimentality and politics: because processes of legitimation cannot do without the production of consent, and empathetic misrecognition is one tactic for creating it. The question is how, and at what cost, different kinds of subjects and contexts of empathy are imagined in the struggle for radical social transformation. See also Jeff Nunokowa, "AIDS and the Age of Mourning," *Yale Journal of Criticism* 4, no. 2 (Spring 1991): 1–12. Judith Butler's work has also been a crucial intertext here, notably its representation of heterosexual melancholia (the disavowed experience of loss heterosexuals endure as a consequence of having to divert ongoing same-sex love/identification/attachments, a condition that expresses itself through gender normativity, heterosexual hegemony, misogyny, homophobia, and other forms of disciplinary order. This opened a space for thinking about the social function of mourning in similar contexts of normative hierarchy in which intimacies appear to have to be constructed, not suppressed. See *Gender Trouble: Feminism and the Subversion of Identity* (New York: Routledge, 1990); and *Bodies That Matter: On the Discursive Limits of Sex* (New York: Routledge, 1993).

7. On the "bottom line" as a site of political articulation and struggle, see Elizabeth Alexander, "'Can You Be BLACK and Look at This?': Reading the Rodney King Video(s)," in *The Black Public Sphere*, ed. Black Public Sphere Collective (Chicago: University of Chicago Press, 1995): 81–98.

utopia nor freedom but survival, which can only be achieved by a citizenry that eats its anger, makes no unreasonable claims on resources or control over value, and uses its most creative energy to cultivate intimate spheres while scrapping a life together flexibly in response to the market world's caprice.[8]

In this particular moment of expanding class unconsciousness that looks like consciousness emerges a peculiar, though not unprecedented, hero: the exploited child. If a worker can be infantilized, pictured as young, as small, as feminine or feminized, as starving, as bleeding and diseased, and as a (virtual) slave, the righteous indignation around procuring his survival resounds everywhere. The child must not be sacrificed to states or to profiteering. His wounded image speaks a truth that subordinates narrative: he has not "freely" chosen his exploitation; the optimism and play that are putatively the right of childhood have been stolen from him. Yet only "voluntary" steps are ever taken to try to control this visible sign of what is ordinary and systemic amid the chaos of capitalism, in order to make its localized nightmares seem uninevitable. Privatize the atrocity, delete the visible sign, make it seem *foreign*. Return the child to the family, replace the children with adults who can look dignified while being paid virtually the same revolting wage. The problem that organizes so much feeling then regains livable proportions, and the uncomfortable pressure of feeling dissipates, like so much gas.

Meanwhile, the pressure of feeling the shock of being uncomfortably political produces a cry for a double therapy—to the victim and the viewer. But before "we" appear too complacently different from the privileged citizens who desire to caption the mute image of exotic suffering with an aversively fascinated mourning (a desire for the image to be *dead*, a ghost), we must note that this feeling culture crosses over into other domains, the domains of what we call identity politics, where the wronged take up voice and agency to produce transformative testimony, which depends on an analogous conviction about the *self-evidence* and therefore the *objectivity* of painful feeling.

---

8. On the structures and rhetorics of coercive flexibility in transnational times, see David Harvey, *The Condition of Postmodernity* (London: Basil Blackwell, 1989); Roger Rouse, "Thinking through Transnationalism: Notes on the Cultural Politics of Class Relations in the Contemporary United States," *Public Culture* 7 (Winter 1995): 353–402; and Emily Martin, *Flexible Bodies: Tracking Immunity in American Culture—from the Days of Polio to the Age of AIDS* (Boston: Beacon Press, 1994).

The central concern of this essay is to address the place of painful feeling in the making of political worlds. In particular, I mean to challenge a powerful popular belief in the positive workings of something I call national sentimentality, a rhetoric of promise that a nation can be built across fields of social difference through channels of affective identification and empathy. Sentimental politics generally promotes and maintains the hegemony of the national identity form, no mean feat in the face of continued widespread intercultural antagonism and economic cleavage. But national sentimentality is more than a current of feeling that circulates in a political field: the phrase describes a long-standing contest between two models of U.S. citizenship. In one, the classic model, each citizen's value is secured by an equation between abstractness and emancipation: a cell of national identity provides juridically protected personhood for citizens regardless of anything specific about them. In the second model, which was initially organized around labor, feminist, and antiracist struggles of the nineteenth-century United States, another version of the nation is imagined as the index of collective life. This nation is peopled by suffering citizens and noncitizens whose structural exclusion from the utopian-American dreamscape exposes the state's claim of legitimacy and virtue to an acid wash of truth telling that makes hegemonic disavowal virtually impossible, at certain moments of political intensity.

Sentimentality has long been the means by which mass subaltern pain is advanced, in the dominant public sphere, as the true core of national collectivity. It operates when the pain of intimate others burns into the conscience of classically privileged national subjects, such that they feel the pain of flawed or denied citizenship as their pain. Theoretically, to eradicate the pain those with power will do whatever is necessary to return the nation once more to its legitimately utopian odor. Identification with pain, a universal true feeling, then leads to structural social change. In return, subalterns scarred by the pain of failed democracy will reauthorize universalist notions of citizenship in the national utopia, which involves believing in a redemptive notion of law as the guardian of public good. The object of the nation and the law in this light is to eradicate systemic social pain, the absence of which becomes the definition of freedom.

Yet, since these very sources of protection—the state, the law, patriotic ideology—have traditionally buttressed traditional matrices of cultural hierarchy, and since their historic job has been to protect universal subject/citizens from feeling their cultural and corporeal specificity as a political vulnerability, the imagined capacity of these institutions to assimilate to the affective tactics of subaltern counterpolitics suggests some weaknesses, or misrecognitions, in these tactics. For one thing, it may be that the sharp specificity of the traumatic model of pain implicitly mischaracterizes what a person is as what a person becomes in the experience of social negation; this model also falsely promises a sharp picture of structural violence's source and scope, in turn promoting a dubious optimism that law and other visible sources of inequality, for example, can provide the best remedies for their own taxonomizing harms. It is also possible that counterhegemonic deployments of pain as the measure of structural injustice actually sustain the utopian image of a homogeneous national metaculture, which can look like a healed or healthy body in contrast to the scarred and exhausted ones. Finally, it might be that the tactical use of trauma to describe the effects of social inequality so overidentifies the eradication of pain with the achievement of justice that it enables various confusions: for instance, the equation of pleasure with freedom or the sense that changes in feeling, even on a mass scale, amount to substantial social change. Sentimental politics makes these confusions credible and these violences bearable, as its cultural power confirms the centrality of interpersonal identification and empathy to the vitality and viability of collective life. This gives citizens something to do in response to overwhelming structural violence. Meanwhile, by equating mass society with that thing called "national culture," these important transpersonal linkages and intimacies all too frequently serve as proleptic shields, as ethically uncontestable legitimating devices for sustaining the hegemonic field.[9]

Our first example, the child laborer, a ghost of the nineteenth century, taps into a current vogue to reflect in the premature exposure of children to capitalist publicity and adult depravity the nation's moral

---

9. One critic who has not underestimated the hegemonic capacities of state deployments of pain is Elaine Scarry, *The Body in Pain: The Making and Unmaking of the World* (New York: Oxford University Press, 1985). This book remains a stunning description of the ways control over actual physical and rhetorical pain provides the state and the law with control over what constitutes collective reality, the conjuncture of beliefs and the material world. See especially part 2, on pain and imagining. Like the legal theorists and jurists whose writing this essay engages, Scarry works a with a fully state- (or institutionally) saturated concept of the subject, a relation more specific and nonuniversal than it frequently seems to be in her representation of it.

and economic decline, citing it as a scandal of citizenship, something shocking and un-American. Elsewhere I have described the ways the infantile citizen has been exploited, in the United States, to become both the inspiring sign of the painless good life and the evacuating optimistic cipher of contemporary national identity.[10] During the 1980s a desperate search to protect the United States from what seemed to be an imminently powerful alliance of parties on the bottom of so many traditional hierarchies—the poor, people of color, women, gays and lesbians—provoked a counterinsurgent fantasy on behalf of "traditional American values." The nation imagined in this reactive rhetoric is dedicated not to the survival or emancipation of traumatized marginal subjects but, rather, to freedom for the American innocent: the adult without sin, the abducted and neglected child, and, above all, and most effectively, the fetus. Although it had first appeared as a technological miracle of photographic bio-power in the mid-1960s, in the post-Roe era the fetus became consolidated as a political commodity, a supernatural sign of national iconicity. What constituted this national iconicity was an image of an American, perhaps the last living American, not yet bruised by history: not yet caught up in the excitement of mass consumption or ethnic, racial, or sexual mixing, not yet tainted by knowledge, by money, or by war. This fetus was an American to identify with, to aspire to make a world for: it organized a kind of beautiful citizenship politics of good intention and virtuous fantasy that could not be said to be dirty, or whose dirt was attributed to the sexually or politically immoral.

By *citizenship* I refer here both to the legal sense in which persons are juridically subject to the law's privileges and protections by virtue of national identity status but also the experiential, vernacular context in which people customarily understand their relation to state power and social membership. It is to bridge these two axes of political identity and identification that Bernard Nathanson, founder of the National Abortion Rights Action League (NARAL) and now a pro-life activist, makes political films starring the traumatically post-iconic fetal body. His aim is to solicit *aversive identifications* with the fetus, ones that strike deeply the empathetic imaginary of people's best selves while creating

---

10. See Berlant, *Queen of America*. The following paragraphs revise and repeat some arguments from this book. For an essay specifically on scandalized childhood in the contemporary United States, see Marilyn Ivy, "Recovering the Inner Child in Late Twentieth Century America," *Social Text* 37 (1993): 227–52.

pressure for the erasure of empathy's scene. First, he shows graphic images of abortion, captioned by pornographic descriptions of the procedures by which the total body is visibly turned into hideous fragmented flesh. He then calls on the national conscience to delete what he has created, an "unmistakable trademark of the irrational violence that has pervaded the twentieth century."[11] The trademark to which he refers is abortion. He exhorts the public to abort the fetal trademark so as to save the fetus itself and, by extension, the national identity form and its future history. In this sense the fetus's sanctified national identity is the opposite of any multicultural, sexual, or classed identity: the fetus is a blinding light that, triumphant as the modal citizen form, would white out the marks of hierarchy, taxonomy, and violence that seem now so central to the public struggle over who should possess the material and cultural resources of contemporary national life.

It will be clear by now how the struggle over child labor takes on the same form as fetal rights discourse: revelations of trauma, incitements to rescue, the reprivatization of victims as the ground of hope, and, above all, the notion that the feeling self is the true self, the self that must be protected from pain or from history, that scene of unwelcome changing. The infantile citizen then enfigures the adult's true self, his inner child in all its undistorted or untraumatized possibility. But to say this is to show how the fetal/infantile icon is a fetish of citizenship with a double social function. As an object of fascination and disavowal, it stands in for (while remanding to social obscurity) the traumatized virtuous private citizen around whom history ought to be organized, for whom there is not a good-enough world. (This currently includes the formerly tacit, or "normal," citizen and the sexually and racially subordinated ones.) In addition to its life as a figure for the injured adult, the fetus has another life as a utopian sign of a just and pleasant socius, both in pro-life, pro-family values rhetoric and in advertisements and Hollywood films about the state of white reproductive heterosexuality in the United States during an era of great cultural, economic, and technological upheaval. Its two scenes of citizenship can be spatialized: one takes place in a traumatized public and the other in a pain-free intimate zone. These zones mirror each other perfectly, and so betray the fetish form of sentimental citizenship, the wish it expresses to signify a political world beyond contradiction.[12]

---

11. Nathanson speaks this line in the film *The Silent Scream* (1984).

12. This intensification of national-popular patriotic familialism has taken place at a time when another kind of privatization—the disinvestment of the state economically

I have elaborated these basic Freudian dicta about mourning, the theory of infantile citizenship, and this account of U.S. political culture to make a context for four claims: that this is an age of sentimental politics in which policy and law and public experiences of personhood in everyday life are conveyed through rhetorics of utopian/traumatized feeling; that national-popular struggle is now expressed in fetishes of utopian/traumatic affect that over-organize and over-organicize social antagonism; that utopian/traumatized subjectivity has replaced rational subjectivity as the essential index of value for personhood and thus for society; and that, while on all sides of the political spectrum political rhetoric generates a high degree of cynicism and boredom,[13] those same sides manifest, simultaneously, a sanctifying respect for sentiment. Thus, in the sentimental national contract antagonistic class positions mirror each other in their mutual conviction about the *self-evidence* and *objectivity* of painful feeling, and about the nation's duty to eradicate it. In the conjuncture "utopian/traumatized" I mean to convey a logic of fantasy reparation involved in the therapeutic conversion of the scene of pain and its eradication to the scene of the political itself. Questions of social inequity and social value are now adjudicated in the register not of power but of sincere surplus feeling: worry about whether public figures seem "caring" subordinates analyses of their visions of injustice; subalternized groups attempt to forge alliances on behalf of radical social transformation through testimonial rhetorics of true pain;[14] people believe that they know what they feel when they feel it, can locate its origin, measure its effects.

The traffic in affect of these political struggles finds validity in those seemingly superpolitical moments when a "clear" wrong—say, the spectacle of children violently exploited—produces a "universal"

---

and culturally in promoting public life—characterizes almost all the activity of the political public sphere. The economic defederalization of citizenship downsizes the public so drastically that it begins to look like "the private," its nineteenth-century antithesis (only this time mass-mediated and thus publicly sutured in a more classic Habermasean sense). Yet all too frequently the analysis of the institutions of intimacy is kept separate from the considerations of the material conditions of citizenship.

13. On cynicism and citizenship, see Slavoj Žižek, *The Sublime Object of Ideology* (London: Verso, 1989), 11–53.

14. On pain's place in forming the political imagination of subjects during the epoch of U.S. identity politics, see Wendy Brown's powerful essay "Wounded Attachments: Late Modern Oppositional Political Formations," in *The Identity in Question*, ed. John Rajchman (New York: Routledge, 1995), 199–227.

response. Feeling politics takes all kinds: it is a politics of protection, reparation, rescue. It claims a hard-wired truth, a core of common sense. It is beyond ideology, beyond mediation, beyond contestation. It seems to dissolve contradiction and dissent into pools of basic and also higher truth. It seems strong and clear, as opposed to confused or ambivalent (thus: the unconscious has left the ballpark). It seems the inevitable or desperately only core material of community.

What does it mean for the struggle to shape collective life when a politics of true feeling organizes analysis, discussion, fantasy, and policy? When feeling, the most subjective thing, the thing that makes persons public and marks their location, takes the temperature of power; mediates personhood, experience, and history; takes over the space of ethics and truth? When the shock of pain is said only to produce *clarity* when shock can as powerfully be said to produce panic, misrecognition, the shakiness of perception's ground? Finally, what happens to questions of managing alterity or difference or resources in collective life when feeling *bad* becomes evidence for a structural condition of injustice? What does it mean for the theory and practice of social transformation when feeling *good* becomes evidence of justice's triumph? As many historians and theorists of "rights talk" have shown, the beautiful and simple categories of legitimation in liberal society can bestow on the phenomenal form of proper personhood the status of normative value, which is expressed in feeling terms as "comfort";[15] and, meanwhile, political arguments that challenge the claim of painful feeling's analytical clarity are frequently characterized as causing further violence to already damaged persons and the world of their desires.

This essay will raise uncomfortable questions about what the evidence of trauma is: its desire is to exhort serious critical, but not cynical, attention to the fetish of true feeling in which social antagonism is, frequently, being worked without being worked through. My larger aim is to bring into being as an object of critique the all-too-explicit "commonsense" feeling culture of national life, evident in the law, identity politics, and mass society generally: it is about the problem of trying juridically and culturally to administer society as a space ideally void of

---

15. On rights talk and normativity, see the volume *Identities, Politics, and Rights,* ed. Austin Sarat and Thomas R. Kearns (Ann Arbor: University of Michigan Press, 1995). See especially Wendy Brown's contribution, an indispensable discussion of the ways "rights talk" enables the production of traumatized political identities: "Rights and Identity in Late Modernity: Revisiting the 'Jewish Question'," 85–130.

struggle and ambivalence, a place made on the model of fetal simplicity. I am not trying to posit feeling as the bad opposite of something good called thinking: as we will see, in the cases to follow politicized feeling is a kind of thinking that too often assumes the obviousness of the thought it has, which stymies the production of the thought it might become.

In particular our cases will derive from the field of sexuality, a zone of practice, fantasy, and ideology whose standing in the law constantly partakes of claims about the universality or transparency of feeling, a universality juridically known as "privacy." We begin by addressing the work of feeling in Supreme Court decisions around sexuality and privacy. But the tendency to assume the nonideological, nonmediated, or nonsocial status of feeling is shared by opponents to privacy as well, with consequences that must equally, though differently, give pause: the following section interrogates the antiprivacy revolution legal radicals have wrought via the redefinition of harm and traumatized personhood. The paradoxes revealed therein will not be easily solved by ignoring or condescending to the evidence of injustice provided by the publicized pain of subordinated populations: the essay's coda focuses on a twelve-step book about reproduction, *Peaceful Pregnancy Meditations,* by Lisa Steele George, whose commitment to therapy for pregnant women and whose paranoia about the world of identity politics in the present moment does *not* produce an image of the just world. Its properly paranoid politics of intimacy rejects the mirroring logics of posttraumatic national subjectivity. It promotes, instead, a deeply felt but stubbornly uncongealed form of personhood whose way of inhabiting politics, publicness, personhood, and power suggests how much work it would take, and what kinds of changes it would bring, to induce a break with trauma's seduction of politics in the everyday of U.S. citizenship.[16]

Privacy

It would not be too strong to say that where regulating sexuality is concerned the law has a special sentimental relation to banality. But to say

---

16. *Intimate discipline* is Richard Brodhead's term for the coercions of sentimental culture in the nineteenth century United States. See "Sparing the Rod: Discipline and Fiction in Antebellum America," *Cultures of Letters: Scenes of Reading and Writing in Nineteenth-Century America* (Chicago: University of Chicago Press, 1993), 13–47.

this is not to accuse the law of irrelevance or shallowness. In contrast to the primary sense of banality as a condition of reiterated ordinary conventionality, banality can also mark the experience of deeply felt emotion, as in the case of "I love you," "Did you come?" or "O' Say, Can You See?"[17] But for an occasion of banality to be both utopian and sublime its ordinariness must be thrust into a zone of overwhelming disavowal. This act of optimistic forgetting is neither simple nor easy: it takes the legitimating force of institutions—for example, the nation form or heterosexuality—to establish the virtue of forgetting banality's banality. Take a classic instance of this process, an entirely forgettable moment in *The Wizard of Oz* that precedes an unforgettable one. Auntie Em says to Dorothy, who has been interfering with the work on the farm (no child labor there: Dorothy carries *books*): "Find yourself a place where you won't get into any trouble." Dorothy, in a trance, seems to repeat the phrase but misrepeats it, sighing, "a place where there isn't any trouble," which leads her then to fantasize "somewhere over the Rainbow." Between the phrase's first and second incarnations the agency of the subject disappears and is transferred to the place: the magic of will and intention has been made a property of property.

The unenumerated relation between *the* place where *you* won't get into trouble and *a* place where, definitionally, *there is no trouble* expresses the foggy fantasy of happiness pronounced in the constitutional concept of privacy, whose emergence in sexuality law during the 1960s brought heterosexual intimacy explicitly into the antagonistic field of U.S. citizenship. Privacy is the Oz of America. Based on a notion of safe space, a hybrid space of home and law in which people will act legally and lovingly toward one another, free from the determinations of history or the coercions of pain, the constitutional theorization of sexual privacy is drawn from a lexicon of romantic sentiment, a longing for a space where there is no trouble, a place whose constitution in law

---

17. Jean Baudrillard posits banality as the affective dominant of postmodern life: see *In the Shadow of the Silent Majorities . . . Or the End of the Social and Other Essays*, trans. Paul Foss, Paul Patton, and John Johnston (New York: Semiotexte, 1983); and "From the System to the Destiny of Objects," in *The Ecstasy of Communication*, ed. Slyvere Lotringer (New York: Semiotexte, 1987), 77–96. See also Achille Mbembe, "Prosaics of Servitude and Authoritarian Civilities," *Public Culture* 5 (Fall 1992): 123-48; Achille Mbembe and Janet Roitman, "Figures of the Subject in Times of Crisis," *Public Culture* 7 (Winter 1995): 323-52; and Meaghan Morris, "Banality in Cultural Studies," in *Logics of Television: Essays in Cultural Criticism*, ed. Patricia Mellencamp (Bloomington: Indiana University Press, 1990), 14-43.

would be so powerful that desire would meet moral discipline there, making real the dreamy rule. In this dream the zone of privacy is a paradigmatic national space too, where freedom and desire meet up in their full suprapolitical expression, a site of embodiment that also leaves unchallenged fundamental dicta about the universality or abstractness of the modal citizen.

Much has been written on the general status of privacy doctrine in constitutional history, a "broad and ambiguous concept which can easily be shrunken in meaning but which can also, on the other hand, easily be interpreted as a constitutional ban against many things other than searches and seizures."[18] Privacy was first conceived as a constitutionally mandated but unenumerated right of sexual citizenship in *Griswold v. Connecticut* (381 U.S. 479 [1965]). The case is about the use of birth control in marriage: a nineteenth-century Connecticut law made it illegal for married couples to use contraceptives for birth control (oral arguments suggest that the "rhythm method" was not unconstitutional in that state);[19] they were only allowed prophylaxis to prevent disease. To challenge this law Esther Griswold, director of Planned Parenthood in Connecticut, and Lee Buxton, the chief physician there, were arrested, by arrangement with the district attorney, for giving "information, instruction, and medical advice to *married persons* as to the means of preventing conception."[20]

The arguments made in *Griswold* stress the Due Process clause of the Fourteenth Amendment, because denying the sale of contraceptives "constitutes a deprivation of right against invasion of privacy."[21] This kind of privacy is allotted only to married couples: Justice Goldberg quotes approvingly a previous opinion of Justice Harlan (*Poe v. Ullman*, 367 U.S. 497, at 533), which states that "adultery, homosexuality, and the like are sexual intimacy which the State forbids . . . but the intimacy of husband and wife is necessarily an essential and accepted feature of the institution of marriage, an institution which the State not only must allow, but which always and in every age it has fostered and protected."[22]

---

18. Justice Hugo Black, concurring, *Griswold v. Connecticut* 381 U.S. 479 (1965), at 509.

19. Stephanie Guitton and Peter Irons, eds., *May It Please the Court: Arguments on Abortion* (New York: New Press, 1995), p. 4.

20. Justice William O. Douglas, Opinion of the Court, *Griswold v. Connecticut*, at 480.

21. Ibid., 5.

22. Justice Arthur Goldberg, concurring, *Griswold v. Connecticut*, at 499.

We can see in Harlan's phrasing and Goldberg's citation of it the sentimental complexities of making constitutional law about sexual practice in the modern United States. The logic of equivalence between adultery and homosexuality in the previous passage locates these antithetical sexual acts/practices in an unprotected public space that allows and even compels *zoning* in the form of continual state discipline (e.g., laws):[23] in contrast, marital privacy is drawn up here in a zone elsewhere to the law and takes its authority from tradition, which means that the law simultaneously protects it and turns away its active disciplinary gaze. At this juncture of space, time, legitimacy, and the law Gayatri Spivak's distinction between *Time* and *timing* will also clarify the stakes of privacy law's optimistic apartheid where sexuality is concerned. Spivak argues that the difference between hegemonic and "colonized" conceptions of imperial legal authority can be tracked by graphing Time as that property of transcendental continuity that locates state power to sustain worlds in the capacity to enunciate master concepts such as liberty and legitimacy in a zone of monumental time, a seemingly postpolitical space of abstraction from the everyday. In contrast, timing marks the always processual, drowning-in-the-present quality of subaltern survival in the face of the law's scrutiny and subject-making pedagogy.[24] Mapped onto sexuality law here, in privacy's early and most happy conceptualization, we see that nonmarital and therefore nonprivate sex exists in the antagonistic performance of the law's present tense, while the marital is virtually antinomian, Time above fallen timing. It is not only superior to the juro-political but also, apparently, its boss and taskmaster.

The banality of intimacy's sentimental standing in and above the law is most beautifully and enduringly articulated in the majority opinion in *Griswold*, written by Justice William O. Douglas. Douglas argues that a combination of precedents derived from the First, Fourth, Fifth, Ninth, and Fourteenth Amendments[25] supports his designation of a

---

23. I borrow this rhetoric of zoning, and specifically its relation to the production of normative sexuality, from Lauren Berlant and Michael Warner, "Sex in Public," *Critical Inquiry* 24 (winter 1998): 547–66.

24. Gayatri Chakravorty Spivak, "Time and Timing: Law and History," in *Chronotypes: The Construction of Time*, ed. John Bender and David E. Wellbery (Stanford: Stanford University Press, 1991), 99–117.

25. Douglas writes: "Various guarantees create zones of privacy. The right of association contained in the penumbra of the First Amendment is one, as we have seen. The Third Amendment in its prohibition against the quartering of soldiers 'in any house' in time of peace without the consent of the owner is another facet of that privacy. The

heretofore unenumerated constitutional right for married persons to inhabit a zone of privacy, a zone free from police access or the "pure [state] power" for which Connecticut was arguing as the doctrinal foundation of its right to discipline immorality in its citizens.[26] The language Douglas uses both to make this space visible and to enunciate the law's relation to it shuttles between the application of *stare decisis* (the rule of common law that binds judicial authority to judicial precedent) and the traditional conventionalities of heteronormative Hallmark-style sentimentality:

> The present case, then, concerns a relationship lying within the zone of privacy created by several fundamental constitutional guarantees. And it concerns a law which, in forbidding the *use* of contraceptives rather than regulating their manufacture or sale, seeks to achieve its goals by means having a maximum destructive impact upon that relationship. Such a law cannot stand in light of the familiar principle, so often applied by this Court, that a "governmental purpose to control or prevent activities constitutionally subject to state regulation may not be achieved by means which sweep unnecessarily broadly and thereby invade the area of protected freedoms" [*NAACP v. Alabama*, 377 U.S. 288, at 307]. Would we allow the police to search the sacred precincts of marital bedrooms for telltale signs of the use of contraceptives? The very idea is repulsive to the notions of privacy surrounding the marriage relationship. We deal with a right of privacy older than the Bill of Rights—older than our political parties, older than our school system. Marriage is a coming together for better or for worse, hopefully enduring, and intimate to the degree of being sacred. It is an association that promotes a way of life, not causes; a harmony in living, not political faiths; a bilateral loyalty, not commercial or

---

Fourth Amendment explicitly affirms the 'right of the people to be secure in their persons, houses, papers, and effects, against unreasonable searches and seizures.' The Fifth Amendment in its Self-Incrimination Clause enables the citizen to create a zone of privacy which government may not force him to surrender to his detriment. The Ninth Amendment provides: 'The enumeration in the Constitution, of certain rights, shall not be construed to deny or disparage others retained by the people.' " *Griswold v. Connecticut*, at 484. Justice Goldberg's concurring opinion, while mainly running a legal clinic on the Founders' relation to unenumerated rights, adds the Due Process clause of the Fourteenth Amendment to this constitutional congeries. Ibid., at 488.

26. Guitton and Irons, eds., *May It Please the Court*, 7.

social projects. Yet it is an association for as noble a purpose as any involved in our prior decisions.[27]

Douglas bases his view that sexuality in marriage must be constitutionally protected—being above the law, prior to it, and beyond its proper gaze—on a sense that "specific guarantees in the Bill of Rights have penumbras, formed by emanations from those guarantees that help give them life and substance."[28] A *penumbra* is generally a "partial shadow between regions of complete shadow and complete illumination," but I believe the sense in which Douglas uses this dreamy concept is more proper to its application in the science of astronomy: "The partly darkened ridge around a sunspot." In other words, privacy protections around even marital sexuality are the dark emanations from the sunspot of explicit constitutional enumeration, and the zone of privacy in which marital sexuality thrives is the shadowland of the "noble" institution of marriage, with its sacred obligational emanations of social stability and continuity, intimate noninstrumentality, and superiority to the dividedness that otherwise characterizes the social. To back him up Justices Harlan's and Goldberg's opinions invoke the state and the Court's propriety in pedagogically bolstering the institutions of traditional American morality and values: after all, the theater of marital intimacy is "older than our political parties, older than our schools."

Justice Hugo Black's dissent in *Griswold* blasts Justices Douglas, Goldberg, Harlan, and White for the unethical emotionality of what he calls the "natural law due process formula [used] to strike down all state laws which [the justices] think are unwise, dangerous, or irrational." He feels that it introduces into constitutional jurisprudence justifications for measuring "constitutionality by our belief that legislation is arbitrary, capricious or unreasonable, or accomplishes no justifiable purpose, or is offensive to our own notions of civilized standards of conduct. Such an appraisal of the wisdom of legislation is an attribute of the power to make laws, not of the power to interpret them." He finds precedent in this critique in a Learned Hand essay on the Bill of Rights that reviles judges' tendency to "wrap up their veto in a protective veil of adjectives such as 'arbitrary,' 'artificial,' 'normal,' 'reason-

---

27. Justice William O. Douglas, Opinion of the Court, *Griswold v. Connecticut*, at 485, 486.

28. Ibid., at 484.

able,' 'inherent,' 'fundamental,' or 'essential' whose office usually, though quite innocently, is to disguise what they are doing and impute to it a derivation far more impressive than their personal preferences, which are all that in fact lie behind the decision."[29] In this view, whenever judges enter the zone of constitutional penumbra, they manufacture euphemisms that disguise the relation between proper law and personal inclination. Patricia Williams has suggested that this charge (and the countercharge that at the heights of feeling it is no different than reason) is at the heart of the fiction of *stare decisis* that produces post-facto justifications from judicial or social tradition for judges who inevitably impose their will on problems of law but who must, for legitimacy's sake, disavow admission of the uninevitability of their claim. The virtually genetic image legal judgment has of itself in history veils not only the personal instabilities of judges but also the madness of the law itself, its instability and fictive stability, its articulation at the place where interpretive will and desire mix up to produce someone's image of a right/just/proper world.[30]

After sexual privacy is donated to the U.S. heterosexual couple in *Griswold* by way of the sentimental reason the Court adopts—through the spatialization of intimacy in a bell jar of frozen history—a judicial and political nightmare over the property of sexual privacy ensued, whose mad struggle between state privilege and private liberty is too long to enumerate here. We can conclude that the romantic banality that sanctions certain forms of intimacy as nationally privileged remains hardwired into the practice of sex privacy law in the United States. Almost twenty years later, however, *Planned Parenthood of Southeastern Pennsylvania v. Casey* (112 S. Ct. 2791 [1992]) recasts the force of its machinery remarkably, replacing the monumentality of sexual privacy that *Roe* had established as a fundamental condition of women's liberty with the monumentality of *Roe* itself as evidence of the Court's very authority.

In their majority opinion Justices O'Connor, Souter, and Kennedy recognize the sovereignty of the zone of privacy as a model for freedom or liberty, returning explicitly to the method of penumbral enumeration and *stare decisis* introduced in *Griswold*. But the real originality of *Planned Parenthood v. Casey* is in the extent to which it supplants *entirely*

---

29. Ibid., at 517 n.10.
30. Patricia J. Williams, *The Alchemy of Race and Rights* (Cambridge: Harvard University Press, 1991), 7–8, 134–35.

the utopia of heterosexual intimacy on which sexual privacy law was based in the first place, putting *women's pain* in heterosexual culture at the center of the story of privacy and legal protections. In this sense the legitimating force of deep juridical feelings about the sacred pleasures of marital intimacy are here inverted and displaced onto the woman, whose sexual and political trauma is now the index of the meaning and value of her privacy and her citizenship.

Briefly, *Eisenstadt v. Baird*, 405 U.S. 438 (1972) extended *Griswold* to unmarried women through the equal protections clause, transforming sexual privacy from its initial scene—the two-as-one utopia of coupled intimacy—into a property of individual liberty. This muted the concretely spatial aspects of the "zone of privacy," dismantling the original homology between the marital/sexual bedroom and the citizen's sense of self-sovereignty. It placed the focus on the space of the woman's body, which includes her capacities, passions, and intentions. But the shift from reframing contraception to adjudicating abortion required the discovery of more emanations from constitutional penumbra: in *Roe v. Wade* (410 U.S. 113 [1973]) the right of privacy remains the *woman's* right but here one that has internal limits at the juncture where state interest over potential "life" and social self-continuity overtake the woman's interest in controlling her sexual and reproductive existence. Gone, from that decision, is *Griswold*'s rhetoric of the Court's moral pedagogy or its chivalry toward sexually sacred precincts: indeed, Justice Blackmun writes that, because of the "sensitive and emotional nature of the abortion controversy," he wants to adhere to "constitutional measurement, free of emotion and predilection."[31] (There is not a sexuality/privacy case in which such a caveat against emotion is not passionately uttered.) *Roe* attempts to achieve its postemotionality by deploying knowledge, plumbing the juridical and historical archive on abortion: its emphasis is not on expanding liberty by thinking through the contexts of its practice but, rather, by massaging precedent and tradition.

Planned Parenthood v. Casey was widely seen as an opportunity for a new set of justices to overturn *Roe*. The Pennsylvania Abortion Control Act of 1982 (amended in 1988–89) did not abolish abortion in the state but intensified the discursive contexts in which it happened, seeking to create around abortion a state-sanctioned, morally pedagogical *zone of publicity*. Provisions included a twenty-four-hour waiting

---

31. Justice Blackmun, Opinion of the Court, *Roe v. Wade* 410 U.S. 113 (1973), at 708.

period, minor notification of parents and wife notification of husbands, and intensified standards of "informed consent" (including a state-authored brochure condemning abortion). The majority opinion has two explicit aims: to affirm the fundamental holdings of *Roe* on behalf of the sovereignty of women's citizenship, the unity of national culture, and the status of the Court's authority; and to enumerate what it felt was underenumerated in *Roe*, the conditions of the state's sovereignty over the contexts of reproduction. In other words, as Justice Scalia's dissent argues, the Court's majority opinion seeks to affirm Roe while also significantly dismantling it. Its technical mechanism for achieving this impossible feat is the substitution of an "undue burden" rule for a whole set of other protections that *Roe* provides: especially by dismantling the trimester framework that determined the woman's sovereignty over reproduction in a pregnancy's first six months and substituting for it a rule that favors the state's right to place restrictions on the woman's reproductive practice (restrictions that can then be weighed by courts that will determine whether a given law mounts egregiously burdensome obstacles to the woman's exercise of her constitutional right to abortion).

Scalia claims that the majority pulls off this impossible feat (in its claim to refuse a "jurisprudence of doubt" while making equivocal legal judgments) by disguising its own muddy impulses in a sentimental and "empty" rhetoric of intimacy:

> The best that the Court can do to explain how it is that the word "liberty" *must* be thought to include the right to destroy human fetuses is to rattle off a collection of adjectives that simply decorate a value judgement and conceal a political choice. The right to abort, we are told, inheres in "liberty" because it is among "a person's most basic decisions," *ante*, at 2806; it involves a "most intimate and personal choic[e]," *ante*, at 2807; it is "central to personal dignity and autonomy," *ibid.*; it "originate[s] within the zone of conscience and belief," *ibid.*; it is "too intimate and personal" for state interference, *ante*, at 2807; it reflects "intimate views" of a "deep, personal character," *ante*, at 2808; it involves "intimate relationships," and "notions of personal autonomy and bodily integrity," *ante*, at 2810.[32]

---

32. Justice Scalia, dissent, *Planned Parenthood v. Casey* 112 S.Ct.2791 (1992), at 2876–77.

Correctly, Scalia goes on to point out that these very same qualities meant nothing to the Justices when they heard *Bowers v. Hardwick* (478 U.S. 186 [1986]), "because, like abortion, they are forms of conduct that have long been criminalized in American society. Those adjectives might be applied, for example, to homosexual sodomy, polygamy, adult incest, and suicide, all of which are equally 'intimate.' "[33]

But Scalia's critique is trivial, in the sense that the majority opinion does not seek to rethink sexual privacy or intimacy in any serious way. The rhetoric of intimacy in the case is part of its argument from *stare decisis*,[34] but the majority justices' originality is located in their representation of the specificity, what they call the "uniqueness," of the material conditions of citizenship for women in the United States. Because the right to sexual privacy has been individuated by *Roe*, privacy no longer takes place in a concrete zone but, rather, a "zone of conscience"—the place where, as Nietzsche tells us, the law is painfully and portably inscribed in subjects.[35] The justices refer to women's "anxieties," "physical constraints," and "sacrifices [that] have since the beginning of the human race been endured by woman with a pride that ennobles her": they contend that a woman's "suffering is too intimate and personal for the State to insist . . . upon its own vision of the woman's role."[36] Therefore, abortion definitively grounds and sustains women's political legitimacy: their "ability to participate equally in the economic and social life of the Nation has been facilitated by their ability to control their reproductive lives."[37]

The justices here concede that femininity in the United States is virtually and generically an undue burden, however ennobling it might be. The de-utopianization of sexual privacy established in *Griswold* and the installation of female citizenship at the juncture of law and suffering is further reinforced by the one part of the Pennsylvania law that

---

33. Ibid. Scalia also blasts Justice Blackmun (n. 2, at 2876) for using the same intimate rhetoric that means nothing, constitutionally, at least to Scalia.

34. A passionate and creative argument about what cases constitute precedent for *Roe* takes place between Justices O'Connor, Kennedy, Souter (ibid., at 2808–16), and Scalia (at 2860–67).

35. Friedrich Nietzsche, *On the Genealogy of Morals*, ed. Walter Kaufmann (New York: Vintage, 1967), 57–96. On the ways Nietzsche reproduces the individuating limits of pain-centered politics, see Wendy Brown, "Wounded Attachments."

36. Justices Sandra Day O'Connor, Anthony M. Kennedy, and David H. Souter, Opinion of the Court, *Planned Parenthood v. Casey*, at 2807.

37. Ibid., at 2809.

the majority finds unconstitutional: the clause that commands women to notify their husbands of their intention to abort. The segment in which this happens exposes women's suffering in the zone of privacy, where, it turns out, men beat their wives. They cite evidence, supported by the American Medical Association, that men are raping their wives, terrorizing them (especially when pregnant), *forcing* them to inhabit a zone of privacy that keeps secreted men's abuse of women. In short, the "gruesome and torturous" conditions of marital domesticity in battering households requires the Court *not to protect privacy* for the couple but to keep the couple from becoming the unit of modal citizenship where privacy law is concerned.[38]

Catharine MacKinnon deems privacy law a tool of patriarchal supremacy:

> Women in everyday life have no privacy in private. In private, women are objects of male subjectivity and male power. The private is that place where men can do whatever they want because women reside there. The consent that supposedly demarcates this private surrounds women and follows us everywhere we go. Men [in contrast], reside in public, where laws against harm exist.... As a legal doctrine, privacy has become the affirmative triumph of the state's abdication of women.[39]

MacKinnon's arguments in these essays—which purport to be about "women" and "men" but which to my ear are more profoundly about heterosexuality as a virtual institution and a way of life—derive from Court practice through the late 1980s and do not consider the work that jurists such as O'Connor have done to deprivatize privacy. But it should be no surprise that the citizen imagined by even moderates these days is no longer a complex subject with rights, needs, reciprocal obligations to the state and society, conflicting self-interests, or prospects for happiness in realms beyond the juridical: the citizen now is a trauma effect who requires protection and political reparation,

---

38. *Ibid.*, at 2827.
39. Catharine A. MacKinnon, "Reflections on Law in the Everyday Life of Women," in *Law in Everyday Life*, ed. Austin Sarat and Thomas R. Kearns (Ann Arbor: University of Michigan Press, 1995), 117–18. See also MacKinnon, *Toward a Feminist Theory of the State* (Cambridge: Harvard University Press), 184–94.

whether or not that citizen can be fully described by the terms in which historically subordinated classes circulate in the United States. The Opinion of the Court in *Casey* answers the dissenters' argument—which asserts that so few women are battered in the United States that the husband notification principle stands within constitutional norms—by arguing that "the analysis does not end with the one percent of women upon whom the statute operates: it begins there."[40] Here their jurisprudence is not so far from Mari Matsuda's when she claims that "looking to the bottom" of social hierarchy and making reparative law from there is the only politically ethical thing to do.[41]

In the twenty years between *Roe* and *Planned Parenthood v. Casey* the general scene of public citizenship in the United States has become suffused with a practice of making pain count politically. The law of sexual privacy has followed this change, registering with symptomatic incoherence a more general struggle to maintain the contradictory rights and privileges of women, heterosexuality, the family, the state, and patriarchalized sexual privilege. The sheer ineloquence of this jumble of categories should say something about the cramped space of analysis and praxis to which the rhetoric and jurisprudence of sexual privacy has brought us—a place where there *is* much trouble: a utopia of law.

Politics

In *Griswold*, I have argued, we see codified the assurance of some jurists that the intimate feelings of married sexual partners represent that zone of privacy and personhood beyond the scrutiny of the law whose value is so absolute that the law must protect its sovereignty. Between *Griswold* and *Roe* these intimate feelings and their relation to liberty were still assumed as the sovereign materials of the law of sexual privacy. Now, however, many of the political and juridical contexts have dissolved that once sustained the fantasy of a core national culture, threatening the capacity of sentimental politics to create feeling cultures of consensus that distract from the lived violences and fractures of everyday life in the polis. The class, racial, economic, and sexual fragmenta-

---

40. *Planned Parenthood v. Casey*, at 2829.
41. Mari J. Matsuda, "Looking to the Bottom: Critical Legal Studies and Reparations," in *Critical Race Theory: The Key Writings that Formed the Movement*, ed. Kimberlè Crenshaw, Neil Gotanda, Gary Peller, and Kendall Thomas (New York: The New Press, 1995), 63–80.

tion of U.S. society has emerged into the vision of the law and the public not as an exception to a utopian norm but as a new governing rule of the present. The legal struggles over affirmative action, welfare, abortion, and immigration the courts currently worry are also about whether the utopian or the traumatic story of national life will govern jurisprudence and the world it seeks to confirm. Trauma is winning.

Central to the legal emergence of the politics of trauma against the scene of liberal-patriotic disavowal has been a group of activists from within (mainly academic) legal studies who speak from feminist, gay and lesbian, antiracist, and anticapitalist movements. They take their different but generally painful experiences of social hierarchy in the United States to require a radical rhetorical and conceptual transformation of legal scholarship that embraces "subjectivity of perspective," asserts the collective nature of subject formation (around stereotypical social identities), and refuses traditional liberal notions that organize the social optimism of law around relatively unimpeded individuality, privacy, property, and conventional values.[42] At stake in this transformation of law is the importance of antinormativity to counterhegemonic critical theory and practice: since liberal law has long recognized a particular and traditionally sanctioned form of universal personhood as that around which society, theory, forms of discipline, and aspirational pedagogies should be organized, antiliberal activism has had strategically to *ground* law in experience (in all senses of the pun) and particular identities.

In this sense critical legal praxis is the opposite of national senti-

---

42. Critical Legal Studies, critical race theory, radical feminist legal theory, and an emergent body of work in gay and lesbian culture, power, and the law encompasses a huge bibliography. Rather than dump a stupidly big omnibus footnote here, let me metonymically signal the archive via a few recent helpful anthologies or extended works: Mary Becker, Cynthia Grant Bowman, and Morrison Torrey, *Cases and Materials on Feminist Jurisprudence: Taking Women Seriously* (St. Paul, Minn.: West Publishing, 1994); Dan Danielsen and Karen Engle, *After Identity: A Reader in Law and Culture* (New York: Routledge, 1995); Lisa Duggan and Nan D. Hunter, *Sex Wars: Sexual Dissent and Political Culture* (New York: Routledge, 1995); Mari J. Matsuda, Charles R. Lawrence III, Richard Delgado, and Kimberlè Williams Crenshaw, *Words That Wound: Critical Race Theory, Assaultive Speech, and the First Amendment* (Boulder, Colo: Westview Press, 1993), 1–15; Kimberlè Crenshaw, Neil Gotanda, Gary Peller, and Kendall Thomas, *Critical Race Theory*; Richard Delgado, *Critical Race Theory: The Cutting Edge* (Philadelphia: Temple University Press, 1995); Patricia Smith, ed., *Feminist Jurisprudence* (New York: Oxford University Press, 1993); Robin West, *Narrative, Authority, and Law* (Ann Arbor: University of Michigan Press, 1993); Patricia J. Williams, *The Alchemy of Race and Rights: Diary of a Law Professor* (Cambridge: Harvard University Press, 1991); and *The Rooster's Egg* (Cambridge: Harvard University Press, 1995).

mentality, which pursues collective cohesion by circulating a universalist currency of distress. At the same time, the structure of reparation central to radical legal politics suggests an unevenness in this general tactic of making legal notions of subjectivity historically and corporeally specific. Subaltern pain is not considered *universal* (the privileged do not experience it, they do not live expecting that at any moment their ordinarily loose selves might be codified into a single humiliated atom of subpersonhood). But subaltern pain is deemed, in this context, universally *intelligible,* constituting objective evidence of trauma reparable by the law and the law's more privileged subjects. In other words, the universal value is here no longer a property of political personhood but, instead, a property of a rhetoric that claims to represent not the universal but the true self. But, if historical contexts are incomparable across fields of simple and complex distinction, how can someone's pain or traumatized identity produce such perfect knowledge? And, if the pedagogies of politics were necessary to reframe a set of experiences, knowledges, and feelings as the kind of pain that exposes injustice, what is "true" about it, exactly?

In this political model of identity trauma stands as truth. We can't use happiness as a guide to the aspirations for social change, because the feeling of it might well be false consciousness; nor boredom, which might be depression, illness, or merely a spreading malaise. Pain, in contrast, is something quick and sharp that simultaneously specifies you and makes you generic: it is something that happens to you before you "know" it, and it is intensely individuating, for surviving its shock lets you know it is your general survival at stake. Yet, if the pain is at the juncture of you and the stereotype that represents you, you know that you are hurt not because of your relation to history but because of *someone else's* relation to it, a type of someone whose privilege or comfort depends on the pain that diminishes you, locks you into identity, covers you with shame, and sentences you to a hell of constant potential exposure to the banality of derision.

Pain thus organizes your specific experience of the world, separating you from others and connecting you with others similarly shocked (but not surprised) by the strategies of violence that constantly regenerate the bottom of the hierarchies of social value you inhabit. In this sense subaltern pain is a public form because its outcome is to make you readable, for others. This is, perhaps, why activists from identity politics generally assume pain as the only sign readable across hierarchies of social life: the subaltern is the surrogate form of cultural intelligibility generally, and negated identities are pain effects. Know me, know my pain—you caused it: in this context paranoia would seem adaptive and would make understandable a desire for law to be both the origin *and* end of my experience of injustice. It might even make a wish that I have to see even subaltern suffering as something more mediated seem, perhaps, cold or an effect of the leisure of privilege. Who has time, after all, to query violence between shock and the moment it becomes true meaning?

These dicta ground much current countertraditional legal argument. Take, for example, an original and impassioned work such as Robin West's *Narrative, Authority, and Law*,[43] which sees as its task the production of moral criticism and transformation of the law from the point of view of its and a society's victims. West wields narratives powerfully throughout the book that reveal the law's fundamental immorality (and therefore its fundamentally immoralizing effect on the subjects who are educated to its standards) where women's lives are concerned, and her powerful feminist arguments for the need to deprivatize women's structurally induced pain testify to the radical changes in the law and other institutions of intimacy that would have to happen if women are to attain legitimacy as social subjects. But West assumes that women's pain is already available as knowledge. To her it *is* meaning and the material for radical pedagogy. To think otherwise is to be either misogynist or guilty of shallow and overacademic postmodernism. Empathy is an ethical rule. Not surprisingly, as it happens, one example of pain's pure force that she uses to summarize her argument comes from a child: "We must be able to say, to quote my two-year-old, 'don't do that—you're hurting me,' and we must be able to hear that utterance as an ethical mandate to change course."[44]

---

43. Robin West, *Narrative, Authority, and Law* (Ann Arbor: University of Michigan Press, 1993).

44. Ibid., 19–20. Much the same kind of respect and critique can be given to Catharine MacKinnon's promotion of juridical reparation on behalf of women's pain under patriarchy: in her work the inner little girl of every woman stands as the true abused self who is denied full citizenship in the United States. For an analysis of antipornography rhetoric's depiction of pain's place in women's citizenship, see Berlant, "Live Sex Acts," *Queen of America*.

Not all radical legal theorists so simplify pain as to make the emblem of true wisdom about injustice and its eradication something as sentimental and fictive (to adults) as a child's consciousness:[45] yet the desire expressed in its seeming extreme clarity signals a lost opportunity for rethinking the relation of critique and culture building at this juncture of identity politics and legal theory. Would the child build a just world from the knowledge he gleans from being hurt? What would the child need to know for that to happen? How could this child learn to think beyond trauma, to make a context for it? It seems hard for this group of legal theorists to imagine the value of such questions, for a few reasons. One may be due to the centrality of "pain and suffering" to tort law, which endorses a construction of the true subject as a feeling subject whose suffering disables a person's ability to live at his full capacities, as he has been doing, and thus requires reparations from the agents who wielded the force. A great deal has been and will be written on this general area, for feminist antipornography and antiracist hate speech litigation borrows much of its legitimation from this hoary jurisprudential domain:[46] their tactic here is to challenge local purveyors of structural violence in order to make racism and misogyny *less profitable,* even symbolically, and meanwhile to use the law to debanalize violence by making illegal that which has been ordinary practice, on the model, say, of sexual harassment law or even more extremely, using the constitutional model of "cruel and unusual punishment" to revoke legitimation from social relations of violence traditionally authorized by the state and the law.

Kendall Thomas has made this latter point, in an essay on privacy

---

45. Another instance in which a generic child's nonideological relation to justice is held as the proper index of adult aspiration is to be found in Patricia Williams, *Alchemy of Race and Rights*. This brilliant book is fully dedicated to understanding the multiple contexts in which (Williams's) legal subjectivity inherits, inhabits, and reproduces the law's most insidious violences: its commitment to syncretic modes of storytelling about these conjunctures leaves open some questions about the relation between what she represents as the madness of inhabiting legal allegories of the self in everyday life and certain scenes of hyperclarity in which children know the true scale of justice and the true measure of pain (in contrast to adults, with their brains twisted by liberal ideologies of property and contract [12, 27, e.g.]). Perhaps this is because, as she says, "Contract law reduces life to fairy tale" (224).

46. See Lucinda M. Finley, "A Break in the Silence: Including Women's Issues in a Torts Course," *Yale Journal of Law and Feminism* 1 (1989): 41–73. See also Scarry, Matsuda, West, and Williams, and MacKinnon, *op. cit.*

after *Bowers*.[47] He takes up Elaine Scarry's model of torture as a vehicle for the legitimating fiction of state power and claims that the Cruel and Unusual Punishment clause of the Eighth Amendment should be applied to state discrimination against gays and lesbians. The strength and clarity of his vision and the sense that his suggestion seems to make brings us to the second reason it seems hard for theorists who equate subjectivity in general with legal subjectivity to work beyond the rule of traumatic pain in imagining the conditions for progressive social change. Thomas's model only works if the agent of violence is the state or the law; it works only if the domain of law is deemed interchangeable with the entire field of injury and reparation, and if the subject of law is fully described by the taxonomies that law recognizes. This position would look awkward if it were rephrased: subjects are always citizens. But the fact is that the notion of reparation for identity-based subordination assumes that the law describes what a person is, and that social violence can be located the way physical injury can be tracked. The law's typical practice is to recognize kinds of subjects, acts, and identities: it is to taxonomize. What is the relation between the (seemingly inevitable) authoritarianism of juridical categorization, and the other, looser spaces of social life and personhood that do not congeal in categories of power, cause, and effect the way the law does? Is the "cruel and unusual punishment" tactic merely a reversal in extremis that points to the sublime banality of state cruelty, or is it a policy aspiration seeking a specific reparation for the specific violation/creation of gay and lesbian identities? Would the homeopathy of law against its own toxins in this domain of state cruelty work for women or the poor African Americans, Hispanics, and immigrants who are currently being economically disenfranchised from the resources that state capitalism manages?

Without making a ridiculous argument that the state is merely a mirage or a fetish that represents networks of inchoate forces that control, without constituting, the realm of society, it should be possible to say that radical counterpolitics needs to contend with notions of personhood and power that do not attain the clarity of state and juridical taxonomy, even across fields of practice and stigma. The desire to find

---

47. Kendall Thomas, "Beyond the Privacy Principle," in Danielsen and Engle, *After Identity*, 277–93.

an origin for trauma, and to rework culture at the violating origin, effectively imagines subjects only within that zone, reducing the social to that zone (in this case the state and the laws that legislate nonnormative sex) and covertly reauthorizing the hegemony of the national. The desire to use trauma as the model for the pain of subordination that gets congealed into identities forgets the difference between trauma and adversity: trauma takes you out of your life shockingly and places you into another one, whereas structural subordination is not a surprise to the subjects who experience it, and the pain of subordination *is* ordinary life.

I have not meant to argue that identity politics has become a mode of "victim politics" too reductive to see the world clearly or to have positive effects. In its most tawdry version this accusation reads that a politics organized around publicizing pain constitutes a further degradation of subaltern selves into a species of subcivilized nonagency. The people who make this argument usually recognize structural social inequality and the devastating impacts it has on persons but continue to believe that the United States operates meritocratically, for worthy individuals. In contrast, Wendy Brown's deconstruction of contemporary U.S. identity rhetorics places skepticism about traumatic identity in the context of imagining a more radical politics. Brown sees people who claim their pain and build collective struggles around it as potentially overidentifying with their pain then identifying with it, becoming passive to it, becoming addicted to seeing themselves as virtuous in the face of bad, unethical power. She follows Nietzsche's dicta against a passive-aggressive politics of *ressentiment:*

> Politicized identity thus enunciates itself, makes claims for itself, only by retrenching, restating, dramatizing, and inscribing its pain in politics, and can hold out no future—for itself or others—which triumphs over this pain. The loss of historical direction, and with it the loss of futurity characteristic of the late-modern age, is thus homologically refigured in the structure of desire of the dominant political expression of the age—identity politics. . . .What if we sought to supplant the language of "I am"—with its defensive closure on identity, its insistence on the fixity of position, its equation of social with moral positioning—with the language of "I want"?[48]

---

48. Brown, "Wounded Attachments," 220, 221.

The critical clarity of a subordinate population's politicized pain has provided crucially destabilizing material that disaffirms the organization of liberal national culture around a utopian form of personhood that lives in zones of privacy and abstraction beyond pain, and, as a counterhegemonic *tactic,* this logic of radical juridicality affirms more powerfully than anything the fragile and violent disavowals that bolster hegemonic worlds of reason and the law.

But to say that the traumatized self is the true self is to say that a particular facet of subjective experience is where the truth of history lies: it is to suggest that the clarity of pain marks a political map for achieving the good life, if only we would read it. It is also to imply that in the good life there will be no pain. Brown suggests that a replacement of traumatic identity with a subjectivity articulated utopianly, via the agency of imagined demand, will take from pain the energy for social transformation beyond the field of its sensual experience. For this to happen *psychic pain experienced by subordinated populations must be treated as ideology,* not as prelapsarian knowledge or a condensed comprehensive social theory. It is more like a capital letter at the beginning of an old bad sentence that needs rewriting. To think otherwise is to assert that pain is merely banal, a story always already told. It is to think that the moment of its gestation is, indeed, life itself.

Coda: Pregnancy, Paranoia, Justice

The world I have tried to telegraph here, in this story about privacy's fall from the utopia of normal intimacy, finds the law articulating its subjects as public and American through their position within a hegemonic regime of heterosexuality, which involves coordination with many other normative social positions that are racially and economically coded toward privilege. I have argued that the split between the patriotic context of national metaculture and the practical fragmentations and hierarchies of everyday life has become powerfully mediated by a discourse of trauma, which imagines "relief" through juridicalized national remedies because, in fighting against the false utopia of privacy, it imagines subjects wholly created by law.

Too often, and almost always in the work of legal radicals, the nation remains sanctified as a political "zone of privacy" in *Griswold*'s sense: it holds out a promise that it can relieve specific subjects of the pain of their specificity, even as the very project of nation formation virtually requires the public exposure of those who do not structurally assimilate to the national norm (so, if population x is relieved of the obstacles to its juridical and cultural citizenship, a given population y will almost inevitably come to bear the burden of surrogacy that expresses citizenship's status as *privilege*). Fighting for justice under the law in the face of these normative strategies is crucial, a tactic of necessity. If it means telling half-truths (that an experience of painful identity shocks a minoritized subject) in order to change juridical norms about that kind of subject, it still must be a good thing. But thinking that the good life will be achieved when there is no more pain but only (your) happiness does nothing to alter the hegemonic structures of normativity and mourning whose saturation of the diminished expectations for liberty in national life I have sketched out in this essay. The reparation of pain does not bring into being a just life.

Usually this point is made in studies of testimony and the Holocaust, the unspeakable national violence that generates horrific evidence that will always fail to represent the brutal totality of its referent and which can never be repaired, reparated.[49] The cases addressed in this essay, in contrast, are ever so banal, cruel but not unusual, an ordinary part of everyday citizenship for subordinate populations in the United States. Such a difference advises replacing the model of trauma I have been critically describing as inadequate material for world or nation building with a model of *suffering,* whose etymological articulation of pain and patience draws its subject less as an effect of an act of violence and more as an effect of a general atmosphere of it, peppered by acts, to be sure, but not contained by the presumption that trauma carries, that it is an effect of a single scene of violence or toxic taxonomy. Thus, where certain ordinary identity forms are concerned, the question of suffering's *differend* might be drawn and drawn out differently, without the danger of analytically diffusing any population's subordination into some parodically postmodern miasma of overdetermination and pseudo-agency. (But even *suffering* can sound too dramatic for the subordinated personhood form I am reaching toward here: imagine a word that describes a constantly destabilized existence that monitors, with a roving third eye, every moment as a potentially

---

49. See Shoshana Felman and Dori Laub, *Testimony: Crises of Witnessing in Literature, Psychoanalysis, and History* (New York: Routledge, 1992); Jean-Francois Lyotard, *The Differend: Phrases in Dispute,* trans. Georges Van Den Abberle (Minneapolis: University of Minnesota Press, 1988).

bad event in which a stereotyped someone might become food for someone else's hunger for superiority and connect that to a term that considers the subjective effects of structural inequalities that are deemed inevitable in a capitalist nation. *Suffering* stands in for that compound word.)

I can provide here only a sketch of this model of pain, subjectivity, and politics. We might start in a place not defined by taxonomic identity, an image of the subject as heterotopic, distracted, or what I have called "loose." Earlier in this essay privacy law was a place of intensified gendering and sexualization: women versus fetuses, wives versus husbands, the law versus the sanctity of the marital couple. Identity was clear; it was bounded; it was opposed to counteridentity. But (as Denise Riley argues), when women are not in any kind of court defending their gender, they experience the relation between their juridicalized femaleness and other scenes of womanhood and identity-style attachment in inconsistent ways.[50] Barbara Duden, Emily Martin, and Rayna Rapp's three ethnographies of the racial, class, and ethnic contexts of reproduction in the United States tell constantly of the minoritization of pregnant women in the face of medical and state expertise about fetuses, health, cleanliness, monitoring.[51] It is as though these women are even more incompetent to the scene of their survival than ordinary consumers, whose desires are at least constantly rerendered as self-expertise by the pedagogies of capitalist culture. Yet the reproducing women have created a sentimental culture of their own, which coexists with the zones of their subordination: it is not that radical, yet it is very critical and, above all, skeptical about the relation between knowing about women's material struggles and making them uninevitable.

I take as an example the book *Peaceful Pregnancy Meditations*. This 1993 book epitomizes much contemporary feminine self-help literature. It merges insights about women's expertise over their bodies from

---

50. Denise Riley, *"Am I That Name?": Feminism and the Category of "Women" in History* (Minneapolis: University of Minnesota Press, 1988).

51. Emily Martin, *The Woman in the Body: A Cultural Analysis of Reproduction* (Boston: Beacon Press, 1987); Rayna Rapp, "Constructing Amniocentesis: Maternal and Medical Discourses," in *Uncertain Terms*, ed. Faye D. Ginsburg and Anna Lowenhaupt Tsing (Boston: Beacon Press, 1990), 28–42; and "Chromosomes and Communication: The Discourse of Genetic Counseling," *Medical Anthropology Quarterly* 2, no. 2 (1991): 143–57; Barbara Duden, *Disembodying Women: Perspectives on Pregnancy and the Unborn* (Cambridge: Harvard University Press, 1993).

the feminist health movements of the 1970s and the sentimental feminine self-help movement of the 1980s, which emphasizes women's expertise over intimate suffering. It takes pregnancy as the condition of ordinary femininity writ large; it uses twelve-step language to partition and make livable the predictable but excruciating changes of pregnancy; it provides on each page space for the reader to become an author through a routine of daily affirmations that enable pregnant women to apportion their anxieties through a life lived one day at a time. It actively disaffirms the political public sphere as the source of emancipatory public making. It is paranoid about the ceaselessness of women's caretaking burdens in the family and affective burdens in society. Its paranoia is entirely banal, about the conditions of women's ordinary lives.

Peaceful Pregnancy Meditations begins with a defensive nod to the world of fetal politics. Day 1, whose title is "Beginnings," begins: "When does pregnancy really begin? At conception? Years ago when we started yearning for a family of our own? Yesterday when our home pregnancy test turned positive? For each mother-to-be, it is different. But no matter where we define our beginning, we know it is truly that: a new beginning."[52] The beautiful tautologies and open questions of this passage provide for the pregnant gender a way of negotiating a complex set of contexts for maternal paranoia and the undue burdens of femininity in the contemporary United States. Pregnancy advice books have long made the woman responsible for fetal health. They have long made the woman feel that the development of her managerial skills is crucial to the happiness of everyone who depends on her to provide clarity for them. But the current public mistrust of women's competence to the maternal service economy has intensified the disciplinary aspects of these discourses and has made women even more defensive.

George's refusal to accede to the priority of fetal personhood or any norm of femininity remains resolute throughout the text. What she does prioritize is ameliorating the shame at the center of the experience of modern pregnancy. She releases women from shame about the ambivalence they feel toward the fetus and the theft of ordinary life that the fetus engenders; she acknowledges women's ambivalence

---

52. Lisa Steele George, *Peaceful Pregnancy Meditations: A Diary for Expectant Mothers* (Deerfield Beach, Fl.: Health Communications, 1993), 3.

toward the couple form and supports their need to build a social world to soften the blows and stresses of a marital intimacy that can only be enjoyed in random moments of repose. Above all, she confirms the rationality of women's ambivalent feelings about the pressure not to have a self that is a part of what structural pain demands of dominated persons.

On each page of the book, which represents one day, pregnant femininity is de-shamed by way of a dialectic between the anger/frustration/discomfort of the reader's complicated social meaning and the assurance and comfort of the poetic affirmation that George writes on each page. The affirmation, a kind of lay prayer, enables the reader to endure that life of which she surely is not master. Formally, this is signified by: a top paragraph (with titles such as "Privacy," "Manly Pride," "Chronic Uncertainty," "Ultrasound") that expresses the zone of discomfort that this day's meditation depicts; a middle paragraph that graphs an affirmation of the reader's desire not to be defeated by today's degree of pain (as in "I try to remain positive toward those around me, seeing their attention as love");[53] and then a bottom third made up of four empty lines for women to write on, which begin with the three words "Today I feel. . . ."

The book does offer the suffering women a dependable space of feeling and temporal freedom from the cramped conditions of social value and everydayness that pregnant women negotiate: women's culture, a survival mechanism that involves forming a relationship with particular commodity forms and, through them, with other women who feel the way they feel, because they are regendered as pregnant women. In this way this book, and the culture of affectivity and opinion that produces other commodities in support of its project of consolation and buttressing, keeps maternity/femininity in the United States from being merely a humiliating, isolating/collectivizing scene of personal struggle, public embarrassment, and alienated nonrepresentation in the political public sphere. This is what makes it a part of sentimental culture. Its aim, however, is not to change the law but to confirm the sheer difficulty of being made its subject while existing in so many strange relations undescribable by the terms *power/powerlessness, pain/happiness, equality/inequality*.

The suffering that George represents neither clarifies into a single

---

53. Ibid., 167.

struggle nor confuses the immediate sources of discomfort as the totality of actual sources. She sees a whole structure and a set of different ideologies in place, situating and destabilizing women and the contexts they inhabit: she cannot imagine freedom in these contexts but merely survival. She suffers gendering, and not just for her married self—but imagines the different contexts of struggle occupied by single mothers-to-be, lesbian mothers-to-be, working mothers-to-be, and the most conventional married mothers-to-be. Linked to one another by a collective experience of being public and scrutinized in pregnancy, they can live the unique change from the positions they were in when they were nonreproducing gendered, sexual, and economic subjects. In their intimacy with and alterity to the reduced versions of their gender, the women imagined in this book imagine no outside to history, no radically different future from the one they are presently suffering (and also finding sustenance in), but an ongoing present in which they are fragmented agents whose strange social value forces a constant improvisation and scraping together of a viable existence.

The binary trauma/reparation would not satisfy the conditions of genuine social oppression that (pregnant) women in the U.S. endure. Their issues are not with the past or with events marked by the scars of trauma. Their issues are with the material conditions of intimacy and the normative ideologies of desire; with having more symbolic than social value, derived from their expertise in realms of feeling; and with having no place for and therefore only a weak commitment to their anger, which pulsates instead as a muffled tone of resigned resentment. The heavily symbolized are always supposed to take whatever social value that status accords and hoard it for an always deferred future, meanwhile coping, if they can, in the everyday.

Sentimental culture takes its strength from this recognition and, in this case, by framing normative femininity and reproduction as processes of labor it establishes gender praxis as a ground of solidarity. But because this labor is so mixed up with intimacy, and therefore with the grounds of optimism, a political response would threaten the only domain of experience that women "control": contemporary national/capitalism has made a bargain with "the personal," after all, which is that people can have dignity in its domains only insofar as they inhabit the world passively, through the negativity of trauma and the optimism held out by that Oz over the mountaintop, a (nation-)state of amelioration. The liberal-radical solution to such positioning has been to deploy an ethics of storytelling about trauma against the normative world of the law, to change the conditions of what counts as evidence, and to make something concrete happen in response, something that pays for the past that is the present. As Derrida has recently argued, however, the dialectic between situated expression that challenges universalist norms and the categorical universalism of law itself constitutes an incommensurateness already within the law that cannot be overcome by law.[54] This sugests why the reparative use of the law I have been tracking is finally, and wearily, sentimental.

Political optimism requires a future, any future that might not be more drowning in the present. This requires a violation of the sentimental contract by an analytically powerful and political rage, a discourse of demand and radical critique, a sacrifice of short-term coalition building to a politics of the long haul. It requires a refusal to be humiliated by its "irrelevance" to policy in an era of transnational capitalist triumphalism, class-bound racism, and sentimental misogyny. It requires a refusal of the seeming rationality of diminished expectations. Most important, at the moment, it requires a refusal of the juro-politics of affect, which uses trauma and stigma to measure injustice through a *feeling* someone has. The everyday struggle is a ground that must be fought for and expanded to include nonsensual experience and knowledge as a part of any "personal" story. This is what was meant by "the personal is the political," a sentence virtually impossible to understand at the present moment. It did not mean that there is only the personal, no such thing as the political. It meant to say that feeling is an unreliable measure of justice and fairness, not the most reliable one; and that new vocabularies of pleasure, recognition, and equity must be developed and taught. And that the everyday of struggle, where people live, is a ground on which ecstasy and theory and unpredicted change can be mapped into a world that will not look like the opposite of the painful one.

Who gave anyone expertise over the meaning of feelings of injustice? I was sympathetic to the cultural politics of pain until I felt the violence of sentimentality: presented as a horror at momentous mass trauma that unifies a fractured society, national sentimentality is too often a defensive response by people who identify with privilege yet

---

54. Jacques Derrida, "Force of Law: The 'Mystical Foundations of Authority,' " in *Deconstruction and the Possibility of Justice*, ed. David Gray Carlson, Drucilla Cornell, and Michel Rosenfeld (New York: Routledge, 1992), 3–67, esp. 61–63.

fear they will be exposed as immoral by their tacit sanction of a particular structural violence that benefits them. I was a wholly sympathetic participant in practices of subaltern testimony and complaint, until I saw that the different stories of trauma wielded in the name of a population's political suffering not only tended to confirm the state and its law as the core sites of personhood but also provided opportunities to isolate further these dominated populations by inciting competitions over whose lives have been more excluded from the "happiness" that was constitutionally promised by national life. Meanwhile, the public recognition by dominant culture of certain sites of publicized subaltern suffering is frequently (mis)taken as a big step toward the amelioration of that suffering. It is a baby step, if that. I have suggested, in contrast, that the pain and suffering of subordinated subjects in everyday life is an ordinary and ongoing thing that is underdescribed by the (traumatic) identity form and its circulation in the state and the law. If identity politics is a literacy program in the alphabet of that pain, its subjects must also assume that the signs of subordination they feel also tell a story that they do not feel yet, or know, about how to construct the narrative to come.

Why Culture Matters to Law: The Difference Politics Makes

Dorothy E. Roberts

Why does culture matter to law? Notice I have not bothered to ask whether culture does in fact matter. As I will soon elaborate, critical legal scholars have definitively shown that neutral legal principles that pretend to disregard culture in fact privilege dominant cultural norms. This has also been the result of court decisions that place culture outside the law's reach. In *Plessy v. Ferguson*[1] the United States Supreme Court upheld the separate but equal doctrine on the ground that the Fourteenth Amendment could not possibly have been intended to abolish social conventions proscribing the commingling of the races. "Legislation is powerless to eradicate racial instincts . . . and the attempt to do so can only result in accentuating the difficulties of the present situation," the Court explained.[2] It therefore concluded that, although the law required blacks' *political* equality, "if one race be inferior to the other *socially*, the constitution of the United States cannot put them upon the same plane."[3]

The Court reasoned, in other words, that the law should not interfere with culture—in this case, the social segregation of blacks from whites. Thus, the Court's separation of culture from politics sanctioned both private and official discrimination against blacks. Culture mattered to the Court's decision, whether to affirm the law requiring blacks to ride in separate railway cars or to overturn it. There was no way to avoid the law's impact on the cultural mores of racial separation. That

---

1. 163 U.S., 537 (1896).
2. 163 U.S., 551.
3. 163 U.S., 552 (emph. added).

settled, the inquiry becomes not whether culture *should* matter to law but, rather, *how* it should matter.

Anthropologists now understand culture in terms of the common meanings, or worldview, that people create and reproduce as members of societies as well as more tangible features such as custom, tradition, and language. Culture is "a set of shared understandings, whether consciously held or not, which makes it possible for a group of people to act in concert with one another."[4] What distinguishes different cultures is not so much their various material artifacts as the different meanings that they attach to things and experiences that are the same across cultures.[5] As one commentator puts it, "culture provides the meaning of and reason for social action."[6] My thesis in this essay is that political action provides the meaning of and reason for culture. I shall attempt to sort through arguments about the importance of culture to law in order to make one central claim: our determination of why culture matters to law must depend on our political objectives. More specifically, I contend that the goal of achieving substantive equality should guide our deliberations about culture's role in creating and interpreting law.

Another possibility is that culture is valuable independent of political objectives and that we should therefore analyze culture's relationship to law without regard to power arrangements. Why not celebrate human cultural difference because it is desirable in and of itself? As Anthony Appiah suggests in his defense of cosmopolitanism, "the reason nations matter is because they matter to *people*. Nations matter morally, when they do, in other words, for the same reason that football and opera matter: as things desired by autonomous agents, whose autonomous desires we ought to acknowledge and take account of, even if we cannot always accede to them."[7] I do not think I would dis-

---

4. Gerald Torres, "Local Knowledge, Local Color: Critical Legal Studies and the Law of Race Relations," *San Diego Law Review* 25 (1988):1043, 1062. For other descriptions of culture as shared meaning, see Ulf Hannerz, *Cultural Complexity: Studies in Social Organization of Meaning* (New York: Columbia University Press, 1992); Jeffrey C. Alexander, "Analytic Debates: Understanding the Relative Autonomy of Culture," in *Culture and Society: Contemporary Debates,* ed. Jeffrey C. Alexander and Steven Seidman (Cambridge: Cambridge University Press, 1990).

5. Linz Audain, "Critical Cultural Law and Economics, the Culture of Deindividualization, the Paradox of Blackness," *Indiana Law Review* 70 (1995): 709, 715–17.

6. Torres, "Local Knowledge," 1061.

7. Kwame Anthony Appiah, "Cosmopolitan Patriots," *Critical Inquiry* 23 (1997): 617, 624. I do not mean to suggest that Appiah's understanding of the moral significance of nations is unrelated to politics, for it supports his defense of liberal democracy that protects the rights of cosmopolitans.

tort Appiah's meaning too terribly if I substituted *culture* for *nations:* culture should matter to law because it matters to people. Now Appiah is not saying that culture matters no matter what, since, in his view, "the fundamental idea that every society should respect human dignity and personal autonomy is more basic than the cosmopolitan love of variety."[8] Other multiculturalists, however, have argued that culture matters virtually no matter what because of its importance to personal identity.[9]

These two approaches raise a related question: Does it matter why we think culture matters to law? In an article advocating affirmative action in legal academia Duncan Kennedy takes both approaches to culture's relationship to law. He first presents a politically progressive understanding and defense of cultural pluralism. At a minimum, he writes, cultural pluralism means that we should "deliberately structure[] institutions so that communities and social classes share wealth and power" and "no community or class is systematically subordinated."[10] It sounds as if his view of culture's role in politics, law, and law school faculties is shaped by his leftist political ideology.

Kennedy nevertheless goes on to say that his argument for affirmative action "includes the idea that cultural diversity and cultural development are good in themselves, even when they do not lead to increased power for subordinated communities in markets and political systems."[11] It is not clear why Kennedy added this point, for the remainder of his essay is characterized by a relentless attention to politics. I suppose Kennedy included this digression to recognize the contribution culture makes to our personal and collective lives even when we do not have politics in mind. He may have also wanted to head off the objection that his defense of academic diversity threatens to "politicize the university" and is, at bottom, anti-intellectual.[12] Whatever his motivation, his article leads me to wonder whether choosing between these two thoughts about why culture matters to law—for political ends or as a good in itself—itself makes a difference.

I lay the foundation for pondering this question by explaining the

---

8. Ibid., 15.
9. See, e.g., Charles Taylor, "The Politics of Recognition," in *Multiculturalism: Examining the Politics of Recognition,* ed. Amy Gutmann (Princeton: Princeton University Press, 1994).
10. Duncan Kennedy, "A Cultural Pluralist Case for Affirmative Action in Legal Academia," *Duke Law Journal* (1990): 705, 712–13.
11. Ibid., 713–14.
12. See Amy Gutmann, intro., in Gutmann, *Multiculturalism.*

problem with pretending that culture does not matter to law, including the dangers of a faith in a universal American culture. Having rejected this integrationist objective, I turn to the nationalist agenda of preserving the cultures of subordinated groups. I consider arguments calling for the law affirmatively to protect subordinated cultures and examine the critical role that politics plays in figuring out how the law might support cultural pluralism. I also pay special attention to the progressive project of using culture as a weapon for social change. I conclude by revisiting the possibility of a unified American culture that links together its diverse cultural communities by a common political commitment. Thus, I see politics as pivotal to the critique of dominant groups' practice of law to impose their cultural perspective on others as well as to the call for subordinated groups to appropriate law to preserve their own cultures. It is only in relation to the struggle to create more equitable arrangements of power that culture matters to law.

The Problem with Pretending Culture Does Not Matter

The traditional approach to the question I have set forth is that culture does not matter very much to law, nor should it. Consideration of culture, the story goes, would contaminate the neutral and objective process by which the law adjudicates conflicts between individuals. The law should recognize that Americans come from different cultures and ensure that the state keeps its nose out of people's customs. But culture should not affect the construction or application of legal principles. In short, law and culture should adopt a stance of peaceful coexistence.

The Fallacy of Cultural Neutrality

The confidence in culture's irrelevance to law has been soundly demolished by critical legal theorists, especially minority scholars. They have powerfully demonstrated that supposedly neutral legal principles mask an underlying white cultural norm that supports white people's way of life and political domination.

In the past whites in the United States used the law brutally to suppress other peoples' cultures. White settlers waged an all-out "cultural genocide" against Indian tribes, for example, by means of legal treaties, followed by executive orders and congressional governance.¹³ The Dawes Act of 1887 divided tribal lands among individual Indians, permitting the collapse of property ownership by sovereign tribes and the transfer of individual allotments to white hands.¹⁴ Whites abolished tribal courts and established "courts of Indian offenses," which punished Indians for practicing their "heathenish" culture. The Rules for Indian Court made it a crime, for example, for any Indian to "engage in the sun dance, scalp dance, or war dance, or any other similar feast."¹⁵ It was a misdemeanor for any Indian to refuse to "adopt habits of industry or to engage in civilized pursuits."¹⁶

Most of the time, however, the law promotes the dominant culture in much more subtle ways. Those in power need not resort to obvious cultural bias because the law's language of neutrality is already weighted in favor of the status quo. The process works like this: whites, as a result of their dominant political position, have been able to incorporate their own cultural perspective into legal principles; they have labeled these legal principles as universal despite their one-sided pedigree; then judges claim to be impartial when they impose these principles without regard to and against the interests of people from minority cultures.

It is hard to notice the law's bias because the dominant perspective has shaped the preexisting language that composes our jurisprudence. Concepts such as merit, the atomized individual, and the reasonable man that make legal rules seem to embody justice actually help to sustain the current order. As Richard Delgado and Jean Stefancic explain, "Long ago, empowered actors and speakers enshrined their meaning, preferences, and views of the world into the common culture and language. Now, deliberation within that language, purporting always to be neutral and fair, inexorably produces the results that reflect their interests."¹⁷

Thus, law, although infused with culture, appears to be without

---

13. Rennard Strickland, "Genocide-at-Law: An Historic and Contemporary View of the Native American Experience," *Kansas Law Review* 34 (1986): 713.
14. Ibid., 724–25.
15. Ibid., 72.
16. Ibid.
17. Richard Delgado and Jean Stefancic, "Hateful Speech, Loving Communities: Why Our Notion of 'A Just Balance' Changes So Slowly," *California Law Review* 82 (1994): 851, 861.

culture. Culture is usually recognized in inverse proportion to power.[18] The more subordinated a community, the more culture it is seen to have. Blacks, Latinos, and Asians have culture—too much culture, some would hasten to add. White people do not. People in power view their way of life not as culture but, rather, as the way things are just supposed to be.

The transparency of white culture is illustrated by judges' frequent refusal in employment discrimination cases to protect black employees' behavior that conflicts with workplace norms. In *Rogers v. American Airlines*, for example, a black woman who wore her hair in cornrows challenged her employer's prohibition against wearing braids on the job based on the policy's discriminatory impact.[19] The court dismissed her claim because the anti-braid policy applied equally to members of all races and did not concern an immutable feature. Rogers, the court pointed out, could easily have changed her hairstyle. The court further opined that the airline's objective to "project a conservative and business-like image" qualified as a bona fide business purpose.[20]

In rejecting the possibility that cornrows might belong in the workplace, the court failed to question whether the airline's, as well as its own, conception of a "business-like image" was derived from white people's culture. It did not see its denial of Rogers' claim as having anything to do with culture at all. But, for black women told to remove their braids or get out, the court clearly declared that their right to work was conditioned on their renunciation of black culture.[21] The employment discrimination law's privileging of one culture over another had serious political ramifications, for it helped to maintain black women's economic subordination.

Here, then, is my first observation about the importance of politics to the question at hand. We cannot explain why culture has mattered to law without referring to relationships of power: the transparent cultural standard hidden in the law got there as a result of social inequities, and it often works to privilege not only white people's way of life but also their position of power.

---

18. Martha R. Mahoney, "Segregation, Whiteness, and Transformation," *University of Pennsylvania Law Review* 143 (1995): 1659, 1664.
19. 527 F. Supp., 229 (SDNY 1981).
20. 527 F. Supp., 233.
21. See Paulette M. Caldwell, "A Hair Piece: Perspectives on the Intersection of Race and Gender," *Duke Law Journal* (1991): 365, 367.

The Problem with a Unified American Identity

Cultural diversity is also made invisible in the integrationist ideal of an American ethnic identity. The unified American identity has historically been pursued as a form of cultural competition—the quest for one superior culture to win out over others. Benjamin Franklin expressed this view when he asked, "Why should Pennsylvania, founded by the English, become a colony of aliens, who will shortly be so numerous as to Germanize us, instead of our Anglifying them?"[22] For many contemporary Americans, as for Franklin, achieving a common culture requires erasing minority cultures by Anglifying them. For decades the project of integrating blacks into the American mainstream has meant discounting the value of black institutions and perspectives. This biased standard is particularly conspicuous in current anti-immigration rhetoric.[23] Proponents of measures to close U.S. borders often defend their position by pointing to the threat that immigration poses for cultural unity. Conservative presidential candidate Pat Buchanan, for example, has proposed "a timeout from illegal immigration so that we can become one nation and one culture. So we can all learn the same customs and traditions."[24]

This view assumes that assimilation is the only model that generates a truly American identity, precluding more inclusive, plural, and sociologically accurate notions of culture in the United States. The assimilationist ideal, moreover, has only operated one way. Underlying whites' appeal to cultural unity is the fear of a loss of cultural preeminence. While whites have demanded that nonwhites assimilate to an Anglo-American way of life, the possibility that whites should assimilate to nonwhite cultures seems downright un-American. This thinking assumes that American culture is synonymous with the culture of white people and that the cultures of Third World immigrants are incompatible with a national identity.

---

22. Quoted in Kenneth L. Karst, "Paths to Belonging: The Constitution and Cultural Identity," *North Carolina Law Review* 64 (1986): 303, 303.

23. For further discussion of the racist meaning of American identity advocated by anti-immigration advocates, see Dorothy E. Roberts, "Who May Give Birth to Citizens? Reproduction, Eugenics and Immigration" in *Immigrants Out! The New Nativism and the Anti-Immigrant Impulse in the United States*, ed. Juan F. Perea (New York: New York University Press, 1996), 205.

24. Lori Rodriguez, "No Justice in Simpson Trial, Buchanan Tells Black Group," *Houston Chronicle*, 8 October 1995, 23.

I want to emphasize that this call for a unified American identity does not arise principally from a distaste for foreign cultures. The objection to a pluralistic conception of American identity is political, not aesthetic. Anti-immigration propaganda often links the cultural threat posed by the United States' changing demographics to a political upheaval. Thus, in an article entitled "This Melting Pot Is Boiling Over" a *Boston Herald* columnist warned that immigration from the Caribbean and Latin America will cause a "multicultural fraying of the social fabric," leading to "riots, cultural separatism, a racialized system of justice . . . and demands for reparations."[25] The author also made it a point to note that these dark-skinned immigrants "immediately qualify for affirmative-action preferences, as will their children and grandchildren."[26]

Multiculturalism is interpreted as balkanization now that the combination of minority groups' insistence on political equality, whites' decreasing numerical predominance, and the country's economic problems threaten to destabilize the social order. These whites celebrate America's cultural diversity as a beautiful mosaic as long as it does not entail any redistribution of wealth and power. When accompanied by political demands, however, cultural pluralism looks like a splintering form of tribalism. This conditional acceptance of diversity without power helps to clarify why Ellen Rooney characterized liberal pluralism as a "heterogeneous yet hegemonic discourse."[27]

Disclosing these modes of cultural bias shows that culture does indeed matter to law. But eliminating cultural *bias* from the law does not necessarily mean eliminating *culture* from the law. Indeed, the fallacy of neutral principles supports the conclusion that culture's influence on the law is unavoidable. Having exploded the myth of cultural neutrality, then, we must proceed to determine how and why culture *should* matter to law.

Is There a Positive Role for Law? The Affirmative Preservation of Cultures

Culture's role in law is as important to nationalists as it is to integrationists. While dominant groups practice law as a tool of cultural sup-

---

25. Don Feder, "This Melting Pot Is Boiling Over," *Boston Herald*, 4 October 1995, 33.
26. Ibid.
27. Ellen Rooney, "Who's Left Out? A Rose by Any Other Name Is Still as Red; or, The Politics of Pluralism," *Critical Inquiry* (Spring 1986): 55.

pression or even extermination, subordinated groups have begun to wield the law as a weapon of cultural preservation. Because culture is practiced in groups, this task belongs to the project of fitting group claims into a legal system founded on individual rights. Identity politics has proclaimed the systemic nature of injustices that once were perceived as aberrational acts of private bias. Eliminating discrimination may require fashioning legal remedies that redress group-wide damage instead of individual injuries. In addition, acting in concert with other members of one's group is more effective than airing isolated grievances. Despite the oppressive incorporation of the dominant culture in law, these may all be benefits of attending to subordinated cultures in legal decision making.

In considering the law's protection of minority cultures, I will adopt as a starting point Kenneth Karst's catalog of the ways constitutional law promotes cultural identification.[28] According to Karst, the principle of equal citizenship affords negative protection against formal discrimination based on a person's membership in a cultural group. It also gives positive protection both to the individual's freedom to choose her own cultural identity and to the group's freedom to exclude outsiders to maintain its own integrity. Thus, Karst sums up, the Constitution "allows an individual to maintain a strong connection to a particular cultural group and still belong to America."[29]

Yet advocates of cultural preservation might find this set of protections inadequate, for they offer primarily, to borrow Michael Walzer's phrase, "opportunities to individuals, not a voice to groups."[30] Political philosophers such as Walzer and Charles Taylor have argued that cultures deserve the law's respect, concern, and recognition in their own right.[31] If there are good reasons to preserve cultures, we might want legal principles that encourage government to take active steps to foster cultural diversity even at the price of interfering with individual interests or a sense of national unity. We might want to protect not only the individual's right to belong to a cultural group but also the cultural group's coercive power over its members.

28. Karst, "Paths to Belonging," 337–40.
29. Ibid., 361.
30. Michael Walzer, "Pluralism in Political Perspective," in *The Politics of Ethnicity*, eds. Michael Walzer, John Higham, and Michael Harrington (Cambridge: Harvard University, Belknap Press, 1982), 14, 22.
31. See Taylor, "Politics of Recognition"; Michael Walzer, "Nation and Universe," in *The Tanner Lectures on Human Values*, vol. 11 (Cambridge: Harvard University Press, 1990).

Congress applied this philosophy when it passed the Indian Child Welfare Act in response to Indian protest against the cultural decimation wrought by welfare agencies' wide-scale removal of Indian children from their families.[32] In explicit recognition of the "unique values of Indian culture" the act gives tribal courts exclusive jurisdiction over child custody proceedings concerning Indian children and establishes preferences to ensure placement with an Indian family. These rules may preempt a mother's choice to shirk tribal authority by placing her child in a non-Indian home, thus giving priority to tribal preservation over tribe members' liberty to make parental decisions.[33] Although the act contains jurisdictional provisions that compromise its recognition of tribal sovereignty, it nevertheless provides important safeguards for Indian cultural survival.[34]

Have we settled the question of culture's relationship to law? Is the answer to use the law consistently to safeguard subordinated cultures from outside intrusion? Closer examination reveals that this simple solution, without added concern for political ends, will yield inadequate and sometimes harmful results.

The controversy surrounding admission of cultural evidence in criminal trials illustrates the limitations of the single-minded objective of cultural preservation. Should defendants be permitted to rely on evidence that their foreign cultural background allows the behavior that the U.S. criminal justice system punishes? In a number of recent cases, usually involving Asian immigrant defendants, courts have mitigated the defendants' liability on the basis of a so-called cultural defense.[35] A New York trial judge, for example, sentenced Chinese immigrant

---

32. 25 U.S.C. SS 1901–63 (1982).

33. See Donna J. Goldsmith, "Individual vs. Collective Rights: The Indian Child Welfare Act," *Harvard Women's Law Journal* 13 (1990): 1, 2; *Mississippi Choctow Band of Indians v. Holyfield*, 490 U.S. 30 (1989) (voiding state court adoption decree involving children born off the reservation to a Choctow mother).

34. See Jeanne Louise Carriere, "Representing the Native American: Culture, Jurisdiction, and the Indian Child Welfare Act," *Iowa Law Review* 79 (1994): 585; Jill E. Adams, "The Indian Child Welfare Act of 1978: Protecting Tribal Interests in a Land of Individual Rights," *American Indian Law Review* 19 (1994): 301.

35. See Holly Maguigan, "Cultural Evidence and Male Violence: Are Feminist and Multiculturalist Reformers on a Collision Course in Criminal Courts?" *New York University Law Review* 70 (1995): 36; Daina C. Chiu, "The Cultural Defense: Beyond Exclusion, Assimilation, and Guilty Liberalism," *California Law Review* 82 (1994): 1053; Leti Volpp, "(Mis)Identifying Culture: Asian Women and the 'Cultural Defense,'" *Harvard Women's Law Journal* 17 (1994): 57.

Dong-Lu Chen to only five years probation after he bludgeoned his wife, Jian-wan, to death with a claw hammer because she had been unfaithful to him.[36] The judge explained that "Chen was the product of his culture.... The culture was never an excuse, but it is something that made him crack more easily."[37] In a California case involving a Chinese immigrant woman, Helen Wu, who strangled her son and then tried to commit suicide after her marriage failed, an appellate court held that the judge should have instructed the jury to consider Wu's cultural background.[38] Although courts have not adopted a formal, free-standing cultural defense, some commentators have advocated one as a way of adding the perspectives of other cultures to the criminal law.

Cultural background will almost always be relevant to a defendant's state of mind and therefore should be admitted in evidence. Without it juries are likely to misunderstand defendants' social context and will therefore be unable to judge their culpability fairly. Absent political insight, however, a cultural defense is at once over- and under-inclusive. It is over-inclusive because the claim "my culture made me do it" could pardon a multitude of crimes that most multiculturalists would agree merit no mercy. For one thing it would absolve many whites for crimes committed against people of minority groups for racist reasons. Bernard Goetz could claim that white cultural images of black criminality made him fear the four black teenagers who approached him on the subway asking for money.[39] The teenagers in Bensonhurst who accosted Yusef Hawkins could claim that their culture taught them to protect their neighborhood against invasion from blacks, especially when the invaders are suspected of dating the group's women. The laid-off autoworker who beat Victor Chin to death with a baseball bat could claim that his culture's historical enmity with the Japanese (he called Chin a "Jap") "made him crack." And any gang of thugs who assault gays and lesbians could certainly point to the deep

---

36. Rorie Sherman, "'Cultural' Defenses Draw Fire," *National Law Journal* (17 April 1989): 3.

37. Nina Schuyler, "Cultural Defense: Equality or Anarchy?" *San Francisco Weekly*, 25 September 1991, 1, 12.

38. *People v. Wu*, 286 Cal. Rptr. 868 (1991).

39. See generally Jody D. Armour, "Race Ipsa Loquitur: Of Reasonable Racists, Intelligent Bayesians, and Involuntary Negrophobes," *Stanford Law Review* 46 (1994): 781 (arguing that fairness to white defendants does not require recognition of racial stereotypes in self-defense law).

homophobia in American culture—and cite the United States Supreme Court's opinion in *Bowers v. Hardwick* for support.[40]

The cultural defense, on the other hand, is equally under-inclusive. The fact that judges have allowed culture to mitigate culpability almost exclusively on behalf of Asian immigrants suggests that this is not a case of cultural pluralism. Courts may be more willing to consider Asian defendants' cultural evidence because they see Asians as a model minority who, by and large, have successfully emulated the American values of family, education, and hard work.[41] Extending a cultural defense to more rebellious minorities such as blacks and Latinos, on the other hand, would likely be perceived as more of a threat to white people's welfare.

I am aware of a handful of cases involving black defendants' attempts to raise a cultural defense. It is no surprise that cultural evidence about the way black people communicate with one another or view white people has been excluded and that the defendants were given no leniency. One court rejected testimony about the cultural significance of the black defendant's shouting at the victim in a rape prosecution on the ground that "to allow a race or any group to set up for itself standards of conduct and reasonableness to apply to nonconsenting individuals in the context of rape is a concept that is unthinkable in our society."[42]

Courts have also rejected cultural evidence proffered by black defendants to challenge white domination. In *People v. Odinga*, for example, the court held cultural evidence irrelevant to the defendant's self-defense claim in his prosecution for killing a police officer.[43] Odinga wanted to explain the reasonableness of his actions through expert testimony on the impact that the history of racial oppression had on his perception of danger posed by the police. Prosecutors, on the other hand, have successfully used similar cultural evidence to damn unruly black defendants. In another prosecution of a black man for killing police officers, *People v. Aliwoli*, the court permitted the prosecutor to refer to black Muslims' characterization of white people as devils and to black Americans' "cultural paranoia" about white people.[44] Ali-

---

40. *Bowers v. Hardwick*, 478 U.S., 186 (1986).
41. See Chiu, "Cultural Defense," 1082–84.
42. *People v. Rhines*, 182 Cal. Rptr. 478, 483 (Cal. Ct. App. 1982).
43. *People v. Odinga*, 143 A.D.2d 202 (N.Y. App. Div. 1988).
44. *People v. Aliwoli*, 606 N.E.2d 347 (Ill. App. Ct. 1992).

woli was sentenced to sixty years in prison. Not only have black defendants been denied the opportunity to present cultural evidence in their favor, but this evidence has been used against them at trial.

Henry Louis Gates Jr. offered a cultural defense of the rap group 2 Live Crew during its obscenity prosecution several years ago.[45] Gates claimed that the group's degrading lyrics embodied a distinctively black style of cultural expression that includes the street tradition called "signifying," or "playing the dozens." According to Gates, this cultural tradition inventively employs "sexual carnivalesque" and parody to contest racial stereotypes about black sexuality by embracing these stereotypes and then exploding them. Black feminists, however, did not get the joke.[46]

To challenge the misogyny of these lyrics does not discount the racism in the Broward County prosecutor's decision to single out 2 Live Crew's music from the ample assortment pornography available on the Florida market.[47] And, although the Supreme Court's test for obscenity excludes material with social or artistic value,[48] the Florida judge did not credit Gates's testimony about the lyrics' cultural significance.[49] Just as significant as Gates's use of culture to defend 2 Live Crew's lyrics is the court's unwillingness to allow the rappers' a cultural defense, despite the artistic merit of rap music, the cultural traditions that it manifests, and its potential for political subversion. My point is not to join the defense of 2 Live Crew's lyrics but, rather, to demonstrate the biased way in which courts have applied cultural defenses. Judges have accepted novel defense theories to mitigate the sentences of immigrant defendants while rejecting a settled First Amendment defense in the case of black rap artists. Although I disagree with Gates's cultural legitimation of 2 Live Crew's sexism, I find the judicial system's racial discrimination even more troubling.

We should eliminate judges' cultural bias from the application of cultural defenses. If courts adopt a rule that permits the admission of cultural evidence to help to demonstrate the defendant's state of mind, the rule should apply to all cultures. Evidence about the antagonistic

---

45. See Henry Louis Gates Jr., "2 Live Crew, Decoded," *New York Times*, 19 June 1990, A23.
46. See, e.g., Kimberlé Crenshaw, "Mapping the Margins: Intersectionality, Identity Politics, and Violence against Women," *Stanford Law Review* 43 (1991): 1241.
47. Ibid., 1292–94.
48. *Miller v. California*, 413 U.S., 15 (1973).
49. Crenshaw, "Mapping the Margins."

relationship between black communities and the police is just as relevant to this limited purpose as is evidence about traditional Chinese views about the family. First Amendment protection of artistic expression should safeguard black people's culture as much as the dominant one. Yet culture should not supersede our political commitment to treat human beings with equal dignity. Culture, then, is not an excuse for violence against women.

Judges seem more willing to accept cultural evidence on behalf of foreigners than on behalf of people who have had time to adapt to "American" culture. Ironically, the very foreignness of Indian culture that once justified its most brutal suppression now supports Congress's policy to sustain that culture through the Indian Child Welfare Act. Indian culture may be preserved because it is isolated on reservations, where it will have no impact on ordinary Americans' daily lives, except perhaps in Americans' fantasizing about Indians' spiritual closeness to nature. Arguments favoring race matching in adoptions of black children on the grounds of black cultural preservation have been far more controversial. The preservation of Indian culture, moreover, has had little effect on Indian poverty and unemployment. This contradiction allowed McGeorge Bundy to declare, "American Indians are by any measure *save cultural heritage* the country's most disadvantaged minority."[50] Preserving minority culture on the basis of its distance from the American mainstream suffers from the same flaw as the assimilationist ideal. Both contain the political presumption that minority cultures deserve no part of structuring systems of power.

Moreover, cultural evidence is usually admitted to defend conduct that does not depart too drastically from the dominant cultural norm. In the cases I have mentioned, courts attributed to foreign culture behavior that conformed to the standard of patriarchal gender relations that characterizes American culture. The court acknowledged Dong-Lu Chen's culture to explain husbands' brutal subordination of their wives; the admission of cultural evidence in the case of Helen Wu supported women's role as self-sacrificing mother. After all, finding one's wife in flagrante delicto is the paradigmatic heat of passion event that mitigates murder to manslaughter in traditional U.S. criminal law and has even excused it.[51] Surely, the prevalence of domestic violence in

---

50. Quoted in Ed Magnuson and Keith Johnson, "The Angry American Indian: Starting Down the Protest Trail," *Time,* 9 February 1970, 14, 15.
51. See Donna K. Coker, "Heat of Passion and Wife Killing: Men Who Batter/Men Who Kill," *Southern California Review of Law and Women's Studies* 2 (1992): 71.

this country and the way that family, neighbors, police, prosecutors, and judges have condoned it demonstrates its prominence in American culture. I would imagine that an American man traveling abroad who shoots his wife to death would have no difficulty eliciting expert testimony on these facts in order to establish an American cultural defense.

Paradoxically, then, cultural evidence usually benefits foreigners whose behavior adheres to patriarchal mandates and poses no threat to white domination. A policy that gives certain cultural minorities the option of assimilating to dominant American norms or preserving their own nonthreatening customs leaves the political order intact. The spectacle of a white anthropologist testifying in court about his stereotyped image of a foreign culture, as occurred in the case of Dong-Lu Chen, is not a very radical picture. A radical pluralism, on the other hand, would seek to incorporate minority cultural perspectives into the criminal justice system that governs everyone. But that would require more than the admission of cultural evidence in criminal trials; it would require the political empowerment of cultural minorities. Another problem with cultural defenses, then, is that they are a weak substitute for a far more important project of ensuring that subordinated groups can participate in the construction and enforcement of the criminal law.

The Relationship between Culture and Political Change

Certainly, recognizing the way in which the law's preference for white people's culture has supported white domination is essential to eradicating that domination. I have just argued as well that political change is required for real incorporation of new cultural perspectives into the law. But is the preservation of subordinate group culture a necessary foundation for political change?

Because the cultures of disempowered groups challenge the dominant culture, they may provide the ingredients for the vision of a just social order.[52] Culture is a weapon of political resistance. The oppressed create their own counterstories that subvert the dominant version of reality.[53] Their subcultures provide a space within the culture of domination in which people who are bombarded daily by degrading images of themselves can celebrate their loveliness and

---

52. Torres, "Local Knowledge," 1068.
53. Richard Delgado, "Storytelling for Oppositionists and Others: A Plea for Narrative," *Michigan Law Review* 87 (1989): 2411, 2413.

moral worth; a space in which people who have been subjugated can transform the oppressive understanding of social relations into more liberating ones. Fostering black culture is a way of loving blackness, something bell hooks calls a revolutionary intervention.[54] Storytelling from minority cultures can help to change the background understandings that determine the interpretation of legal decisions, giving law reform efforts a greater chance of success.[55]

Subordinated cultures may even appropriate for their own purposes the very ideologies intended to oppress them. For example, African slaves reinterpreted conservative Christianity as an affirmation of their humanity and a call to revolutionary action.[56] Far from understanding the Bible as a legitimating text, slaves saw in Scripture divine condemnation of their earthly subjugation: "To the surprise and fear of many whites, slaves transformed an ideology intended to reconcile them to a subordinate status into a manifesto of their God-given equality."[57] The black jazz musician's improvisational skill has come to symbolize for minority scholars the remarkable cultural technique of transforming ordinary notes into something extraordinary, distinctive, and rebellious.[58] Just as John Coltrane or Archie Shepp could turn a standard melody into a radically new composition, minority cultures might reinvent a vision of justice out of their experience with oppression and the remnants of washed-out legal doctrine.

It makes sense that the best insight for eradicating systemic injustices and defining the contours of a just society will flow from the cultures that have suffered most. We should "look to the bottom," in Mari Matsuda's words, because groups who have experienced discrimination "speak with a special voice."[59] Minority culture is indispensable to

---

54. bell hooks, "Black Looks: Race and Representation" (Boston: South End Press, 1992), 20.

55. Richard Delgado, "Rodrigo's Final Chronicle: Cultural Power, the Law Reviews, and the Attack on Narrative Jurisprudence," *Southern California Law Review* 68 (1995): 545, 563.

56. Anthony E. Cook, "Beyond Critical Legal Studies: The Reconstructive Theology of Dr. Martin Luther King, Jr.," *Harvard Law Review* 103 (1990): 985, 1018.

57. Ibid.

58. See, e.g., Mari J. Matsuda, "Looking to the Bottom: Critical Legal Studies and Reparations," *Harvard Civil Rights Civil Liberties Law Review* 22 (1987): 323, 336–37, 388; John O. Calmore, "Critical Race Theory, Archie Shepp, and Fire Music: Securing an Authentic Intellectual Life in a Multicultural World," *Southern California Law Review* 65 (1992): 2129.

59. Matsuda, "Looking to the Bottom," 323.

the process of social change: the concrete experience of oppression cannot be replicated in the imagination of moral philosophers who fashion theories of justice from abstract social positioning.[60]

The insight that minority cultures provide extends beyond ways to ameliorate specific systemic flaws; these cultures may be guided by a wholly different perspective that contests the individualism, materialistic greed, and alienation of the Western worldview. Minority cultures are also a source of inspiration, for they have miraculously survived the onslaught of supremacist ideology, every form of marginalization imaginable, and sheer brute terror. "Cultures have a spirit," writes Indian law scholar Rennard Strickland.[61] And that spirit can be tapped to revitalize America's decaying social order. Paying attention to culture may be necessary not only for minority group survival but for the survival of America itself.

Thus, black nationalist Harold Cruse, finding that the Negro problem in the United States was "primarily a cultural question," centered his program for black liberation on attacking white control of the country's cultural apparatus and fostering the vitality of black cultural life.[62] For Cruse social change required a cultural revolution designed to achieve "the complete democratization of the national cultural ethos."[63]

Yet the thesis that the cultures of subordinated groups are necessarily radical or that all aspects of these cultures challenge the dominant mind-set is fallacious. As we saw with cultural defenses, some features of these cultures may reproduce the oppressive status quo. Nor can the culture of subordinated groups be reduced to their struggle against oppression. As Patricia Williams has pointed out, "battling discrimination, although a generalizable group experience, is not the same as or the whole of what I am calling culture."[64] Resistance theorists have acknowledged that subordinate groups respond to power in both reactionary and progressive ways, both supporting the dominant social structure and subverting it. As Henry A. Giroux observed in his study of students' oppositional acts, "Put simply, not all oppositional behav-

---

60. Ibid., 324.
61. Strickland, "Genocide-at-Law," 752.
62. Harold Cruse, *Rebellion or Revolution?* (New York: Morrow, 1968), 66.
63. Harold Cruse, *The Crisis of the Negro Intellectual* (New York: Morrow, 1967), 456.
64. Patricia J. Williams, "*Metro Broadcasting, Inc. v. FCC*: Regrouping in Singular Times," *Harvard Law Review* 104 (1990): 525, 529 n. 23.

ior has 'radical significance,' nor is all oppositional behavior a clear-cut response to domination."[65] Only political principles can distinguish between those aspects of culture that are truly subversive and liberatory from those that reproduce the dominant mind-set.

Nationalism that centers on cultural unity rather than political allegiance tends to become obsessed with cultural purity or authenticity, often devolving into outlandish claims about members' primordial superiority and irrational beliefs about outsiders' evil nature. This type of nationalism leads to calcification of the group's boundaries and intolerant enforcement of the official view of authentic group characteristics. Elizabeth Kiss points out that cultural nationalists in postcommunist East-Central Europe claim that Jews are culturally "alien" and cannot be "authentic" Poles or Hungarians.[66] During the 1960s some black nationalists, such as Ron Karenga, similarly prescribed images of authentic black culture that exaggerated the inherent cultural distance between blacks and whites and put women in a subordinate role.[67] Kenneth Karst fears that a gay nationalist strategy risks reducing the group's individual members to the single dimension that defines the group, creating intolerance of diversity among its presumed members, and reinforcing the binary view that defines everyone in society as gay or straight.[68] Based on these concerns, we could take the postmodernist position that all identity categories are a myth and therefore seek to explode rather than fortify them.[69]

The reason why we should not take this course again derives from politics. Black nationalism, for example, is a political strategy that offers the only hope of liberation for the masses of black people in the United States. Indeed, it may offer the only hope of real social progress in the United States, whose revolutionary will has been perpetually stymied by the country's racial deadlock.[70] White Americans' unwillingness to

---

65. Henry A. Giroux, "Theories of Reproduction and Resistance in the New Sociology of Education: A Critical Analysis," *Harvard Education Review* 53 (1983): 257, 285.

66. Elizabeth Kiss, "Is Nationalism Compatible with Human Rights? Reflections on East-Central Europe" in *Identities, Politics, and Rights,* ed. Austin Sarat and Thomas R. Kearns (Ann Arbor: University of Michigan Press, 1995).

67. Robert Allen, *Black Awakening in Capitalist America* (Garden City, N.Y.: Doubleday, 1969), 139–44; Gary Peller, "Race Consciousness," *Duke Law Journal* (1990): 758, 819.

68. Kenneth Karst, "Myths of Identity: Individual and Group Portraits of Race and Sexual Orientation," *UCLA Law Review* 43 (1995): 263, 363.

69. Ibid.

70. I elaborate this point in Dorothy E. Roberts, "Welfare and the Problem of Black Citizenship," *Yale Law Journal* 105 (1996): 1563 (book review).

grant full citizenship rights to blacks has persistently blocked efforts toward radical social change. The United States still suffers from the malady Harold Cruse diagnosed three decades ago: "White America has inherited a racial crisis that it cannot handle and is unable to create a solution for that does not do violence to the collective white American ego."[71] Black nationalism, including the nurturing of black culture, recognizes the futility of appeals to whites' self-interest and goodwill as remedies for racial subordination.

Concerns about essentialism should be dealt with, but they do not supersede the advantages of developing strong black political, economic, and cultural institutions as a liberation strategy. Our task is to apply politics to eliminate the black community's internal inequities and the exclusionary aspects of black culture, not to deny the importance of black culture and community altogether.

The political allegiance to a cultural group, moreover, can be a powerful rejection of biological definitions of identity.[72] I see identifying as black as at least as much a political choice as a biological destiny. It was whites who defined enslaved Africans as a biological race and whites who "were charged with the responsibility of maintaining racial purity" through the mandates of laws punishing interracial sex and marriage.[73] Blacks, in contrast, have resisted this racial ideology by defining themselves as a political group. True, being born to a parent with dark skin creates a presumption of group membership. But each black individual born in the United States must make the conscious decision whether or not to claim an affiliation with black culture and black people. She must resolve for herself the "two warring ideals in one dark body" that W. E. B. Du Bois so poignantly described in *The Souls of Black Folk*.[74] Stephen Carter says that the choice to identify with other black people "is partly cultural, partly social, and partly political, but it is mostly affectional."[75] Cultural identity can best avoid the pit-

---

71. Cruse, *Rebellion or Revolution*, 104.
72. For further discussion of genetics and racial identity, see Dorothy E. Roberts, "The Genetic Tie," *University of Chicago Law Review* 62 (1995): 209.
73. A. Leon Higginbotham Jr. and Barbara Kopytoff, "Racial Purity and Interracial Sex in the Law of Colonial and Antebellum Virginia," *Georgetown Law Journal* 77 (1989): 1967, 1968.
74. W. E. B. Du Bois, *The Souls of Black Folk* (New York: Signet, 1969), 45.
75. Stephen L. Carter, "The Black Table, the Empty Seat, and the Tie," in *Lure and Loathing: Essays on Race, Identity, and the Ambivalence of Assimilation*, ed. Gerald Early (New York: Allan Lane, 1994), 55, 64.

falls of essentialism if it is embraced partly as a political act and if it remains open to political critique.

Black cultural nationalist thinking displayed another fatal flaw: it held that black cultural expression itself could serve as a mechanism of black liberation. The harshest repudiation of this view came from black revolutionary nationalists such as the Black Panther's minister of defense, Huey Newton, who charged that these "pork chop nationalists" suffered from "having the wrong political perspective.... They feel that the African culture will automatically bring political freedom."[76] In *Black Awakening in Capitalist America* Robert Allen distinguished Harold Cruse's support for cultural revolution from cultural nationalists' mystical fascination with black art and culture. Yet Allen nevertheless questioned Cruse's reliance on democratic cultural pluralism to launch the black revolution. Allen argued that cultural nationalism as a separate ideology had no hope of bringing about social change unless it were incorporated into a revolutionary political movement.

Culturalism without ideological direction or as its own ideology will also fail to produce social change because its forms of expression are easily appropriated and rearticulated by the dominant culture in an effort to derail social struggle. Cultural symbols of political resistance may be packaged for mass consumption and stripped of their power to inspire collective political action. Movies about Malcolm X and the Black Panthers are box office hits, and songs from the civil rights movement sell products as background jingles in television commercials.[77] Indian cultural images have met a similar fate in movies such as the Oscar-winning *Dances with Wolves* and the antipollution advertisement displaying a tearful Indian elder.

In his analysis of Afro-Brazilian social protest in the 1970s Michael Hanchard highlights how the culturalist tendencies of Brazilian activists made their creative practices vulnerable to conversion into commodified leisure.[78] The Black Soul movement's music and dances, for example, which originated as a source of black cultural identity and solidarity, were soon incorporated by the Rio de Janeiro tourist and

---

76. Huey Newton, "The Movement" (August 1968), quoted in Allen, *Black Awakening in Capitalist America*, 141.

77. Michael Hanchard, "Culturalism versus Cultural Politics: Movimento Negro in Rio de Janeiro and São Paulo, Brazil" in *The Violence Within: Cultural and Political Opposition in Divided Nations*, ed. Kay B. Warren (Boulder: Westview Press, 1993), 57, 80. See also hooks, *Black Looks*, 33.

78. Hanchard, "Culturalism versus Cultural Politics," 80.

entertainment industry for profit. Hanchard observes that "the distinction between meanings attributed to social struggle and meaning enveloped by social struggle is consequential for the *movimento*. . . . Language and signification are indissoluble elements of cultural and material life; yet unless they are bound up with nondiscursive practices, they are politically self-limiting."[79] For this reason it is crucial to distinguish between *culturalism,* in which culture becomes an easily appropriated end in itself, and *cultural politics,* which employs culture as one facet of a more comprehensive political movement for social change.

The Question of a Unified American Culture Revisited

The objective of social change brings us back to the question of the form of nation-state we are striving for. How will the political structure we work to establish accommodate the diverse cultural groups we want the law to recognize and respect?

While seeking the law's protection of distinct cultural groups, cultural pluralists advocate some type of unifying theme that ties these groups together. Cultural pluralism, unlike legal pluralism, "assumes the fact or desirability of cultural or social diversity within a single sovereign state."[80] If we are all to live together peaceably in a single nation-state, cultural pluralists argue, then we cannot afford to abandon the ideal of a unified community that embraces our cultural differences. Even Edward Said's concept of the resistance culture of formerly colonized peoples ultimately evolves to a stage characterized by a "noticeable pull away from separatist nationalism towards a more integrative view of human community and human liberation."[81] The goal is to fashion a unitary law that will garner citizens' national allegiance yet respect their identification with cultural subgroups, permitting each to "belong to America and at the same time keep that particularlized identification if she wants it."[82]

To be sure, these revisited ideals of legal universalism and unified

---

79. Ibid., 81.
80. Carol Weisbrod, "Family, Church and State: An Essay on Constitutionalism and Religious Authority," *Journal of Family Law* 26 (1987–88): 741, 743.
81. Edward W. Said, *Culture and Imperialism* (New York: Knopf, 1993), 216.
82. Karst, "Myths of Identity," 369.

American identity are radically more respectful of cultural differences than the racist versions I described earlier. Yet how can we guarantee that the cultural pluralists' ideal of a unitary political culture does not replicate the ethnic version's masquerade of dominant cultural norms? Attention to the political subordination of minority cultures raises serious questions about cultural pluralists' hope in a unified American civic culture.

Some writers advocate a unified American identity because they believe that it is a prerequisite for racial harmony. They criticize cultural separatists for hindering cross-racial understanding by claiming a unique cultural experience that only group members can comprehend. This perspective, these pluralists argue, threatens civic unity by denying the possibility of interethnic empathy. Federal appellate judge J. Harvey Wilkinson III warns:

> To speak of the inaccessible racial experience is to surrender to the somber role of race in human history and to foreclose a future based on the productive potential inherent in individual diversity. Belief in the notion of inaccessible racial cultures elevates the supposed racial differences in the human persona above all else.[83]

The conservative dissenters in *FCC v. Metro Broadcasting* similarly rejected the Federal Communications Commission's minority set-aside program designed to increase broadcast diversity because it "embodies the related notions that a particular and distinct viewpoint inheres in certain racial groups."[84] The justices contended that the government's policy impermissibly valued certain applicants based on the presumption that their perspective was determined by their race and that other applicants could not represent that perspective in broadcast programming. Randall Kennedy made this point as well in his critique of critical race theory when he asked: "But what, as a function of race, is 'special' or 'distinct' about the scholarship of minority legal academics? Does it differ discernibly in ways attributable to race from work produced by white scholars?"[85]

---

83. J. Harvie Wilkinson III, "The Law of Civil Rights and the Dangers of Separatism in Multicultural America," *Stanford Law Review* 47 (1995): 993, 1004–5.

84. 110 S. Ct. 2997, 3037 (1990) (O'Connor, J., joined by Rehnquist, C.J., and Scalia and Kennedy, J.J., dissenting).

85. Randall Kennedy, "Racial Critiques of Legal Academia," *Harvard Law Review* 102 (1989): 1745, 1778.

For these writers the nationalist vision not only misperceives human nature; it also prevents human interaction that transcends racial and ethnic differences. By placing undue weight on distinct racial experiences, the worry goes, demands for separate cultural institutions block channels of mutual understanding. Judge Wilkinson thus contends that "to accept the inaccessibility of racial experience is also to deny the value of empathy."[86] This conclusion parallels Martha Nussbaum's fear that, by "conceding that a morally arbitrary boundary such as the boundary of the nation has a deep and formative role in our deliberations, we seem to be depriving ourselves of any principled way of arguing to citizens that they should in fact join hands" across the "boundaries of ethnicity and class and gender and race."[87] By this logic it is black nationalists' preoccupation with race that prevents progress toward racial harmony.

Judge Wilkinson offers the Civil Rights Act, drafted by white congressmen, as an example of interracial empathy: "They had not personally experienced what it was like to be denied service at a restaurant or to be rejected for employment, only because of one's race. Yet they understood the injustice involved; they could empathize."[88] According to this thinking, the path to a unified American identity lies in cultural understanding. But the reliance on empathy to achieve social change has helped to stymie progressive movements. Empathy alone is not powerful enough to overcome the allure of white social privilege, a privilege that provides a powerful incentive to leave the social order intact. Besides, many whites who believe that they are victims of reverse discrimination feel that they deserve empathy as well.

There is no reason to believe that cultural appreciation has much effect on political arrangements. The increasing infusion of black lifestyle into mainstream commercial culture has not meant a commensurate improvement in the material status of black Americans. While white consumers listen to gangsta' rap, braid their hair in cornrows, and mimic a ghetto stance, the unemployment rate among blacks has remained about twice that among whites for the last thirty years.[89] Elementary schools across the country celebrate Kwanzaa, but black chil-

---

86. Wilkinson, "Law of Civil Rights," 1005.
87. Martha Nussbaum, "Patriotism and Cosmopolitanism," *Boston Review* 19 (October–November 1994): 3, 6.
88. Wilkinson, "Law of Civil Rights," 1005.
89. Derrick Bell, "Political Reality Testing: 1993," *Fordham Law Review* 61 (1994): 1033, 1034.

dren still receive an inferior education. Contemporary mass culture promotes racial difference and nostalgia for the primitive as a titillating departure from boring white lifestyles. As bell hooks notes, advertising exploits images of dark-skinned people to add "'a bit of the Other' to enhance the blank landscape of whiteness."[90] The fantasy of Otherness, however, does not undermine the assumed superiority of whiteness. To the contrary, whites point to black cultural traits as the reason for black people's disempowerment. Current welfare reform proposals designed to change recipients' behavior, for example, stem from the view that economic disparities can be traced to deviant black culture.

Cultural understanding, then, although better than cultural bigotry, falls short of changing the inferior political position of minority cultural groups. The solution to the United States' racial impasse must be based on a shared *political* commitment to overturn systems of domination, not on mutual experience or empathy.

Of course, those in power cling to the romantic possibility of cultural harmony without political change. E. M. Forster's English character Fielding similarly chided his Muslim companion, Assiz, for his dream of an independent India. When Assiz cried out to Fielding, "Yes, we shall drive every blasted Englishman into the sea, and then ... you and I shall be friends," Fielding responded, embracing Assiz affectionately, "Why can't we be friends now?"[91] "Why can't we be friends now?" is the plaintive refrain of romantic multiculturalists who view nationalism as a stumbling block to cultural interaction. But the stumbling block is really their own unwillingness to part with their privileged social position.

Another view relies on a universal political culture instead of empathy to unify the United States' diverse citizenry. American civic culture transcends ethnic cultural differences, permitting individual citizens to identify as Americans while preserving their separate cultural identities.[92] Thus, Anthony Appiah argues that we can be cosmopolitans who celebrate the variety of human cultures at the same time that we are patriots, committed to the institutions of the state that "provide the over-arching order of our common life."[93] Many cultural pluralists see the civic principles of liberty and equal citizenship as the

---

90. hooks, *Black Looks*, 21.
91. E. M. Forster, *A Passage to India* (New York: Harcourt, Brace and Company, 1924), 322.
92. Karst, "Paths to Belonging," 363.
93. Appiah, "Cosmopolitan Patriots," 629.

bedrock of a common political culture that can achieve the twin ends of diversity and unity. This notion of a unitary polity does not violate cultural pluralists' concern for diversity because it does not require individuals to abandon the particular traditions, customs, and mind-set of their respective cultures. As long as these diverse groups adopt the same legal "ground rules," they can "retain their distinct identities yet continue to coexist."[94]

Although this view resolves the problem of the dominant group's cultural imperialism, it takes as unproblematic the state's legal and political authority over minority cultures. Thus, Nomi Maya Stolzenberg and David N. Myers note that "the very idea that coexistence is obtainable suggests that cultural groups are not seen as posing the same sort of threat to the state as a rival sovereign."[95] By focusing on the unitary civic culture's accommodation of diverse cultural perspectives, cultural pluralists overlook some minorities' difficulty with claiming U.S. citizenship and consequent demands for greater political self-determination.

For many blacks living in the United States the discomfort with U.S. citizenship does not stem from cultural incompatibility but from political opposition. To them the essence of American civic culture is the reality of political exclusion, surveillance, and repression, not the ideals of liberty and equality. The symbols of American nationhood are not the Bill of Rights and the Liberty Bell but, rather, the noose, the white hood, and the "Whites Only" sign, supplemented by more contemporary emblems such as the overcrowded housing project, jail, and welfare office. This portrait of a deeply regressive American culture leaves little to rally around. Identification with a political order that has betrayed black people's interests at every turn would be an act of self-destruction. Citizenship in a *multicultural* America that preserves "traditions, observances, parades, rituals, creeds, customs, and cuisines"[96] while maintaining its profound disparities in wealth and privilege is no less repugnant. Appiah recognizes this conflict between the experience of oppression and the ideal of a unified culture and offers a possible reconciliation: he points out that sharing a common political culture

---

94. Robert C. Post, "Cultural Heterogeneity and Law: Pornography, Blasphemy, and the First Amendment," *California Law Review* 76 (1988): 297, 302.

95. Nomi Maya Stolzenberg and David N. Myers, "Community, Constitution, and Culture: The Case of the Jewish *Kehilah*," *University of Michigan Journal of Law Reform* 25 (1992): 633, 660.

96. Arthur Schlesinger Jr., "Multiculturalism and the Bill of Rights," *Maine Law Review* 46 (1994): 189, 198.

does not require that the culture mean the same thing to all citizens.[97] That resolution will work only if each culture's meaning has a real chance of contributing to the structures that govern people's lives.

I am not sure whether or not a notion of national community that rejects completely the ideal of a unitary political culture in favor of one that accords cultural subgroups greater sovereignty is either feasible or desirable. Some black nationalists might contend that my argument leads inexorably to advocacy of an independent black nation. Some cultural pluralists might contend that it underestimates the unifying potential of liberal democratic principles properly applied. But I am sure that we cannot adopt ready-made the existing American political culture premised largely on the disenfranchisement and poverty of blacks and other minorities.

Conclusion

My focus on politics may seem to take all the fun out of culture; surely, we love our own culture and appreciate others for more than political reasons. Some will object that I have dragged the delightful topic of cultural diversity down to the grubby level of battles for political power. Perhaps one day we will live in a country in which we can enjoy cultural differences for their aesthetic value and the spice they add to our lives. But, until we achieve that utopian world, culture matters to law mostly for political reasons. And we must be sure of our political objectives before we place any importance on culture at all. People who proclaim that politics cheapens discussions about culture usually do so from a preeminence they would like to see undisturbed.

I have not taken the position that either culture or politics is all that matters but, rather, that the two are very much related. Without a political agenda discussions about cultural diversity threaten to become no more than an intriguing sideshow, a tonic to soothe the white psyche—a luxury we can ill afford in the face of the social misery that plagues this country. Without a commitment to radical political change, an interest in cultural preservation is likely to create a smokescreen for the preservation of the current order beset by race, class, and gender inequities. Guided by a revolutionary political theory, however, culture can be a powerful force for imagining and creating a just way of life in the United States.

---

97. Appiah, "Cosmopolitan Patriots," 629–30.

Civil Rights Rhetoric and White Identity Politics

George Lipsitz

> The discourses of race and nation are never very far apart, if only in the form of disavowal.
>
> Etienne Balibar

In their 1993 book, *The Scar of Race,* Paul M. Sniderman and Thomas Piazza mobilize scholarly arguments in support of neoconservative understandings of the changing nature of race in the United States. "A generation ago" they argue, "the issue of race was, through and through, a matter of right versus wrong. It was wrong—unequivocally wrong, unambiguously wrong—to make it a crime for a black to drink from the same water fountain as a white, or to play in the same public park, or to attend the same school."[1] Because of the civil rights movement, society reached a consensus on those issues, and today "race prejudice no longer organizes and dominates the reactions of whites."[2]

A new race problem has come into existence, however, according to Sniderman and Piazza, one caused by civil rights advocates themselves. They contend that since the passage of the 1964 Civil Rights Act black leaders have abandoned "the highest ambition of civil rights activists that the state be neutral on race" to demand, instead, a system

---

Epigraph: Etienne Balibar, "Race and Nationalism," in *Race, Nation, and Class,* by Etienne Balibar and Immanuel Wallerstein, trans. Chris Turner (London and New York: Verso, 1991), 37.
    1. Paul M. Sniderman and Thomas Piazza, *The Scar of Race* (Cambridge and London: Harvard University Press, 1993), 1.
    2. Ibid., 5.

of racial preferences in the form of affirmative action.[3] Sniderman and Piazza charge civil rights leaders with abandoning "a larger crusade on behalf of what Americans, white as well as black, agreed is just" in favor of race-conscious "separatism" and self-interested "pork barrel" politics.[4] They claim that affirmative action programs violate the American creed of fairness to which whites are committed, and whites have come to dislike blacks, not because whites are racists but because they dislike affirmative action so much that they have come to dislike blacks as a result.[5]

The story that Sniderman and Piazza tell replicates the commonsense wisdom of contemporary political discourse about race. But is it true? These arguments make empirical claims that can be tested through research. Was the main goal of the civil rights movement to make the state neutral on issues of race? Did civil rights leaders abandon integration in favor of race-conscious separatism? Have blacks abandoned broader principles of justice in favor of self-interest? Do affirmative action remedies offend white people's sense of fairness so sharply that they have come to dislike black people as a result? Has the pursuit of short-sighted "identity politics" on the part of people of color undermined a national consensus in favor of integration? An examination of the history of "civil rights" struggles over fair housing, school desegregation, and fair hiring follows as a way of subjecting the Sniderman and Piazza thesis to evaluation based on evidence.

Fair Housing

The National Housing Act of 1934 made home ownership a possibility for millions of U.S. families by putting the resources of the federal government behind home loans characterized by low down payments, extended loan maturities, and regulated interest rates. The Home Owners Loan Corporation offered these loans on a racially discriminatory basis, however, giving highest priority to loans in areas that were all white and all Christian, while systematically denying loans to neighborhoods with minority residents. At the same time, the federal government encouraged local authorities to locate public housing develop-

---
3. Ibid., 67.
4. Ibid., 129.
5. Ibid., 8.

ments in segregated neighborhoods and to allocate tenants to projects on the basis of race.[6]

The General Services Administration channeled the government's rental and leasing business to realtors who routinely engaged in racial discrimination, while federally subsidized urban renewal plans reduced the already limited supply of housing for communities of color through "slum clearance" programs. Of the 400,000 housing units lost to urban renewal by 1963, less than 3 percent were replaced. More than 60 percent of those displaced by urban renewal were African American, Puerto Rican, or members of other minority racial groups.[7] The Federal Housing Administration and the Veterans Administration financed more than $120 billion of new housing between 1934 and 1962, but less than 2 percent of this real estate was available to nonwhite families, and most of that small amount was located in segregated areas.[8] In 1968 lobbyists for the banking industry helped draft the Housing and Urban Development Act, which allowed private lenders to shift the risks of financing low-income housing to the government, thereby creating a lucrative and completely unregulated market for themselves. The Federal Housing Authority (FHA) allowed banks to use one part of the act for blockbusting—for financing the flight of whites from central cities to suburbs—while using another part of the act to sell homes that did not meet FHA standards to blacks at exorbitant rates. Lenders profited greatly from the many sales and mortgage foreclosures on substandard housing that resulted from these policies, but the attendant price fixing and inflation increased costs of inner-city housing between 200 and 300 percent between 1968 and 1972. Then a wave of foreclosures on uninspected and substandard dwellings destroyed the value of inner-city housing and ruined neighborhoods. In response, the Department of Housing and Urban Development essentially redlined inner cities, destroying their housing markets.[9] Thus, federal and local governments have historically devoted enormous resources toward skewing opportunities for decent housing along racial lines, toward giving

---

6. Jill Quadagno, *The Color of Welfare: How Racism Undermined the War on Poverty* (New York: Oxford University Press, 1994), 24.

7. Arlene Zarembka, *The Urban Housing Crisis: Social, Economic, and Legal Issues and Proposals* (New York, Westport, Conn., and London: Greenwood Press, 1990), 104.

8. Quadagno, *Color of Welfare*, 92, 91.

9. Ibid., 105, 113; Douglas S. Massey and Nancy A. Denton, *American Apartheid: Segregation and the Making of the Underclass* (Cambridge and London: Harvard University Press, 1993), 204–5.

white people a possessive investment in their whiteness, yet they did nothing to challenge the systematic and pervasive racial discrimination of the real estate industry.

The 1948 *Shelley v. Kraemer* case culminated a long struggle by African Americans to get the Supreme Court to rule on the constitutionality of "restricted covenants"—deed restrictions that required whites to sell their homes only to other whites. The Court decided that it violated the constitutional rights of African Americans for state courts to enforce these restrictions, a verdict that seemed to outlaw this widely used discriminatory practice. The decision, however, only banned state court *enforcement* of restrictive covenants; it did not make it illegal for property owners to adhere to these covenants voluntarily or to register them with local authorities. Consequently, victims of restricted covenants had to initiate legal action themselves and bear the complete effort and expense of securing justice without government assistance.[10] Even after the Supreme Court's ruling in *Shelley v. Kraemer* the Federal Housing Administration continued to recommend restrictive covenants as a condition for receiving federally secured home loans.[11] In addition, the Court's ruling left in place most of the crucial mechanisms of real estate discrimination including redlining (denying loans to areas inhabited by racial minorities), steering (directing minority buyers exclusively to homes in minority neighborhoods), and blockbusting (using fears of "racial incursion" to get white home owners to panic and sell, at bargain rates, homes that could then be sold to minority home buyers at exorbitant prices).[12]

In 1962 President Kennedy issued Executive Order 11063, requiring federal agencies to prevent discrimination in federally supported housing. But federal officials did not press the order on local housing authorities, and the Federal Housing Administration refused to apply the order to its own loans. When Congress passed the 1964 Civil Rights Act, it specifically exempted federal mortgage insurance programs from the law, guaranteeing continued discrimination in home lending.[13] That same year California voters, by an overwhelming margin, decided to repeal that state's fair housing law. California governor Pat

---

10. David Theo Goldberg, *Racist Culture: Philosophy and the Politics of Meaning* (London and Cambridge: Blackwell, 1993), 195.
11. Massey and Denton, *American Apartheid*, 188.
12. *Urban Housing Crisis*, 101–3.
13. Massey and Denton, *American Apartheid*, 189–90, 191–92.

Brown, who supported open housing, reflected back on that defeat years later and admitted, "I was completely out of tune with the white citizens of the state who felt that the right to sell their property to whomever they wanted was a privileged right, a right of ownership, a constitutional right."[14]

When Lyndon Johnson asked Congress to pass a fair housing bill in 1966, his request produced "some of the most vicious mail LBJ received on any subject," according to White House aide Joseph Califano.[15] Republican minority leader Everett Dirksen lambasted the bill as a threat to the nation, claiming that white opposition to fair housing stemmed not from racial prejudice by whites but from bad behavior by blacks moving into white areas. The House of Representatives did pass a bill in response to Johnson's request, but that legislation acknowledged the "right" of individuals to discriminate in selling their homes and to require their realtors to discriminate as well. Martin Luther King Jr. argued that the bill was not worth passing, and a filibuster by its opponents in the Senate prevented it from becoming law.[16]

It was not until 1968 that Congress passed a comprehensive Fair Housing Act, but this law contained provisions that made it virtually unenforceable. Under Title VIII of the law the Department of Housing and Urban Development (HUD) could investigate complaints made directly to the HUD secretary but could not initiate its own studies. The law gave the HUD secretary only thirty days to decide whether to pursue or dismiss complaints, but, even if the department pursued the case, it had no enforcement power and was limited to "conference, conciliation, and persuasion." The law allowed the Department of Housing and Urban Development to refer to the attorney general those cases in which it found discrimination, but Title VIII allowed the attorney general to act only if cases "raised an issue of general public importance" or revealed "a pattern or practice" of discrimination.[17] Under the aegis of this act aggrieved parties had to file lawsuits within six months of the alleged violation or within thirty days of the end of mediation. They had to bring action on their own behalf, hire their own lawyers, assume their own legal fees, pay court costs, and bear the burden of proof to establish that serious acts of discrimination had taken place. The act

---

14. Quadagno, *Color of Welfare*, 98–99.
15. Ibid., 99.
16. Ibid.
17. Massey and Denton, *American Apartheid*, 196.

then restricted the punitive damages they could collect to a maximum of a thousand dollars.[18]

Despite the severe limitations of the 1968 law, the Department of Housing and Urban Development received thousands of complaints each year. But during the 1970s less than 30 percent of cases filed with HUD reached the mediation stage, and close to 50 percent of those remained in noncompliance. A 1980 study showed that only 35 percent of cases brought to HUD reached agreement and that half of those were settled in favor of the party accused of discrimination. A total of only four hundred fair housing cases have been decided since 1986; by 1980 only five victims of discrimination had received damages in excess of thirty-five hundred dollars. Most experts believe that more than two million cases of housing discrimination occur each year, but the law is so weak that no action can be taken. As former HUD secretary Patricia Roberts Harris noted, our society does not often respond to crime by limiting authorities "to asking the discovered lawbreaker whether he wants to discuss the matter."[19]

Advocates of fair housing opportunities for African Americans and other minorities persevered in the face of relentless opposition from whites. Every judicial, legislative, and executive victory in the fight against housing discrimination fell victim to subterfuge and subversion by defenders of discrimination. When a federal judge in Chicago found that city's housing authority culpable for historic patterns of segregation in 1969, he ordered the city to build seven hundred new units of public housing in white neighborhoods and to locate 75 percent of new construction outside the ghetto. But the Chicago Housing Authority responded by ceasing all new housing construction.[20] When a St. Louis suburb reincorporated itself and changed its zoning laws in 1970 in order to block construction of a low- and middle-income integrated housing development, secretary of Housing and Urban Development George Romney filed a lawsuit against the action in federal court. But Attorney General John Mitchell ordered Romney to drop the suit, while the White House announced it would suspend civil rights laws for a year while it studied the situation. In that time hundreds of grants were approved without scrutiny to see if they complied with federal civil rights law. President Nixon conceded that denying

---

18. Ibid., 196–200.
19. Ibid., 196.
20. Ibid., 190.

housing to people because of their race was wrong, but he added that he found it equally wrong for cities opposed to federally assisted (and therefore integrated) housing to "have it imposed from Washington by bureaucratic fiat."[21] Nixon's tactic of affirming support for integration in the abstract while acting to undermine the mechanisms that might make it actually possible in reality became a standard response to desegregation demands by white politicians during the civil rights and post–civil rights eras.

Yet chronic, pervasive, and persistent discrimination continued to deny fair housing opportunities to African Americans and other "minority" groups. These practices artificially limited the supply of housing for people of color, forcing them to pay more for less, and secretly subsidized white Americans who could select houses from a broader and therefore more competitive market. A Housing Market Practices Survey conducted by the Department of Housing and Urban Development in the 1970s revealed that black "testers" got less information on the availability of for-sale housing than white testers did 15 percent of the time and less information about the availability of rental housing than did whites 27 percent of the time.[22] As late as 1970, examiners for the Federal Home Loan Bank Board consistently redlined postal zip code areas where the black population was increasing.[23] In 1977 training manuals for private appraisers continued to use "100 percent Caucasian" as a description of desirable neighborhoods "without adverse effects from minorities."[24] Yet the federal and state officials remained largely uninterested in enforcing fair housing laws.

Every triumph by fair housing advocates has turned out to be a victory without victory. For example, urban renewal opponents won a long-sought victory in 1970, when the Uniform Relocation Assistance and Real Property Acquisition Act mandated for the first time that local housing authorities replace the low-income units they destroyed (most often occupied by racial minorities). Congress responded by eliminating the urban renewal program and replacing it with community development block grants that emphasized luxury housing for upper- and middle-class home owners. In St. Louis the city evicted five hundred families (almost all of them African American) from the Pershing

---

21. Quadagno, *Color of Welfare*, 109–10.
22. Zarembka, *Urban Housing Crisis*, 16–17.
23. Massey and Denton, *American Apartheid*, 105.
24. Zarembka, *Urban Housing Crisis*, 103.

Waterman Redevelopment area, gave developers $5.8 million in tax abatements, demolished nine buildings at city expense, secured $1.4 million in federal block grant funds, and sold 106 parcels of land to the developers for $122 per parcel. Because the Pershing Redevelopment Company was a private enterprise and because the funding came from block grants rather than urban renewal funds, none of the dislocated families received a single dollar in relocation assistance.[25]

In 1974 Congress adopted the Equal Credit Opportunity Act, expressly prohibiting discrimination in real estate lending. The law required banks to keep track of the racial identities of applicants accepted and rejected for loans. But no such data was collected. Ten civil rights groups filed suit in 1976, asking the courts to order the comptroller of the currency, the Federal Deposit Insurance Corporation (FDIC), and the Home Loan Bank Board to obey the 1974 law. The agencies signed a court order agreeing to collect the required information, but the comptroller of the currency and the FDIC ceased keeping records based on race in 1981, when the court order expired. Home Loan Bank Board records revealed that blacks continued to face rejection rates several times that encountered by white applicants.

The 1975 Home Mortgage Disclosure Act and the 1977 Community Investment Act required banks to identify the neighborhoods in which they granted home improvement and mortgage loans and to demonstrate their willingness to supply capital to worthy borrowers in low-income areas.[26] But the Reagan Administration rendered these acts of Congress moot by ignoring the information available and, in fact, filing no fair housing suits in 1981 and only two in 1982. At a time when the number of housing discrimination complaints filed with HUD doubled, the Reagan Justice Department neglected serious complaints but, instead, initiated frivolous suits against plans that actually maintained integrated housing and prevented blockbusting by regulating the racial balance in housing developments. One action by the administration aimed to invalidate deed restrictions in one of the few genuinely integrated areas of Houston, the Houston Oaks subdivision, because the original deeds contained restrictive covenants that were neither enforced nor honored by the residents. The administration also used

---

25. Ibid., 129.
26. Massey and Denton, *American Apartheid*, 206.

the Paperwork Reduction Act as an excuse to stop HUD from gathering data on the racial identities of participants in its housing programs.[27]

Similarly, when a 1980 amendment to the Housing and Community Development Act provided language that would allow local housing authorities to address directly the urgent housing needs of racial minorities, the Reagan Administration rendered the victory a hollow one by virtually eliminating all federal funding for subsidized housing.[28] The subsidized housing program has the highest percentage of black recipients of any federal benefit program—38.5 percent black in 1979. The Reagan Administration reduced the funding allocated to subsidized housing from $26.1 billion in 1981 to $2.1 billion in 1985.[29] Yet, while cutting allocations for these programs aimed at providing simple subsistence and income maintenance for a significantly black clientele, the Reagan Administration made no effort to raise federal revenue by ending the home owner mortgage deduction, an aspect of federal housing policy infinitely more costly to the government but one that provides aid for asset accumulation that is disproportionately accessible to whites.

The 1988 Fair Housing Amendments Act addressed many important shortcomings in previous fair housing legislation, but it came at a time when increased housing prices made entry into the market prohibitive for many people of color. In addition, housing in the United States has become so hypersegregated, loan procedures so discriminatory, and enforcement of fair housing laws so infrequent that federal law acknowledging the rights of all people to secure housing on a fair basis may have no effect on their ability actually to do so. In addition, whites who first attained home ownership under blatantly discriminatory circumstances condoned and protected by the judicial, legislative, and executive branches of government have also become more formidable competitors for housing as a result of the increased value of their homes due to appreciation and inflation. Median sales prices on new homes and on sales of existing homes increased by almost 230 percent between 1970 and 1985, while the consumer price index in general rose by 177 percent.[30]

---

27. Ibid., 207–8.
28. Zarembka, *Urban Housing Crisis*, 106.
29. Quadagno, *Color of Welfare*, 114.
30. Zarembka, *Urban Housing Crisis*, 8.

The possessive investment in whiteness generated by failure to enforce fair housing legislation has concrete costs for people of color. In their comprehensive new study Melvin L. Oliver and Tom Shapiro estimate that discrimination in the home loan industry alone costs black home owners $10.5 billion in extra payments and that every black home owner is deprived of nearly $4,000 as a result of the .54 percent higher rate they pay on home mortgages. The costs for those who cannot enter the housing market, who consequently build up no equity and do not qualify for the home owners' tax deduction, is, of course, much higher.[31] The appreciated value of owner-occupied homes constitutes the single greatest source of wealth for white Americans. It is the factor most responsible for the fact that the disparity between blacks and whites in the realm of wealth is far greater than the disparity between the two groups at the level of income. It is the basis for intergenerational transfers of wealth that enable white parents to give their children financial advantages over the children of members of other groups. Its value stems not from the wisdom of white home buyers or the improvements they have made on their property but, rather, from the ways in which patterns of bad faith and nonenforcement of antidiscrimination laws enable the beneficiaries of past discrimination to protect their gains and pass them on to their families.

School Desegregation

In its 1954 *Brown v. Board of Education* ruling the Supreme Court culminated sixteen years of school desegregation decisions by acknowledging that the state played a central role in promoting and preserving racial differences by relegating black students to separate and therefore inherently unequal educations. While refusing to sanction de jure segregation in the future, the decision nonetheless provided no means for dismantling the structures that crafted advantages for white students out of the disadvantages of students of color. The plaintiffs in *Brown* sought more for their children than mere physical proximity to whites; they pursued desegregation as a means of securing for black students the same educational resources and opportunities routinely provided to whites. But the *Brown* decision helped frustrate their aims because it outlawed only one technique of inequality—de jure segregation—with-

---

31. Melvin L. Oliver and Tom Shapiro, *Black Wealth/White Wealth* (New York: Routledge, 1995), 142.

out addressing the ways in which discrimination in housing, employment, and access to public services enabled whites to resegregate the schools by moving to suburban districts. In addition, as Cheryl I. Harris argues, by calling for change with all deliberate speed, *Brown I* and *Brown II* preserved the power of whites "to control, manage, postpone, and if necessary, thwart change."[32]

Just as the absence of enforcement mechanisms made violations of fair housing laws into an unusual class of criminal offenses—violations of the law that carried virtually no penalties—*Brown I* and *Brown II* pioneered new kinds of constitutional rights. In most previous decisions the Supreme Court considered constitutionally protected rights as "personal and present" so that their violation required immediate redress. But the rights of black children in *Brown I* and *Brown II* received no such protection. The level of white resistance to desegregation dictated the remedy, an approach that Harris correctly concludes invited "defiance and delay."[33] School desegregation efforts faced massive resistance in the North and the South, but, even with clear evidence of refusal to respond to *Brown*, the courts did not begin to evaluate proposed remedies for segregation critically until the 1968 *Green v. County School Board of New Kent County, Virginia*.[34] Federal courts did not direct school districts to adopt specific remedies such as busing until 1971, with the *Swann v. Charlotte-Mecklenberg Board of Education* case, and the Supreme Court did not announce that the time for "all deliberate speed" had run out until the 1975 and 1977 *Bradley v. Milliken* cases. By inviting more than two decades of delay, the Supreme Court condoned the systematic denial of black children's constitutional rights and, instead, responded to white parents and their representatives, who argued that remediation inconvenienced them and interfered with their expected privileges as whites.[35]

In the 1973 *San Antonio Independent School District v. Rodriguez* case

---

32. Cheryl I. Harris, "Whiteness as Property," *Harvard Law Review* 106, no. 8 (June 1993): 1754.

33. Ibid., 1755.

34. Nathaniel R. Jones, "Civil Rights after *Brown*: 'Stormy the Road We Trod,'" in *Race in America: The Struggle for Equality*, ed. Herbert Hill and James E. Jones Jr. (Madison: University of Wisconsin Press, 1993), 100.

35. Wiley A. Branton, "Race, the Courts, and Constitutional Change in Twentieth Century School Desegregation Cases after Brown," in *African Americans and the Living Constitution*, ed. John Hope Franklin and Genna Rae McNeil (Washington and London: Smithsonian Institution Press, 1995), 86; Harris, "Whiteness as Property," 1756.

the Supreme Court acknowledged that the education provided to Mexican-American children in San Antonio was inferior to that offered to Anglo children, but the Court then claimed that education was not so fundamental a right that it enjoyed constitutional protection, and consequently the courts could not order equalization of resources.[36] In *Bradley v. Milliken I* and *II*, the Court ruled against cross-district city-suburb busing as a remedy for segregation. In this case the Court received evidence that various governments and government agencies participated in the construction and maintenance of discriminatory policies in the Detroit school system. It received the findings of a federal court that private sector actions in real estate and home lending led to residential segregation that made school integration by district impossible. But by a 5–4 decision the justices ruled against cross-district busing, apparently persuaded by Justice Potter Stewart's stupefyingly innocent conclusion that racial segregation in Detroit's schools was caused by "unknown and unknowable factors."[37]

White political leadership played an important role in solidifying resistance to school desegregation. In 1964 close to 70 percent of Northern whites supported the Johnson Administration's efforts to desegregate the South, but, when urban riots, fair housing campaigns, and efforts to end de facto school segregation hit the North, public opinion changed. By 1966, 52 percent of Northern whites told pollsters that they felt that the government was pushing integration "too fast."[38] Richard Nixon secured Strom Thurmond's support in the 1968 presidential campaign in return for a promise to lessen federal pressure for school desegregation.[39] As president, Nixon abandoned the school desegregation guidelines issued in the 1964 Civil Rights Act, nominated opponents of busing to the Supreme Court, and in his 1972 reelection campaign urged Congress to pass legislation overturning court-ordered busing.[40]

Opposition to school desegregation has enabled whites to preserve advantages they held as a result of overt de jure segregation in an earlier era. As Gary Orfield argues, the superiority of suburban schools is

---

36. Jones, "Civil Rights after Brown," 103.
37. Ibid.; Harris, "Whiteness as Property," 1756.
38. Quadagno, *Color of Welfare*, 30.
39. Ibid., 127.
40. Gary Orfield, "School Desegregation after Two Generations: Race, Schools, and Opportunity in Urban Society," in Hill and Jones, *Race in America*, 240.

taken for granted as a right attendant to home ownership, while desegregation is viewed as a threat to a system that passes racial advantages from one generation to the next. In Orfield's words, "Whites tell pollsters that they believe that blacks are offered equal opportunities, but fiercely resist any efforts to make them send their children to the schools they insist are good enough for blacks." At the same time, "the people who oppose busing minority students to the suburbs also tend to oppose sending suburban dollars to city schools."[41]

Efforts at desegregating higher education also provoked white resistance. In the 1978 *Regents of the University of California v. Bakke* case an unsuccessful white applicant to the University of California–Davis medical school charged that he had been denied admission to the school because of his race. Allan Bakke charged that he had a higher undergraduate grade point average than the average GPA of minority students admitted through a special admissions program. Bakke did not challenge the legitimacy of the thirty-six white students with GPAs lower than his who secured acceptance to the UC-Davis medical school the year he applied, nor did he challenge the enrollment of five students admitted because their parents had attended or given money to the school. Bakke did not challenge his exclusion from the other medical schools to which he applied that did not have minority special admissions programs but favored younger applicants over the thirty-six-year-old Bakke. But he did claim that the sixteen minority special "admits" to UC-Davis took spots that he deserved, even though the graduation rate for special admission students in the past had ranged from 91 to 95 percent, and at least one of the minority special admits the year Bakke applied had an undergraduate GPA of 3.76, a score much higher than Bakke's.[42]

Cheryl Harris notes that Bakke's case rested upon the expectation "that he would never be disfavored when competing with minority candidates, although he might be disfavored with respect to other more privileged whites."[43] While conceding the legality of the UC-Davis minority special admissions program, the Supreme Court nonetheless ordered Bakke's admission to medical school. Justice Powell ruled that universities could not use race as a factor in admission procedures

---

41. Ibid., 245, 240.
42. Carter A. Wilson, "Exploding the Myths of a Slandered Policy," *Black Scholar* (May–June 1986): 20; Harris, "Whiteness as Property," 1770.
43. Harris, "Whiteness as Property," 1773.

merely to correct past injustices, but they could use it if they decided that using race as a factor would enhance the educational environment for other (meaning white) students. In this case the California Supreme Court used the standard of strict scrutiny that had traditionally been used only on behalf of "discrete and insular minorities" likely to suffer "invidious discrimination." In his deciding opinion supporting the state court's level of scrutiny, Justice Lewis Powell did not argue that whites actually were part of a discrete and insular minority likely to suffer invidious discrimination, but he did say that white individuals might be so upset by what they viewed as preferential treatment for Chicanos and blacks that they might *perceive* a denial of equal rights amounting to invidious discrimination.[44] In this case, as in many others, guesses about the perceptions and expectations of whites superseded the constitutional rights and empirical realities facing blacks.

The value attached to white perceptions by Justice Powell was not an aberration; it has played an important role in juridical approaches to a variety of racial issues, especially employment, as we shall see in the next section. Its centrality to educational issues is best illustrated by a comparison of the litigation over Bakke with the universally recognized legality of special admissions plans that routinely benefit whites such as "legacy" admits at elite institutions including Harvard, Yale, Dartmouth, the University of Pennsylvania, and Stanford. These programs give special preference to children of alumni and children of large donors to the schools. At the University of California and the University of Virginia alumni children from out of state secure the advantage of being treated as if they were in-state students. Since the 1950s, 20 percent of the undergraduate students entering Harvard have secured admission because their parents were Harvard alumni.[45] A Department of Education study discovered that the average legacy admit to Harvard between 1981 and 1988 had significantly lower grades and scores on standardized tests than the average nonlegacy candidate admitted to that institution.[46] Legacy admits, who are mostly white, are twice as likely to be admitted to Harvard as black or Hispanic students. A study by Jerome Karabel and David Karen discov-

---

44. David W. Bishop, "The Affirmative Action Cases: Bakke, Weber, and Fullilove," *Journal of Negro History* 67, no. 3 (Fall 1982): 231.

45. John Larew, "Why Are Droves of Unqualified, Unprepared Kids Getting into Our Top Colleges?" *Washington Monthly* (June 1991): 10.

46. Ibid., 11.

ered that, if legacy admits faced the same standards by which other students are judged, there would have been two hundred fewer of them in the Harvard class of 1992. Those two hundred legacy admits outnumbered their class's combined total of Puerto Rican, Mexican-American, Native American, and African-American students.[47] This system, which routinely channels rewards to the beneficiaries of past discrimination and their children, has never been found to disadvantage minority students by the same judicial system that found it necessary to intervene on behalf of Allan Bakke, nor has it met with disfavor from the conservative foundations, politicians, and university regents who attacked and dismantled the University of California's commitment to race- and gender-based affirmative action policies in 1995.

By extending to Bakke a level of constitutional protection routinely denied to black children trapped in inferior and segregated schools, the Court's decision reveals much about the politics of school desegregation in the aftermath of *Brown*. As Cheryl Harris astutely concludes, "When the law recognizes, either implicitly or explicitly, the settled expectations of whites built on the privileges and benefits produced by white supremacy, it acknowledges and reinforces a property interest in whiteness that reproduces Black subordination."[48]

Fair Hiring

Just as the government's housing policies and educational assignments have systematically advantaged whites over blacks and other minorities, federal labor policies have also played a role in creating and preserving a possessive investment in whiteness. The Social Security Act of 1935 exempted from coverage the job categories most likely to be filled by racial minorities—farm workers and domestics—while the National Labor Relations Act put the force of federal law behind racially restrictive union rules and regulations. When the National Association for the Advancement of Colored People proposed that the Wagner Act contain a prohibition against racial discrimination by trade unions, the American Federation of Labor announced that it would not support the legislation if it contained such a provision. Thus, organized labor was willing to forgo federally sanctioned collective bargaining in order to preserve its more important privilege of racial monopolies for

---

47. Ibid.
48. Harris, "Whiteness as Property," 1731.

white workers, but, ultimately, the New Deal sided with the unions and gave them recognition of collective bargaining *and* racial exclusivity.[49]

President Roosevelt's Executive Order 8802 mandated fair hiring by holders of federal defense contracts in 1941, and by 1964 thirty-four states had fair hiring laws on the books.[50] But little enforcement power stood behind federal or state laws, and, consequently, racially based hiring remained the norm rather than the exception in the U.S. economy. Employer preferences and trade union discrimination consistently relegated minority workers to the worst jobs with the lowest rewards. By the 1950s black workers aged twenty-four to forty-four faced unemployment levels three times that confronting their white counterparts. Only 50 percent of black workers worked full-time, while the percentage of white workers in year-round employment approached 67 percent. Compared to whites, black workers endured lower median incomes, a greater likelihood of layoffs, less access to medical and pension plans, and more injuries at work.[51] Small wonder, then, that grassroots mobilization in African-American communities in the 1950s and 1960s often coalesced around struggles for fair and full employment.

In the early 1960s blacks in Philadelphia, Newark, and New York staged nonviolent direct action protests against tax-supported construction projects that hired few, if any, black workers.[52] In St. Louis activist Percy Green temporarily halted construction on the federally funded Gateway Arch by climbing up one leg of the structure and chaining himself to it in order to dramatize his complaints against the project's all-white construction crew.[53] In Cambridge, Maryland, the militant Cambridge Nonviolent Action Committee conducted a survey of the black community and found that 42 percent considered unemployment their most pressing problem, as opposed to 26 percent who

---

49. Quadagno, *Color of Welfare*, 23.

50. Herbert Hill, "Black Workers, Organized Labor, and Title VII of the 1964 Civil Rights Act: Legislative History and Litigation Record," in Hill and Jones, *Race in America*, 263.

51. William H. Harris, *The Harder We Run: Black Workers since the Civil War* (New York: Oxford University Press, 1982), 123, 130, 131, 133, 137.

52. Quadagno, *Color of Welfare*, 64.

53. George Lipsitz, *A Life in the Struggle: Ivory Perry and the Culture of Opposition* (Philadelphia: Temple University Press, 1995), 84–85.

expressed concern about housing and 6 percent who considered access to public accommodations their top priority.[54] In 1960 a study by the U.S. Commission on Civil Rights discovered "persistent and undeniable" racial discrimination and rebuked the AFL-CIO for its inaction on the problem.[55] The massive March on Washington in August 1963, most often remembered as the occasion for Martin Luther King Jr.'s "I Have a Dream" speech, was officially titled a march for jobs and justice, with signs prominently displayed calling for stronger fair employment practices legislation. An investigation by Attorney General Ramsey Clark into the causes of the Watts riots found employment issues paramount in the minds of community residents.[56]

Confronted with direct action protests and indirect political pressure, the AFL-CIO threw its support behind Title VII of the 1964 Civil Rights Act, a section of the bill designed to promote fair hiring. But, as has often been the case in desegregation issues, AFL-CIO leaders supported this bill because they believed that a commitment to integration in principle might be enough to ward off measures that might actually bring it about. A leading lobbyist working on behalf of the Civil Rights Act later recalled that the unions "had just been so beaten for their racism that they wanted a bill and then they could blame it on the bill if it wasn't enforced."[57] In order to achieve that end they helped craft a statute that resembled many of the existing ineffective state fair hiring laws replete with their assumptions that discriminatory hiring was an individual act and an individual problem rather than a systemic feature of the economy.

Just as the 1968 Fair Housing Act and the 1954 *Brown* decision established principles about housing and education that could not be implemented, Title VII of the 1964 Civil Rights Act contained provisions that undermined its stated goals. In addition to weak enforcement it also provided explicit special protection for the beneficiaries of past discrimination. As a condition of its support, the AFL-CIO insisted that the bill had to protect current seniority rights—even those obtained through overtly discriminatory practices—and that the man-

---

54. Peter B. Levy, "The Civil Rights Movement in Cambridge, Maryland during the 1960s," *Viet Nam Generation* 6, nos. 3–4 (1995): 101.
55. Quadagno, *Color of Welfare*, 63.
56. Ibid., 67.
57. Hill, "Black Workers," 267.

date for fair hiring applied only to future rather than present appointments.[58] Section 703(h) of the bill offered these guarantees, and in the judgment of Herbert Hill, former National Labor director of the National Association for the Advancement of Colored People, these provisions offered protection to "the racial status quo of seniority systems for at least a generation."[59]

Like changes in the laws governing school segregation and real estate discrimination, the fair hiring laws met with massive resistance by white employers and workers. The St. Louis unions targeted by Percy Green's direct action protests at the Gateway Arch responded to Title VII by adding a "grandfather clause" to their apprenticeship regulations, giving extra points on an exam to applicants whose fathers were journeyman construction workers. Construction unions in Philadelphia initiated confidential oral interviews as prerequisites for admission to apprenticeship programs in plumbing, pipefitting, sheet metal work, roofing, and electrical work. All of the black applicants failed this section of the "exam." Forty percent of the apprentices in the Philadelphia Plumbers Union were the sons of union plumbers. One construction worker in that city bristled when told that blacks considered these practices discriminatory, explaining: "Some men leave their sons money, some large investments, some business connections and some a profession. I have none of these to bequeath to my sons. I have only one worthwhile thing to give: my trade. . . . For this simple father's wish it is said that I discriminate against Negroes. Don't all of us discriminate? Which of us when it comes to choice will not choose a son over all others?"[60] This worker understood very well the value of his whiteness and what it would be worth to his son to pass it across generations. Like white parents able to leave suburban homes to their children or provide them with exclusive educations, he understood that whiteness is property, to borrow a term from legal scholars Derrick Bell and Cheryl Harris. Perhaps he also knew that government officials, union leaders, and employers would help him protect that property.

Title VII of the 1964 Civil Rights Act charged the Department of Labor's Bureau of Apprenticeship Training with the responsibility of breaking down discrimination in building trades unions. Staffed by individuals with long histories in the trade union movement, the

---

58. Ibid., 269–70.
59. Ibid., 170.
60. Quadagno, *Color of Welfare*, 64–65.

Bureau disregarded most of the complaints it received and failed to take any action when several of its very few investigations revealed clear evidence of discrimination. Three years after the bill became law the agency was still in the process of compiling a list of apprenticeship programs that had been "warned" about discrimination, but even those unions notified of violations of the law needed only to issue a statement announcing their intention to comply with the law to get back into the good graces of the government. While the agency dawdled, unions developed a vast proliferation of tests, oral interviews, and new "education" requirements as a means of continuing to discriminate under the guise of raising standards. In 1968 an exasperated secretary of labor ruled that in the future government contractors would not receive any contracts unless they took "affirmative action" to guarantee fair hiring.[61]

The provisions in Title VII designed to protect the seniority rights of those workers who benefited from racial discrimination before 1964 had an enormous impact in the 1970s, when deindustrialization, downsizing, and economic restructuring produced large numbers of layoffs. A 1977 study for the U.S. Commission on Civil Rights found that seniority-based layoffs worked particular hardships on black workers during the 1973–74 recession. In areas where blacks made up only 10 to 12 percent of the workforce, they accounted for 60 to 70 percent of the workers laid off.[62] Unprotected by seniority in the present because they had been discriminated against in the past, they paid disproportionate costs for the economic restructuring of the 1970s and 1980s. In addition, because discrimination in hiring did not magically cease with the passage of the 1964 bill, those employees who benefited from discrimination since 1964 also got to retain the seniority rights they accrued, while others had to struggle against overt and covert discrimination in order to get jobs with lesser seniority. Along with plant closings, layoffs have devastated black communities. One study found that 50 percent of black males in durable goods manufacturing in five Great Lakes cities lost their jobs between 1979 and 1984.[63]

---

61. Ibid., 73–75.
62. Gertrude Ezorsky, *Racism and Justice: The Case for Affirmative Action* (Ithaca: Cornell University Press, 1991), 25.
63. Richard Child Hill and Cynthia Negry, "Deindustrialization and Racial Minorities in the Great Lakes Region, USA," in *The Reshaping of America: Social Consequences of the Changing Economy*, ed. D. Stanley Eitzen and Maxine Baca Zinn (Englewood Cliffs, N.J.: Prentice-Hall, 1989), 168–78.

Efforts to find fair solutions to the ways in which seniority-based layoffs impacted unfairly against blacks have been thwarted by the Supreme Court. In the 1986 *Wygant v. Jackson Board of Education* case the Court overturned a collective bargaining agreement that called for laying off some senior white teachers before junior black teachers in order to remedy previous discrimination and to prevent budget crises from causing the district to lose all of its minority teachers. In deciding that this agreement violated the constitutional rights of white workers, Justice Powell posed the decision as a "color-blind" defense of the principle of seniority, arguing "the rights and expectations surrounding seniority make up what is probably the most valuable capital asset that the worker 'owns,' worth even more than the current equity in his home."[64] Using arguments similar to those employed by the Philadelphia construction worker defending nepotism in his union, Powell's comparison to home equity is an appropriate one but perhaps not for the reasons he intended. Like the equity in homes secured in discriminatory housing markets, white seniority rights secured in discriminatory labor markets routinely receive protection from the courts as if they were constitutional rights. In addition, race, not seniority, stood at the center of this case. Thurgood Marshall observed in his dissent in the *Wygant* case that all layoffs burden someone, but they are rarely treated as violations of constitutional rights. Marshall noted that the plan the Court rejected did more to protect seniority rights than random layoffs would have, but, by the Court's reasoning, random layoffs would have been constitutional. The violation here was not of seniority but of white expectations that their past advantages will be secured by the courts. As Cheryl Harris explains, "Although the existing state of inequitable distribution is the product of institutionalized white supremacy and economic exploitation, it is seen by whites as part of the natural order of things that cannot legitimately be disturbed."[65]

The Supreme Court brought its protection of white expectations full circle in the 1989 *City of Richmond v. J. A. Croson Co.* decision overturning Richmond City Council legislation setting aside 30 percent of construction contracts for minority-owned businesses. The Court ruled that the requirement violated the constitutional rights of white contractors, who previously had secured 99.33 percent of city contracting busi-

---

64. Harris, "Whiteness as Property," 1783.
65. Ibid., 1778; Derrick Bell, "Remembrances of Racism Past: Getting beyond the Civil Rights Decline," in Hill and Jones, *Race in America,* 80.

ness. In this case the Court applied to white male business owners the "strict scrutiny" standard originally developed in the 1938 *United States v. Carolene Products Co.* case to protect "discrete and insular" minorities subject to pervasive discrimination.

Justice Sandra Day O'Connor's majority opinion ignored evidence about systematic discrimination in the construction industry, including the fact that between 1973 and 1978 minority businesses received only .67 percent of construction contracts in a city whose population was virtually evenly divided between white and black. Like Justice Stewart in *Bradley v. Milliken I* and *II* Justice O'Connor could not fathom why blacks had not received construction contracts from the city of Richmond prior to the set-aside program. "Blacks may be disproportionately attracted to industries other than construction," she mused, dismissing national statistics on discrimination in the industry because she claimed that they proved nothing about discrimination in the industry in Richmond.[66] Yet, while finding no pattern of discrimination against blacks that might compel remedial action, the majority of the Court did find that the claim by a white contractor that he might be relegated to competing for 70 percent of Richmond's construction work instead of 99.33 percent to be sufficiently serious to warrant strict scrutiny and to overturn the policy of Richmond's democratically elected but predominately black city council. Unlike the city council of the all-white municipality of Blackjack, Missouri, whose desires to be free of outside "bureaucrats" caused Richard Nixon to suspend enforcement of civil rights laws in 1970, the Richmond city council's actions were overturned as a violation of constitutional rights.

This special sensitivity to potential civil rights violations against whites has served as part of a broader pattern. The Court ruled in *Martin v. Wilks* that white male firefighters in Birmingham were entitled to reopen a collective bargaining agreement containing a court approved affirmative action promotion plan many years after the original case because they now felt they experienced "reverse discrimination." But in the *Lorance v. ATT Technologies, Inc.* case the same year the Court told female employees that they could not file claims against discriminatory policies in their place of employment because they had waited too long to complain. In fact, they filed suit as soon as they were aware of the policy's adverse effect on them, but the Court ruled they should have

---

66. Robert L. Carter, "Thirty-five Years Later: New Perspectives on Brown," in Hill and Jones, *Race in America*, 86, 88.

questioned the procedures at the precise moment when they were adopted, even though they could not have possibly known then what results the policies would bring.[67] The same Supreme Court that granted "suspect-class" status to Birmingham's white male firefighters and Richmond's white contractors denied that status in other cases to women and to persons with below-average incomes.[68]

Derrick Bell aptly sums up the state of "civil rights" law in the 1990s in a two-part formulation:

> 1. Because most policies challenged by blacks as discriminatory make no mention of race, blacks can no longer evoke the strict-scrutiny shield in absence of proof of intentional discrimination—at which point, strict scrutiny is hardly needed. 2. Whites challenging racial remedies that usually contain racial classifications are now deemed entitled to strict scrutiny without any distinction between policies of invidious intent and those with remedial purposes.

Thus, for equal protection purposes, whites have become the protected discrete and insular minority.

Race and Disavowal

Close examination of the historical record reveals the factual shortcomings of the history presented by Sniderman and Piazza. It is not correct to say that the highest ambition of civil rights activists was to make the state neutral on race. Mass mobilization by African Americans and their allies in the postwar period sought concrete and material gains—housing, education, jobs, and political power. They actively sought state intervention, not neutrality. Yet, because of massive resistance by whites opposed to desegregation of neighborhoods, schools, and places of employment, the state has more often been an antagonist than an ally of antiracism.

It is not correct to condemn civil rights leaders for abandoning integration in favor of race-conscious separatism. The most separatist and race-conscious citizens of our society have been suburban whites and their elected representatives; the most persistent and powerful pol-

---

67. Ibid., 86.
68. Bell, "Remembrances of Racism Past," 76.

itics of the past five decades have been white efforts to use the courts, the executive branch, and the private sector to structure white advantage systematically out of the disadvantages imposed on racial "minorities." Whites express support for integration in theory but not in practice. They oppose black separatism but cling to all-white residential enclaves, schools, and hiring practices. Faced with their traditional dilemma of trying to integrate into a country that does not want them or trying to separate from a country that finds their exploitation too valuable to let them go, black citizens and their leaders routinely vote for candidates of other races, try to live in integrated neighborhoods, favor desegregated schools, and oppose racially discriminatory hiring. To accuse them of abandoning integration assumes that physical proximity to whites or color-blind legislation was their primary goal and, furthermore, that whites have been willing to integrate. Neither assumption conforms to the evidence.

It is not correct to say that blacks have abandoned broader principles of justice in favor of selfish "pork barrel" politics. This formulation implies that whites have ideals but that blacks have interests. It absolves whites of responsibility for their own actions and ignores the material advantages they continue to accrue because of white supremacist practices. It implies that black parents in the 1960s let their children be hit with bottles and bricks in Cicero and Marquette Park, Illinois, or to be bitten by dogs and blasted by firehoses in Birmingham, Alabama, just so whites could practice de facto segregation rather than de jure segregation. It imagines that Rosa Parks went to jail so that whites could pass on to their children the benefits of past discrimination in housing, education, and employment without fear of race-based remediation. It blasphemes the memory of Dr. King, a man who told us that fighting injustice was even more important than being nonviolent, by appropriating his desire for a day when race would not matter and implying that he meant that identifying people by race in order to address and redress the ways in which racial identities affect access to homes, education, and jobs would be wrong.

It is not correct to say that white people have such a strong sense of fairness that they have come to dislike blacks as a result of affirmative action. Affirmative action came into existence because whites did not obey the law, did not comply with fair housing laws, desegregation orders, and fair hiring regulations. Where is the sense of fairness among whites when inherited wealth enables young whites to reap enormous benefits from past discrimination, when federal laws protect seniority systems established under unfair hiring practices, and when housing discrimination and unequal school funding give children of different colors access to very different and very unequal educations?

It is not correct to claim that the United States reached a consensus in favor of civil rights a generation ago. Black protest, white fears of disruption, and efforts by the Democratic Party to expand its voting base in a South that was becoming increasingly Republican led to changes in civil rights law. But each of the laws and court decisions contained protection for white privileges and white expectations. Even so, whites have mobilized consistently to resist those changes, to maximize their own historic racial advantages, and to make communities of color pay a disproportionate price for structural changes in the economy. That they then sanctimoniously blame this whole process on blacks does not speak well for the sense of responsibility that whites so often salute themselves for possessing.

By defining African-American self-activity during the 1950s and 1960s as a "civil rights movement" seeking to make the state neutral on matters of race rather than as a "freedom movement" raising radical and far-reaching critiques of U.S. society, Sniderman and Piazza distort the historical record and deploy a familiar and ideologically charged weapon. Just as political leaders of that era attempted to contain the wide-reaching and radical demands for democracy and opportunity raised by popular protest and channel them into necessary but narrow reforms such as the right to eat at a previously segregated lunch counter or the right to vote, neoconservative commentary in the present attempts to suppress social memory about the 1960s by retrospectively rewriting the goals of the movement. As Malcolm X used to remind his followers: "If they can't beat you, they'll join you. But when they join you, you'll head off in a direction you never intended to go."

Sniderman and Piazza's *Scar of Race* is not so much a serious scholarly study of the changing nature of race as it is a cynical exercise in spin control, an effort to appeal to white identity politics by obscuring the material advantages that accrue to whites because of their whiteness. But, while not useful as an explanation of how race affects life chances or political culture in the United States, *The Scar of Race* does have utility as an example of the ways in which civil rights rhetoric serves to obscure social relations, how it permits racist practices by prohibiting racist proclamations. This linkage of racist behavior with disavowal of racist principles reflects more than the personal hypocrisy of individuals or the duplicity of well financed neoconservative publicists and politicians. It is a long-standing and essential component of U.S. racism.

When Ronald Reagan campaigned to be governor of California in 1966, he rode the crest of a wave of opposition to the state's fair housing law, which had been repealed in a referendum two years earlier by an overwhelming white vote. Reagan attacked legislation making it illegal to refuse to sell a home to someone because of their race as "an infringement on one of our basic individual rights." When his opponent in the Republican primary claimed that Reagan's opposition to fair housing laws and to the 1964 Civil Rights Act put the Republicans on the wrong side of the defining moral issue of the day, Reagan angrily retorted, "I resent the implication that there is any bigotry in my nature."[69] In that campaign and later, as president, one of Reagan's great skills was the use of disavowal to disarticulate racist policies from the stigma of openly racist beliefs. He drew upon long-standing traditions in U.S. history in doing so.

For example, in a statement on 1 February 1943 announcing the establishment of the 442d combat team, a military unit composed of Japanese-American soldiers, President Franklin D. Roosevelt proclaimed that

> no loyal citizen of the United States should be denied the democratic right to exercise the responsibilities of citizenship, regardless of his ancestry. The principle on which this country was founded and by which it has always been governed is that Americanism is a matter of the mind and heart; Americanism is not, and never was, a matter of race or ancestry. A good American is one who is loyal to this country and to our creed of liberty and democracy.[70]

Roosevelt's claims about Americanism as a matter of the mind and heart rather than of race and ancestry came in the context of a decision to establish a segregated unit for Japanese-American sol-

---

69. Quoted in Thomas Byrne Edsall with Mary D. Edsall, *Chain Reaction: The Impact of Race, Rights, and Taxes on American Politics* (New York: Norton, 1992), 139.

70. Quoted in Takashi Fujitani, "Nisei Soldiers as Citizens: Japanese Americans in U.S. National, Military and Racial Discourses" (paper delivered at the Conference on the Politics of Remembering the Asia/Pacific War," at the East-West Center, Honolulu, 8 September 1995), 5.

diers in a military that already segregated African Americans. It came from the same president who less than a year earlier had issued Executive Order 9066 mandating the forced incarceration and compulsory sale and confiscation of property of close to 120,000 loyal Japanese Americans. The president's statement did not close the internment camps, offer reparations to internees, challenge U.S. laws restricting naturalized citizenship to "white" immigrants, or contest state laws denying Japanese Americans the right to vote, to marry freely, or to own property. Instead, he offered the members of the 442d combat team the responsibilities of citizenship without its rewards—the opportunity to fight, and possibly die, for a country that kept them in second-class status precisely because of their race and ancestry. Yet Roosevelt framed a decision completely concerned with issues of race and ancestry as proof that race and ancestry have never been important in the United States. As Takashi Fujitani argues, "the systematic disavowal of racism coupled with its ongoing reproduction lies at the heart of the treatment of Japanese Americans during the war."[71]

Roosevelt's rhetoric about race no doubt reflected the pressures of practical politics as well his own personal predisposition. He served as the leader of a political coalition composed of open white supremacists as well as representatives of communities of color. Creating the 442d combat team offered an opportunity to include Japanese Americans directly in the war effort without undercutting the expectations or offending the interests of whites. Roosevelt's words on 1 February 1943 may well have been aimed at putting his enemies off balance by establishing racial inclusion as a venerable principle of Americanism rather than as a radical departure from the past.

Yet the combination of disavowal of racism and its ongoing reproduction that Fujitani finds in Roosevelt's formulation has a long history. The U.S. Constitution coyly avoids direct references to race, but its passages about ending the slave trade and representation of persons held in servitude acknowledge racist realities too threatening to be mentioned directly. The Immigration and Naturalization Act of 1790, the Chinese Exclusion Act of 1882, and the Immigration Restriction Act of 1924 all put the power of law behind defining the United States in terms of race and ancestry. Roosevelt's own key legislative achieve-

---

71. Fujitani, "Nisei Soldiers as Citizens."

ments, the Wagner Act and the Social Security Act, had no overt racial provisions, but, by denying coverage to domestics, farmworkers, teachers, social workers, and librarians, New Deal legislators knew that they restricted most of the benefits of the emerging welfare state to white males.

The combination of disavowal of racism with its ongoing reproduction forms such a central component of past and present U.S. political rhetoric, public policy, and law, that we might be better served by seeing Roosevelt's (and Reagan's) rhetoric as a node in a larger network, as an emblematic illustration of the role of antiracist rhetoric in the construction of racist policies. By avoiding direct endorsement of white supremacy, by denying the existence and salience of race, or by declaring racism nonexistent or existent only in the past, certain strains of civil rights rhetoric serve to sanction the production and extension of racist practices. Seen in this light, Roosevelt's language about the 442d combat team tells us less about the political contradictions of the New Deal coalition or about the personal hypocrisy or duplicity of the president himself than it does about the connection between a civil rights rhetoric ostensibly about inclusion and the production, maintenance, and extension of white supremacy.

We might be tempted to ask several related questions that Sniderman and Piazza don't ask: Why do white people act this way? What enables the recipients of unearned privilege to pose as put-upon victims? If we were to apply their own color-blind standards, we might ask about them the same kinds of questions that Charles Murray and Richard Hernstein asked about blacks in *The Bell Curve*, questions about their genes, synapses, and intelligence, their capacity for complex thought or their predilection for plunder. But we know better. We know that playing into the idea of essentialist differences between blacks and whites would hide concrete social relations just as thoroughly and just as destructively as the conservative argument that racism no longer exists does. The problem with white people is not our whiteness but our possessive investment in it. Created by politics, by culture, and by conduct, it can be changed, but only if it is addressed and assessed honestly and thoroughly, as a matter of the distribution of resources and life chances as well as matter of feelings and emotions.

Not all believers in white supremacy are white. Not all whites are white supremacists. But racism is a matter of behavior as well as of belief. Material conditions as well as mental attitudes structure the ways in which race affects life chances. In the years ahead each of us will be asked many times to collaborate with the regime of white supremacy so poisonously rooted in our past and so pervasive in the present for its own sake as well as a way of hiding the consequences of twenty years of neoconservative economic policies and the inequitable and inhuman system of transnational capitalism that it has created. None of us chooses our parents, but each of us can choose our politics. None of us chooses our color, but each of us can determine our conduct. Disavowal does not make racism disappear; it only works to obscure its causes and consequences. To paraphrase the neoconservatives' favorite paraphrase of Dr. King, our ability to tell the truth about race, power, and life chances and to do something about them will not depend upon the color of our skin but, rather, on the content of our character.

Does Integration Have a Future?

Kenneth L. Karst

I invite the reader to join in a little experiment. Following is a list of six terms, all of which appear regularly in our journals of opinion. About each item on the list, please ask yourself, "Are you for it or against it?"

cultural nationalism
cultural assimilation
identity politics
color blindness
multiculturalism
integration

Now I do understand that every one of these abstractions can bear more than one meaning.[1] But, even without any further specification of meanings, a great many Americans—including those who use the terms in debating public issues—are pretty sure they are for some of these policies or practices and against others, perhaps even strongly for or strongly against. These reactions tend to be polarized. That is, those who say they support cultural nationalism, identity politics, and multiculturalism are likely to reject assimilation, color blindness, and inte-

---

This chapter is a modified version of the inaugural William and Anne Krupman Lecture, given at Amherst College on 15 April 1996.

1. My list does not even exhaust the relevant vocabulary. For example, Bill Ong Hing distinguishes between *cultural pluralism* (which he advocates) and *separatism,* either as a policy goal or as a social fact. See his article "Beyond the Rhetoric of Assimilation and Cultural Pluralism: Addressing the Tension of Separatism and Conflict in an Immigration-Driven Multiracial Society," *California Law Review* 81 (1993): 863. On separatism, see 890–902.

gration, and vice versa. On each side the opposing view may seem not just wrongheaded but scary.

What seems wrongheaded to me is the polarity itself, the false assumption that the United States is faced with an either/or choice between two competing futures, each with its own policy program defined around one of the two sets of abstractions I have listed. Some Americans currently engaged in these polarized polemics may not know they are staging a revival; this show, first produced in colonial times, has had more remakes than *A Star Is Born*. It is a mystery how otherwise clever people in so many different generations have convinced themselves that social life is so simple—but I leave that question to students of psychohistory.

At least since the first Europeans set foot on these shores, American society has been characterized by a dynamic process involving both cultural pluralism and assimilation, both separation and integration. If today's thinking about race and ethnicity emphasizes complexity and change, that just means that our understanding is catching up to the cultural untidiness and flux that have been always present in American life. Surely, from now on, any sensible discussion of culture—any culture—must come to grips with what Clifford Geertz calls "belatedly appreciated commotion and muddle."[2]

My objectives here are both descriptive and normative. I want to inquire into the factors, including law, that may contribute to the integration or separation of cultural groups. Then I shall argue that it is a mistake of considerable magnitude to try to force the ideas of integration and multiculturalism into polar opposition and to seek to use law to promote one and suppress the other. In suggesting how a limited use of law can help us to accommodate both of these impulses, I shall make clear two preferences of my own. First, America's cultural complexity and dynamism, far from being in conflict with nationhood, are good for the nation. Second, the American nation is worth preserving, and that implies preserving our national civic culture. In particular, given our cultural variety, America's nationhood depends on ensuring equal citizenship for all Americans. To put these normative points in a nutshell: I live in southern California, and I am an American, and I make both of these statements with gratitude and with hope.

---

2. Clifford Geertz, *After the Fact: Two Countries, Four Decades, One Anthropologist* (Cambridge, Mass.: Harvard University Press, 1995), 63.

Los Angeles, following the pattern of New York in the early twentieth century and a series of European capitals much earlier, has become a world city. Mike Nichols has been credited with the phrase, "the Los Angelesisation of the world."[3] No doubt the people who repeat this expression mean not just that Hollywood projects its version of America on theater screens all over the globe but also that many peoples in many places seem to follow cultural paths blazed in southern California: here a certain style, there a celebration of youth, everywhere an insatiable passion for the new. Recently, Los Angeles has become a world city in a second sense: a gathering place for people—and peoples—from every continent except Antarctica. About 24 percent of the people presently living in California are foreign-born.[4] As early as 1984, students at Hollywood High School spoke thirty-five different native languages at home.[5] Today the world's diverse cultures are projected on Los Angeles television screens, not just by satellite from abroad but also during the local news.

One result of this influx has been a resurgence of nativist sentiments, and political operatives have been quick to tap into those feelings. In California in 1994 the governor's successful campaign for reelection was highlighted by an encoded appeal to nativism. In the meantime two recent nationally publicized books have called for a radical reduction of immigration. This position is readily understandable when it comes from a writer who deplores the imminent crumbling of "the racial hegemony of white Americans."[6] The other writer, who has nothing but scorn for the idea of white hegemony, nonetheless calls for immigration restrictions in the (illusory) hope of tightening the domestic labor market and raising wages. This proposal, coupled with the same writer's repeated denunciations of what he chooses to call multi-

---

3. Tom Shales, "Hollywood," *Washington Post*, 18 May 1986, E1. I first heard the phrase attributed to the late Alan Watts but do not know who is borrowing from whom. Here, in a footnote, we have a metaphor for cultural interaction.

4. This percentage describes 7.7 million Californians. Robert A. Rosenblatt, "California Population Rises a Modest 0.6%," *Los Angeles Times*, 27 January 1995, A15, col. 1.

5. Stehen Braun, "Hollywood High: Strangers in a Strange Land," *Los Angeles Times*, 16 September 1984, sec. 9, p. 18, col. 1.

6. Peter Brimelow, *Alien Nation: Common Sense about America's Immigration Disaster* (New York: Random House, 1995), 122. The quoted words were first used by a critic to characterize Brimelow's position, but Brimelow here adopts the words as his own and italicizes them for emphasis.

culturalism,[7] recalls the 1920s, when immigration restrictions were linked to the force-fed assimilation of the Americanization movement.[8] Talk like this gives integration a bad name.

In civil rights law, too, the tides have been running against the integrationist impulse. A majority in the Supreme Court, after doing its best to retract the reach of federal employment discrimination law,[9] has all but stifled the prospects for judicial contributions to school integration[10] and has sharply limited the power of Congress and the state legislatures to use race-conscious remedies for past discrimination in voting[11] and in public contracting.[12] In the fall of 1996 the voters of California adopted an initiative measure forbidding any state agency to use race or ethnicity as an element in the selection of persons for any program. The regents of my university had given the initiative campaign its send-off by adopting a similar policy a year earlier. In all, these are disquieting times for Americans who share the ideal of one nation, indivisible.

---

7. See Michael Lind, *The Next American Nation: The New Nationalism and the Fourth American Revolution* (New York: The Free Press, 1995). For the term *multiculturalism* Lind has a particular cluster of meanings in mind: (1) the view that America is a multinational federation, not (as Lind himself calls it) a nation state with a unified national culture; and (2) support for a system of sharply defined racial/ethnic entitlements, as opposed to Lind's expressed preference for strictly "color-blind" public policies. He considers other common uses of *multiculturalism* to be misleading: e.g., as a synonym for *multiracial* or *multiethnic* or as a name for a program to educate school children about the nation's cultural diversity. See, e.g., 97 n*. This lack of consensus about the meaning of *multiculturalism* is one feature that makes it so unwieldy a banner for mobilization and so inviting a target for attack.

8. The main purposes and effects of this movement were to impose "Anglo-conformity" on immigrants from Southern and Eastern Europe. John Higham, *Send These to Me: Immigrants in Urban America* (Baltimore: Johns Hopkins University Press, 1984), 235–50; William G. Ross, *Forging New Freedoms: Nativism, Education, and the Constitution 1917–27* (Lincoln: University of Nebraska Press, 1994).

Lind (*Next American Nation,* 322 n.*) explicitly rejects the goal of forced conformity, but he also specifies a thoroughgoing cultural assimilation as a central feature of his program of "liberal nationalism" (esp. 285–88).

9. See, e.g., *Wards Cove Packing Co., Inc. v. Atonio,* 493 U.S. 802 (1989). Congress saved Title VII by enacting the Civil Rights Act of 1991 (105 Stat. 1071).

10. The latest in this series of restrictive decisions are *Board of Education v. Dowell,* 498 U.S. 237 (1991); *Freeman v. Pitts,* 503 U.S. 467 (1992); and *Missouri v. Jenkins,* 515 U.S. 70 (1995).

11. See *Shaw v. Reno,* 509 U.S. 630 (1993); *Miller v. Johnson,* 515 U.S. 900 (1995).

12. *Adarand Constructors, Inc. v. Peña,* 518 U.S. 200 (1995); *Richmond v. J. A. Croson Co.,* 488 U.S. 469 (1989).

Some of these developments will seem to civil rights advocates to originate from "the devil we know." The political agenda emphasizing the social issues and calling for cultural counterrevolution began in the 1960s as an appeal to a constituency that saw racial integration as a threat to white supremacy.[13] More recently, though, integration has confronted a different kind of challenge from within various minority communities. Contemplating the loss of momentum of the movement to integrate American institutions, some members of racial and ethnic minorities are turning inward, embracing separatist views of community and politics.[14] Indeed, some public policies advanced in the name of cultural nationalism are hard to distinguish from policies that used to be promoted by White Citizens' Councils from Richmond to Dallas. Some, but not all, of these newer challengers wave the banner of multiculturalism—a banner that is unwieldy, and not just because the word is so long.[15] Whatever the label may be, the fear is that integration means the submersion of minority cultures in a standardized majority culture that is largely defined by America's inheritance from Europe. These minority critics and the constituency for cultural counterrevolution have almost nothing else in common; the two groups become political bedfellows only when the subject is integration. Now that a politics of resentment has encountered a politics of recognition,[16] any effort to explore the future of integration will touch a sore spot in the American body politic.

Well, then: *Does* integration have a future? When a question like this is raised by a lawyer, you will expect the ensuing discussion to be variations on the theme of "Yes and no"—and I intend to fulfill that expectation.

---

13. On the origins of that agenda, see generally Kenneth L. Karst, *Law's Promise, Law's Expression: Visions of Power in the Politics of Gender, Race, and Religion* (New Haven and London: Yale University Press, 1993), chaps. 1–2.

14. The point has been noted by social scientists and journalists alike. See, e.g., Christine H. Russell, "The Convergence of Black and White Attitudes on School Desegregation Issues during the Four Decade Evolution of of the Plans," *William and Mary Law Review* 36 (1995): 613, 637–51; Sam Fulwood III, "Black Atttitudes Shift Away from Goal of Inclusion," *Los Angeles Times*, 30 October 1995, A1, col.1.

15. See n. 7; and text at nn. 72–73 infra.

16. See Charles Taylor, "Multiculturalism and the Politics of Recognition," in *Multiculturalism and "The Politics of Recognition": An Essay by Charles Taylor*, ed. Amy Guttman (Princeton: Princeton University Press, 1992).

Plural Identities, Heterogeneous Cultures, and Nationhood

Imagine three Americans: one who traces his ancestry to the Plymouth Plantation, one with ancestors who were brought to this country in slavery, and one who arrived from Vietnam as a permanent immigrant fifteen years ago. These people may define themselves in three different racial groups. But the lines that divide every modern society into social groups are multiple and crisscrossing. Among the many potential lines of division, here are just a few: age, sex, parenthood, sexual orientation, primary language, religion, race, ethnicity, occupation, economic class, political affiliation, even preferences about leisure activity. Each line of division is a potential basis for identifying social groups and defining individual identities. So, no one is *just* a black or white American or *just* a Native American or an Asian American; no one is *just* a member of an ethnic group defined by ancestral origins in Hungary or Haiti, in Greece or Guatemala. In every modern society an individual has a number of diverse personal identities—that is, "identifications with" different groups.[17] Although our three Americans may self-identify as racially diverse, for some purposes they will be members of the same group. Often such a group will have its own symbolic world, and to exactly this degree it can be called a subculture.

Beyond this plurality of identities for each of us, a further complication is that some lines of division are not lines at all, but blurry boundary zones that make a great many people hard to classify. For example, millions and millions of Americans have racially mixed ancestry. (Even to refer to "racially mixed ancestry" is misleading if it be taken to imply that race is intrinsic to an individual. That story is a fiction; what I mean by racial mixture is that an individual's ancestors were, by social convention, assigned to different racial groups.) The overwhelming majority of black Americans have some ancestors who were socially identified as white, and our Mayflower Society member

---

17. An early discussion of this notion of "multiple personality" is George Herbert Mead, *Mind, Self and Society*, ed. Charles Morris (1934; reprint, Chicago: University of Chicago Press, 1962), 142–44. On the division of the self into diverse roles in diverse institutions, see Peter L. Berger and Thomas Luckmann, *The Social Construction of Reality* (New York: Doubleday Anchor, 1966), 72–79. On modern uses of the term *identity*, see Philip Gleason, "Identifying Identity: A Semantic History," *Journal of American History* 69 (1983): 910.

may have some ancestors who were socially identified as black.[18] For this reason, among others, perceptions of racial difference in this country are blending more and more into perceptions of cultural difference.[19]

Although some writers say they deny the existence of an American national culture,[20] that culture is visible all around us.[21] True enough, the national culture is itself a multicultural potpourri. Within this mix, undoubtedly, the predominant cultural strands are European American and African American.[22] The black American contributions to the national culture are pervasive. Consider the music written by white composers—not just popular music but "serious" music, from George Gershwin and Aaron Copland to Leonard Bernstein and John Adams. Consider the continuing creative infusion of black American language into everyone's everyday speech and the continuing influence of black American styles on popular fashions in dress. Consider the sharply increased share of black American writers—novelists and scholars, journalists and poets—in the national literary output. There is much

---

18. For a short discussion of this theme and a number of supporting references, see Kenneth L. Karst, "Myths of Identity: Individual and Group Portraits of Race and Sexual Orientation," *UCLA Law Review* 43 (1995): 263, 267–74, 296–311.

19. See Dorothy Roberts, "The Genetic Tie," *University of Chicago Law Review* 62 (1995): 209; Karst, "Myths of Identity," 311–18.

20. Michael Walzer is one of these. See his comment, in Guttman, *Multiculturalism*, 110–11; and his book, *What It Means to Be an American: Essays on the American Experience* (New York: Marsilio Pubs., 1992), esp. 49.

21. Although I disagree with Michael Lind's critique of "multiculturalism" and with his proposals for restricting immigration, I think he is right in asserting the existence of a national culture. When disagreement is found at such a high level of abstraction, however, it is more than possible that the dispute concerns the definition of *culture*.

For a wise and balanced discussion of the interrelations of the national culture and our separate ethnicities, see David A. Hollinger, *Postethnic America: Beyond Multiculturalism* (New York: Basic Books, 1995), esp. 131–63. For a set of stimulating essays on the potential meanings of citizenship and nationhood in a culturally diverse nation, see Gary Jeffrey Jacobsohn and Susan Dunn, *Diversity and Citizenship: Rediscovering American Nationhood* (Lanham, Md.: Rowman and Littlefield, 1996).

22. Other cultural influences should be obvious to anyone. Asian-style food and clothing are common, and many Americans are either members of religions with Asian origins or influenced by those religions. Many Americans are conscious of a Native American influence on our feelings about the natural world and our concerns about the influence in our society of greed—the basic deadly sin. Even so, it is accurate to say that the strongest influences on the national culture up to now have been European and African.

more—medicine, religion, architecture, you name it—but we need not belabor the point.[23]

If we look in the other direction and think of some particular black American writers whose contributions to the national culture we know and admire, the process of mutual acculturation is unmistakable. Whoever our writers of choice may be—and however strongly they may advocate views identified as racial nationalism or multiculturalism—their cultural inheritance is not purely African. English is their native language, and they think in vocabularies influenced by what they see in the books and periodicals and television programs that Americans everywhere see.[24] As for clothes—well, there are some writers, including scholars, who consistently wear traditional African dress. But only some. Malcolm X went to Africa in search of community, but when he returned to America the sign at the airport read, "Welcome Home, Malcolm."[25]

These recitals of the obvious are encapsulated in two quotations. The first is from Reginald McKnight, a black American fiction writer and scholar, on the complexity that attends any effort to define culture or individual cultural identity by focusing narrowly on race. After discussing the elusive qualities that add up to what he calls "blackness-as-performance" and "whiteness-as-performance," he goes on to say:

> when one straddles the interstices of culture and history one begins to trace all the borrowings, the purchases, the thefts, the loans, the imitations that lead to the artifacts that one group or another claim as theirs, . . . when we are honest with ourselves, the best we can say is that this thing or that thing is a product of our species.[26]

McKnight describes himself as a "cultural mulatto."[27]

---

23. On the inheritance of white Americans from black American culture, see William D. Piersen, *Black Legacy: America's Hidden Heritage* (Amherst: University of Massachusetts Press, 1993).

24. The same point can be made about black artists and musicians who make use of Western cultural forms and transform them. See, e.g., Henry Louis Gates Jr., *Loose Canons: Notes on the Culture Wars* (New York: Oxford University Press, 1992), esp. xvi–xvii.

25. Malcolm X, *The Autobiography of Malcolm X*, paperback ed. (epilogue by Alex Haley) (New York: Ballantine, 1966), 419.

26. Reginald McKnight, "Confessions of a Wannabe Negro," in *Lure and Loathing: Essays on Race, Identity, and the Ambivalence of Assimilation,* ed. Gerald Early (New York: Viking Penguin, 1993), 95, 107–8.

27. Ibid., 103, borrowing the term from Trey Ellis.

The second quotation comes from the closing paragraph of a distinguished history of the American South since 1865, written by Joel Williamson, a historian who is socially identified as white:

> The simple fact is that white America is married to black America by the space of national geography and by centuries of time. More importantly, they are married because each has given to each so much, and taken so much. Culturally, black America is so much white; and white America, in its stubborn and residual racial egotism, resists the realization of how very deeply and irreversibly black it is, and has been. The struggle against that awareness, the rage against the realization of their blackness and its legitimacy is the struggle of white people in race relations. To recognize and respect the blackness that is already within themselves would be to recognize and respect the blackness that is within the nation, and, [functionally], to surrender the uses, physical and psychological, that they have learned to make of blacks as a separate people.[28]

These wise words grew out of the writer's Southern experience, but he properly addresses them to all Americans who self-identify as white. Every individual American is the cultural product of a multicultural environment. Every reader of this essay is a cultural mulatto.

Of Time and the Streams of Culture

Human groups are heterogeneous; always, and everywhere, cultural purity is a chimera.[29] Furthermore, human groups are in flux; always, and everywhere, cultures are in a process of change.[30] The prevailing view among scientists today is that racial categories are not given in

---

28. Joel Williamson, *The Crucible of Race: Black-White Relations in the American South since Emancipation* (Oxford and New York: Oxford University Press, 1984), 522. The bracketed word is misprinted in the original as *functually;* what I have rendered as *functionally* might also be *finally.*

29. In Osaka, Japan, on a summer afternoon in 1987, Smiley (my wife) and I saw a first-rate production of *Madame Butterfly*—not the opera *Madama Butterfly* but David Belasco's Broadway play, from which Puccini took the story. The play we saw was done by Bunraku puppeteers, clad in black and manipulating puppets that were almost life-size. At the end of the play many in the audience, mostly Japanese women, were crying into their handkerchiefs. For us it was a cultural bath—but part of the charm of the moment lay in the unresolved questions: Whose culture? Whose bath?

30. See, e.g., Renato Rosaldo, *Culture and Truth* (Boston: Beacon Press, 1989), 102–5 (105: "cultural life is both inherited *and* always being changed").

nature but are imposed by observers on a series of streams of continuous variation in physical characteristics, appearing as successive generations of humans spilled out of Africa to Asia and Europe and then to what Europeans, much later, would presume to call the New World.³¹ Variations in culture, or ethnicity, are also the results of migration; they, too, tend to be gradual and continuous, lacking sharp divisions. Not only do streams of culture diverge over time; they influence one another; they merge.³² For example, to trace the linguistic tributaries of modern American English would take us to a multitude of tongues—mostly, but not entirely, European.³³ The blending of those languages resulted from a continuous flow of interactions among peoples, prominently featuring the contributions of immigrants. Was the first "English only" movement born of resentment against the Norman French? And what was English, anyway? Ask the Germans who came to East Anglia in the fifth century or the Danes who came to the Midlands in Alfred's time or the Norwegians who came to Scotland and Yorkshire. Ask the Romans or the Celts. Cultural assimilation has been going on as long as humans have lived in groups and moved from place to place, with cultures flowing like the tides. Someone should pass the word to our present-day King Canutes.³⁴

Once Irish Americans and Italian Americans were called "unassimilable," but now, with the passage of the generations, the integration of European American groups is the norm rather than the excep-

---

31. See the sources cited in Karst, "Myths of Identity," 300 n. 162, 306 n. 194.

32. In today's world it is hard to find any culture with definite boundaries. Even cultures that seem timeless or primitive or isolated turn out, on examination, to be historical and sophisticated and connected with the world "outside." See Robert Paul Wolff, "A Critique of the Concept of Culture" (MS, 1992). Anthropologists soldier on, and I am glad they do. But, as one of my favorite authors says:

> Questions . . . continue to rain down, on the very idea of a cultural scheme. Questions about the coherence of life-ways, the degree to which they form connected wholes. Questions about their homogeneity, the degree to which everyone in a tribe, a community, or even a family (to say nothing of a nation or a civilization) shares similar beliefs, practices, habits, feelings. Questions about discreteness, the possibility of specifying where one culture, say the Hispanic, leaves off and the next, say the Amerindian, begins. (Geertz, *After the Fact*, 42–43)

Anyone who is interested in "the Hispanic" and "the Amerindian" should read Richard Rodríguez's meditation on the theme in *Days of Obligation: An Argument with My Mexican Father* (New York: Viking Penguin, 1992), 1–25.

33. Britons imported a great many words from the empire (*jodhpur, boomerang*), and white Americans appropriated a vocabulary along with the lands of the West (*powwow, rodeo*).

34. Remember, the real Canute, king of England, was a Dane.

tion. The historic indicia of ethnic cohesion among Italian Americans are the preference of immigrants for Italian over English, concentration of residence in distinctively "Italian" neighborhoods, ethnic concentration in certain working-class job categories. The immigrant generation typically has limited facility in English and thus may have difficulty moving out of low-paying work. The second generation, with its command over English, has better job prospects. Many third-generation families can send their children to college, and "the grandchildren of the immigrants are moving into the professions and the higher white-collar fields." Increasingly, they marry outside the ethnic group and move to ethnically integrated suburbs.[35]

Shall we label this progression as the assimilation of an ethnic group? Assuredly not—at least not in the sense of the death of a culture. Precisely because the identity of every individual is multifaceted, even among the third generation the "varieties of ethnic experience" are apt to range widely over a scale of intensity.[36] The term *assimilation* is used awkwardly in relation to an individual; it is visible mainly as a change that a group undergoes as the generations pass. Even among European ethnic groups seen to be most widely assimilated in the United States—say, the Dutch—it would be an exaggeration to say that the process of assimilation is complete. Just over a decade ago John Higham remarked that "every one of the racial and national groupings that was created in America has stubbornly persisted."[37] What these intergenerational changes do represent is the integration of American institutions, families included.

When we look for causes of this integration history, we are drawn irresistibly to the topic of economic opportunity. If ethnic intermarriage is correlated positively with levels of education, one reason is that young people of the middle class, college students in particular, have access to social markets that were largely closed to their parents. The

---

35. These patterns were noted in Nathan Glazer and Daniel Patrick Moynihan, *Beyond the Melting Pot: Jews, Italians and Irish of New York City* (Cambridge: University of Massachusetts Press, 1963), see 206. For more recent documentation, see Richard D. Alba, "Assimilation's Quiet Tide," *Public Interest* 119 (Spring 1995): 3, 5–8.

36. See, e.g., Micaela di Leonardo, *The Varieties of Ethnic Experience: Kinship, Class, and Gender among California Italian-Americans* (Ithaca: Cornell University Press, 1984); William C. McCready, "The Persistence of Ethnic Variation in American Families," in *Ethnicity in the United States: A Preliminary Reconnaissance*, ed. Andrew M. Greeley (New York: John Wiley, 1974), 157. See also Herbert J. Gans, "Symbolic Ethnicity: The Future of Ethnic Groups and Cultures in America," *Ethnic and Racial Studies* 2 (January 1979): 1.

37. Higham, *Send These to Me*, 178.

chances are high that any reader of this essay is the child or grandchild of ethnic intermarriages.

But what about race? If the word *integration* makes you focus on race, you may be thinking, "Never mind the future of integration; the question is whether it has a past." After four decades of constitutional decisions and civil rights laws, in our largest cities black and white Americans mostly live in racially identifiable separate neighborhoods,[38] and their children mostly attend racially identifiable separate schools.[39] Many job opportunities are affected by just such social networks as the school or the neighborhood.[40] More significant integration is to be found in schools in the South and in smaller cities,[41] in higher education,[42] and in the armed forces[43]—but not even in these areas can the successes be called complete.

What can be said is that economic opportunity appears to play a central role in the process of racial integration, just as it has in the integration of members of European ethnic groups. A racial case in point is

---

38. See Douglas S. Massey and Nancy A. Denton, *American Apartheid: Segregation and the Making of the Underclass* (Cambridge, Mass.: Harvard University Press, 1993), 222. My colleague Richard Sander has criticized Massey and Denton for some of their methodological choices, but he agrees with this general point. Richard H. Sander, book review, *Journal of Legal Education* 44 (1994): 143, 147.

39. It is not clear how much "white flight" from the public schools has resulted from desegregation orders. See James S. Liebman, "Desegregating Politics: 'All-Out' School Desegregation Explained," *Columbia Law Review* 90 (1990): 1463, 1622–23, and nn. 669–74. White flight to the suburbs might have been slowed by a more ambitious Supreme Court majority. That is, *Milliken v. Bradley I*, 418 U.S. 717 (1974), might well have been decided another way. But flight to private schools could have been controlled only if the Court were willing to abandon a major strand of constitutional doctrine protecting parental freedom in the field of education. See, e.g., *Pierce v. Society of Sisters*, 268 U.S. 510 (1925). The Court did interpret the 1866 Civil Rights Act to forbid racial discrimination in the admission of pupils to private schools (*Runyon v. McCrary*, 427 U.S. 160 [1976]), but the private "segregation academies" formed in response to public school desegregation remain segregated. How many black parents would choose to send their children to those academies?

40. See, e.g., Gerald David Jaynes and Robin M. Williams Jr., *A Common Destiny: Blacks and American Society* (Washington, D.C.: National Academy Press, 1989), 319–23.

41. For a breakdown of integration results by region, see Liebman, "Desegregating Politics," 1465–71.

42. By 1977 the percentage of black students entering college was approximately the same as that of white students; since 1977, however, there has been a marked drop-off in black students' college entry (Jaynes and Williams, *Common Destiny*, 338–45).

43. The U.S. Army in particular has been an integration success story—and this despite the recently publicized pockets of white supremacy crazies in the ranks. For sources, see Kenneth L. Karst, "The Pursuit of Manhood and the Desegregation of the Armed Forces," *UCLA Law Review* 38 (1991): 499, 510–22.

the experience of Japanese Americans. I grew up in Los Angeles, and I remember well the open expression of racist attitudes toward "the Japanese" and the low incomes and the residential concentration of Japanese immigrants and their children. But I remember, too, that my Japanese American classmates at Virgil Junior High spoke English at least as well as I did. In 1942 those classmates were taken away from us, swept along in the burst of official racism that uprooted scores of thousands of American families and sent them off to camps in the desert. When the families returned, a new residential convergence was out of the question. In impressive proportions those families managed to send their children to college. Today it is the middle-class grandchildren who are of marrying age, and about two-thirds of them are marrying persons who have no Japanese ancestry.[44] There are lessons here concerning the relation of economic class to the potential integration of black Americans, and the lessons are not exactly subtle. Black-white intermarriage, for example, is also strongly correlated with educational levels,[45] and higher-income black families, on the average, live in neighborhoods with higher levels of integration.[46] I do intend to return to the subject of race relations, but for now I want to consider another aspect of the historic processes of integration of European Americans: the role of ethnic politics.

One frequent comment about cultural identity politics is that it treats complex people as abstractions, reducing them to the single dimension of race or ethnicity.[47] This pattern is not unusual in politics. The Sierra Club has a diverse membership, but in politics the members

---

44. See sources cited in Karst, "Myths of Identity," 265 n. 7, 298 n. 154.

45. Matthijs Kalmijn, "Trends in Black/White Intermarriage," *Social Forces* 72 (1993): 119, 132.

46. Middle-class black Americans do largely live in racially identifiable black neighborhoods. But black families with annual incomes over $75,000 have an average .49 index of exposure to whites. In the aggregate, that is, their neighbors are distributed half-and-half between white and black families. Sander, book review, 148 and n. 13.

I do not mean to minimize the differences in social conditions between black Americans and the descendants of white immigrants. Nathan Glazer is right when he remarks that "the most troubling aspect of American life" is not the integration of immigrants but the social distance that remains between white and black Americans ("Reflections on Citizenship and Diversity," in Jacobsohn and Dunn, *Diversity and Citizenship*, 85, 97). For contrasts of the histories of white "ethnics" and black citizens, see Ronald Takaki, *A Different Mirror: A History of Multicultural America* (Boston: Little, Brown, 1993); Jennifer L. Hochschild, *Facing Up to the American Dream: Race, Class, and the Soul of the Nation* (Princeton: Princeton University Press, 1995), 225–49.

47. I have said something like this myself (Karst, "Myths of Identity," 364–66).

are seen as one-dimensional supporters of environmental preservation; the American Legion, in its political activity, sees its members as veterans and little more.[48] What is crucial to any political mobilization is the sense of individuals that they are members of a group. In the case of racial or ethnic identity politics, identification with the group typically has grown out of a need for defense against the "slights and prejudice" of the larger society.[49]

This defensive solidarity is a persistent feature in political movements emphasizing separate development. A century and a half ago, in the cities of the Northeast, the American parochial school movement gathered steam when Catholic parents withdrew their children from public schools in response to systematic Protestant indoctrination.[50] In the 1960s, before Malcolm X visited Africa, he scorned the ideal of racial integration, calling it a disguised way to perpetuate white supremacy.[51] This remark was an echo of the defensive separatism of Marcus Garvey a generation before.[52] In this forum I note that Charles Hamilton Houston was an admirer of Garvey; indeed, he arranged for Garvey to be honored at a luncheon of black students at Harvard Law School.[53] But Houston devoted much of his professional life to achieving the integration of American institutions.[54] Like Martin Luther King Jr., Houston taught us that we can embrace solidarity politics without embracing separatism.[55]

Furthermore, American history suggests that even a cultural politics that does begin in a separatist spirit will probably lead to political integration and a considerable measure of social assimilation. Think of the separatist stances once taken by American Catholics or Mormons

---

48. The complexity of individual identities implies the heterogeneity of groups and thus complicates the task of a political leader who seeks to mobilize a "single-issue" group.

49. Wilson Carey McWilliams, *The Idea of Fraternity in America* (Berkeley and Los Angeles: University of California Press, 1974), 102.

50. See, e.g., Ray A. Billington, *The Protestant Crusade, 1800–1860: A Study of the Origins of American Nativism* (1938; reprint, Chicago: Quadrangle, 1963), 142–58, 220–34.

51. E.g., Malcolm X, *Autobiography*, 275–81.

52. Garvey was not the first to argue for separate development, but he was the first to organize a national movement for that purpose. See generally Gary Peller, "Race Consciousness," *Duke Law Journal* (1990): esp. 758, 783–811.

53. Genna Rae McNeil, *Groundwork: Charles Hamilton Houston and the Struggle for Civil Rights* (Philadelphia, University of Pennsylvania Press, 1983), 8–9.

54. Ibid., esp. 111–27, 131–55.

55. Peller's discussion ("Race Consciousness," 811–20) illuminates this point.

and how integrated the members of these two groups are today.[56] Organization around ethnic solidarity has led to similar destinations; once the "unassimilable" Irish Americans were mobilized as an inward-looking political group, they rather quickly took command of local politics in a number of cities, including New York and Boston.

The politics of ethnic solidarity may often have seemed its own justification, given the prominent role played by the system of patronage. From an early time, though, this politics had a strong expressive content. Consider the massive rallies in this country for Irish independence from Great Britain. The New York columnist Peter Finley Dunne, in the voice of "Mr. Dooley," remarked that, if Ireland "cud be freed by a picnic, it'd not only be free today, but an empire."[57] But the rallies of Irish Americans said more about them as Americans than as Irish. The solidarity they asserted carried a message: they were not merely peasant immigrants but "independent Americans to be reckoned with; they were affirming their right to a full measure of self-respect."[58] Their dominance of big-city politics allowed the Irish to look beyond their own group for alliances with other groups—in short, to integrate, politically.[59]

To achieve influence in a political world larger than the city, an ethnic group's leaders necessarily make these coalitions. In this process the leaders integrate themselves into institutions outside the group—even though this behavior may cause some members of the group to say they are "losing touch" with the community. On the other hand, the leaders risk working themselves out of their jobs. The more successful they are in achieving gains for their constituency, the more likely is that constituency to dissolve, for every success of the group's individual members in the larger society weakens their need for the solidarity of the ethnic group.[60] Even insular groups such as the Amish, who try to avoid politics, find it hard to escape the cultural influence of the larger

---

56. These stories are vividly told in R. Laurence Moore, *Religious Outsiders and the Making of Americans* (Oxford and New York: Oxford University Press, 1986).

57. Quoted in Robert D. Cross, "The Irish," in *Ethnic Leadership in America*, ed. John Higham (Baltimore: Johns Hopkins University Press, 1978), 176, 185.

58. Ibid., 185.

59. Ibid., 189.

60. See Kenneth L. Karst, "Paths to Belonging: The Constitution and Cultural Identity," *North Carolina Law Review* 64 (1986): 330–32; and sources cited.

society.[61] But active political participation *is* integration. It is only a small exaggeration to say that the expression *separatist politics* eventually becomes a contradiction in terms.

Cultural Preservation, Cultural Change, and Law

In offering these accounts of the integration process, I have not identified the law as a major causative factor. This is not to say that law has played no part in shaping the American nation's responses to cultural difference. But the harsh fact is that, at least until the middle of this century, the coercive powers of law were employed mainly to exclude whole groups of people from membership in the nation or to offer membership only on the condition of cultural conformity. This sad history is one reason why some Americans glower at the very word *integration* and want to direct the law's coercive powers toward keeping a particular subculture intact.

To speak of exclusion calls to mind legal restrictions on immigration—for example, the Chinese Exclusion Act, a late-nineteenth-century law designed to do just what its name suggested. But in speaking of exclusion I mean to refer more broadly to two other uses of law. First, some laws have categorically denied various "outsider" groups their claims to full citizenship—such as the Jim Crow laws or the state laws that once prohibited Jews from voting or the World War II regulations that ordered my Japanese American classmates to the camps. Second,

---

61. A poignant example emerged in the aftermath of *Board of Education of Kiryas Joel Village School Dist. v. Grumet*, 512 U.S. 687 (1994). In that case the Supreme Court held as unconstitutional New York's special law establishing a school district to offer special education in a village established as a religious enclave for Satmar Hasidim, a group that sets a stern face against assimilation into the larger society. The justices virtually invited the state to allow such a district to be incorporated under a general law; the legislature adopted such a law; and the village incorporated itself as a school district. State funding, of course, came with strings: the district schools must be secular. Some of the more zealous separatists among the Satmar were particularly upset that the menorah could not be used "for any purpose other than to teach Jewish students height and depth perception" (*Forward*, 18 August 1995, p. 1). I am indebted to Sanford Levinson for this story.

The case of Kiryas Joel has stimulated an unusually strong body of commentary. A persistent theme in these writings is this question: To what degree is government obligated to support an insular group's efforts to maintain its insularity? See Martha A. Minow, "The Constitution and the Subgroup Problem," *Indiana Law Journal* 71 (1995): 1. Cf. Abner S. Greene, "Kiryas Joel and Two Mistakes about Equality" (1); with Christopher S. Eisgruber, "The Constitutional Value of Assimilation" (87); and Ira C. Lupu, "Uncovering the Village of Kiryas Joel" (104), all in *Columbia Law Review* 96 (1996).

some laws and government policies have been designed to suppress cultural difference—for example, by wiping out Native American religions or, during World War I, by eliminating the teaching of German in the schools. Every one of these episodes illustrates how the law can exclude not only by what it does but also by what it says—separating Americans from one another by direct coercion as well as by officially expressing that some cultural forms are "American" and others are not.[62]

The exclusionary uses of law are by no means the whole story. Even in the dismal days preceding *Brown v. Board of Education*,[63] here and there the Supreme Court found ways to use law as an instrument of inclusion.[64] By the mid-1960s the Congress joined in the civil rights cause.[65] What the Court and the Congress mainly achieved through law during that remarkable decade was not racial integration but the elimination of barriers to integration. Equally important to the themes of cultural difference and cultural change was Congress's virtual elimination of restrictive racial and cultural qualifications for immigration, a move that would produce, in the next generation, a noticeable cultural diversification in America's community of equal citizens.[66]

In this field as elsewhere the law is the most flexible of instruments, capable of deployment in the service of disparate policies: separation or integration, diversity or conformity. But deployment of the law is no guarantee that the law's announced purpose will be achieved. We ought to be skeptical about the capacity of law to channel American society in some definitive way toward either integration or cultural separatism.

It is, for example, the gravest folly to try to use the power of government to "Americanize" people by forcing them into cultural molds chosen by a political majority. I say "try," because attempts like these are usually ineffectual. Some of them—for example, the law forbidding

---

62. On some recent efforts to capture government as a way of exploiting the expressive powers of law, see Karst, *Law's Promise*.

63. 347 U.S. 483 (1954).

64. The bright moments included *Buchanan v. Warley*, 245 U.S. 60 (1917); *Smith v. Allwright*, 321 U.S. 649 (1944); *Shelley v. Kraemer*, 334 U.S. 1 (1948); *Takahashi v. Fish and Game Commission*, 334 U.S. 410 (1948).

65. Here I refer to the Civil Rights Act of 1964, 78 Stat. 241, and the Voting Rights Act of 1965, 79 Stat. 427.

66. This change was wrought by the Immigration and Nationality Act of 1965, 79 Stat. 911.

the teaching of German—have been struck down by the courts,[67] and under today's constitutional doctrine the whole legislative package of Americanization would be invalid. As the Supreme Court has remarked, it is too late for the nation to turn its back on those interpretations.[68] Even in the absence of judicial invalidation, other attempts to use law to coerce conformity have simply failed. Peyote religion has survived the federal government's onslaught,[69] and, even after an indecently enthusiastic Supreme Court upheld the act of Congress that criminalized polygamy in the Utah Territory, devout Mormons in substantial numbers have continued to practice plural marriage to this day.[70]

If it is unwise to use law to coerce cultural assimilation, relying on law to prevent assimilation is also foolish. Although the modern fate of the Jim Crow laws shows the futility of any overt use of law to achieve a stigmatizing separation of a racial or ethnic group, today we hear calls from a different direction for laws to maintain cultural separation. A current example is the claim that laws or administrative regulations should limit the adoption of black children to would-be parents who are black.[71] Proponents of this position make two kinds of arguments. One is that black parents as a group generally can do a better job than white parents in preparing black children for life in a society that has not put racism aside. The second argument is that interracial adoptions threaten the preservation of black American culture—or, as it is sometimes put, are the instruments of "genocide." The child welfare argument is debatable, but it deserves to be taken seriously. The culture maintenance argument, though, deserves to be dismissed out of

---

67. *Meyer v. Nebraska*, 262 U.S. 390 (1923).

68. See, e.g., *Bob Jones University v. United States*, 461 U.S. 574, 593 (1983) ("a firm national policy to prohibit racial segregation and discrimination in public education"). See also *Plyler v. Doe*, 457 U.S. 202, 218 (1982) (referring to "the kind of 'class or caste' treatment that the 14th Amendment was designed to abolish").

69. See generally Omer C. Stewart, *Peyote Religion: A History* (Norman: University of Oklahoma Press, 1987).

70. See, e.g., Eugene Linden, "The Return of the Patriarch," *Time*, 1 February 1988, 1, estimating that some forty thousand polygamists live in Utah alone. Other estimates for the western states have ranged from ten thousand to thirty thousand, but no one can make an accurate count. See, e.g., Brandon Griggs, "Rising From the Myths," *Salt Lake Tribune*, July 27, 1997, J1 (estimating "20,000 ex-communicated mormons" practicing polygamy in Utah).

71. This is the position of the National Association of Black Social Workers. This issue has spawned a heated debate, an act of Congress, and a growing literature. For one brief discussion and citations to others, see Karst, "Myths of Identity," 345–52.

hand—and not just because it is unconstitutional. Doctrine aside, the argument should be rejected. It asks government to pick out one particular meaning of race or culture and to write that meaning into law. In this realm—where meanings are, to say the least, contested—government has no legitimate business. It is no favor to any social group to try to preserve some supposed cultural essence in a bottle. No living culture stands still. In culture as well as biology there is wisdom in the motto Adapt or Die.

So, the first general lesson for both multiculturalists and assimilationists is easy: do not think you can use the compulsion of law to force American society down your favored cultural path; the law you enact will likely be both unconstitutional and ineffective. The second lesson may be harder for our polarized antagonists to accept, but it is a corollary of the first lesson: relax; your opponents are not going to wreak havoc, because they, too, will be ineffective when they try to use law to stamp out your own cherished cultural vision. I address these messages first to the assimilationists and then to the cultural separatists.

To those who favor a strong form of assimilationism: When you bemoan multicultural education in the schools, be sure not to let the abstraction *multiculturalism* obscure the range of different educational projects that can go by that name. It is true that some critics of what they call Eurocentric education have intensified cultural nationalism to the level of cultural chauvinism. One who seeks to focus social studies education narrowly on the history and culture of a single racial or ethnic group simply swaps one form of ethnocentrism for another.[72] But there is considerable variation among the curricula that have resulted from these initiatives, and mostly they do not seek to prevent exposure to the common American culture.[73] Even if a few schools do offer the

---

72. See, e.g., Molefi Kete Asante, "Racism, Consciousness, and Afrocentricity," in Early, *Lure and Loathing,* 127, 138–43. When Asante was my colleague at UCLA, he was known as Arthur Smith. The name change is consistent with his dictum that "one can have only one heritage despite the multiplicity of cultural backgrounds that go into that heritage" (139–40). He defines a heritage as "a unified field of culture, that is, one whole fabric of the past rather than split sheets or bits and pieces" (140). My own view is that a unified field of culture is even harder to find than its elusive analogue in physics (see Wolff, "Critique"). On the relation of theories of Afrocentricity to "the American dream," see Hochschild, *Facing Up,* 136–40, 212–13.

73. See generally Kevin Brown, "African-American Immersion Schools: Paradoxes of Race and Public Education," *Iowa Law Review* 78 (1993): 813. As Brown makes clear, Afrocentric teaching can be incorporated into a curriculum without going all the way to the view of Asante ("Racism") that a child has only one cultural heritage.

narrowest of cultural perspectives, their students inevitably imbibe large doses of the common culture outside the school—notably from television and the movies—and those infusions are at least as powerful as any curriculum. Most educational movements bearing the name of multiculturalism are not discarding Shakespeare or Walt Whitman. Rather, they have the more modest goal of expanding teaching materials over a wider cultural spectrum, in recognition of the many sources of the American national culture. Our whole history suggests that, if this sort of inclusion has any social effects, they will be integrating effects, not just for minority students but for all students.

It seems important, too, to remind the assimilationists that the existence of a number of robust subcultural groups, far from threatening "balkanization,"[74] is and always has been a strength of American nationhood, not a weakness. One who gave early voice to this insight was James Madison, who understood that the worst of all possible political worlds was one in which the populace was divided into two sharply defined factions, each seeking to dominate the other. That was the lesson of seventeenth-century England, where the political fabric had been torn by just such a two-sided cultural conflict. Madison foresaw that a multiplicity of religions and other factions would dampen conflict, for the factions would be aligned differently as the polity moved from one set of issues to another.[75] The wisdom of Madison's view has been confirmed not only by social theorists such as Georg Simmel and Lewis Coser[76] but, more important, by generations of political experience in the nation that Madison helped to found. As we have seen, "separatist" politics in this country has led, not to disintegration, but to inclusion.

Antidiscrimination laws, and even race-conscious and ethnicity-conscious affirmative action programs, are similarly aimed at inclu-

---

74. In the 1990s this old scare word has found new favor with Patrick Buchanan, Norman Podhoretz, George Will, and Newt Gingrich, to name just a few. See "Dole, Forbes Sustain the Most Hits" (UPI dispatch from Des Moines, Iowa, 13 January 1996) (quoting Buchanan); William A. Henry III, "Beyond the Melting Pot," *Time,* 9 April 1990, 28 (quoting Podhoretz); George F. Will, "Nothing like This Tuesday," *Washington Post,* 6 November 1994, C7; Newt Gingrich, "Remarks at National Conference of State Governors," Federal News Service, 8 February 1966. For a book-length rendering of the theme, see Arthur M. Schlesinger Jr., *The Disuniting of America: Reflections on a Multicultural Society* (Knoxville: Whittle Communications, 1991).

75. *The Federalist* no. 51 (Madison).

76. Georg Simmel, *Conflict and the Web of Group Affiliations* (New York: Free Press, 1955); Lewis A. Coser, *The Functions of Social Conflict* (New York: Free Press, 1956), 139–49.

sion—which is to say, integration.[77] Yet some of the same people who talk up the virtues of cultural assimilation also argue for narrowing the reach of the civil rights laws and altogether reject the idea of race-conscious remedies, although they may be just the remedies needed to make integration possible. Let me say it directly: even when an affirmative action program considers race or ethnicity as a factor in hiring or in university admissions, it is in no sense equivalent to Jim Crow's subordination of a racial group.

To the self-styled multiculturalists: It is true that every integration implies some disintegration. For example, over the past generation the improvement of prospects for many black Americans has produced a growing class division, with resulting strains within the black community.[78] Even so, the preservation of American nationhood need not threaten the survival of a black subculture or any other. To recognize that every individual in a complex society has multiple identities and multiple group ties is to say that every community—including the nation—has only a partial claim on the individual's attachments. The nation may, indeed, seek to enforce its claims by using the power of government, and the Americanization movement reminds us to be wary about nativist impulses to deploy that power for the purpose of suppressing cultural difference. But, as we have seen, that movement's legal instruments mostly did not work and in any case cannot pass constitutional muster today.[79]

---

77. See, e.g., Justice John Paul Stevens, dissenting, in *Wygant v. Jackson Board of Education*, 476 U.S. 267, 313, at 316 (1986).

78. On class divisions, see Roy L. Brooks, *Rethinking the American Race Problem* (Berkeley and Los Angeles: University of California Press, 1990), 14–128; Roy L. Brooks, "Race as an Under-Inclusive and Over-Inclusive Concept," *African-American Law and Policy Review* 1 (1994): 2, 20–27. For the view that "the black community" is today more of a political aspiration than a reality, see Regina Austin, "'The Black Community,' Its Lawbreakers, and a Politics of Identification," *Southern California Law Review* 65 (1992): 1769. See also Angela P. Harris, "Race and Essentialism in Feminist Legal Theory," *Stanford Law Review* 42 (1990): 581, 584, 608; Regina Austin, "Left at the Post," *Law and Society Review* 26 (1992): 751.

79. By this statement I mean to say that today's constitutional doctrine would require a different result in *New Rider v. Board of Education*, 480 F.2d 693 (10th Cir.), cert. denied, 414 U.S. 1097 (1973). The Tenth Circuit upheld the application of an Oklahoma school district regulation of student hairstyles to forbid the wearing of braids by high school boys; the boys in question, members of the Pawnee tribe, wore braids as an expression of cultural and religious tradition. The school superintendent provided a caricature of the forced-conformity point of view when he "stated that the integrated school system cannot countenance different groups and remain one organization" (480 F.2d at 698).

On the positive side multiculturalists who object to "integrationism"[80] should recognize that integration implies cultural change not only for those who used to be excluded from an institution but also for the longtime members who used to assume, unconsciously, that the institution was their own subculture's preserve. All over the land, from the city council chamber to the halls of the academy, white Americans are being re-acculturated, learning to assign new meanings to behavior. Among the prominent bearers of those new meanings are the colleagues of color who have arrived in the last generation.

One serious cost of the polarization of debate is that the advocates of cultural preservationism and the advocates of cultural assimilationism too often assume the worst about their opposite numbers, demonizing them as extremists. This development lends urgency to the search for goals on which the debaters can find some agreement. Let me suggest two goals that offer this possibility. One is centered on status, and the other is centered on material concerns.[81] I shall discuss the two goals separately, but in the end they are intertwined.

The status goal is to make the constitutional guarantee of equal citizenship into a reality for all Americans.[82] Some hard-core cultural nationalists surely will reject this goal as illusory—either because they think that citizenship implies conformity or because they see the very

---

80. I take this word from Alex M. Johnson Jr., "Bid Whist, Tonk, and United States v. Fordice: Why Integrationism Fails African-Americans Again," *California Law Review* 81 (1993): 1401, but Johnson does not quite fit the label "multiculturalist." When Johnson says that the decision in *Brown v. Board of Education* was a mistake (1402, 1409), he risks being understood not just as an opponent of "integrationism" in the sense of forced assimilation but, more generally, as an opponent of the integration of American institutions. One who reads his whole article will see that this is *not* his message. Jerome Culp similarly sees the *Brown* decision as resting on an "assumption that all blacks seek or should seek assimilation" in the strong sense that would "make black people white people with black skin" (Jerome McCristal Culp Jr., "Black People in White Face: Assimilation, Culture, and the *Brown* Case," *William and Mary Law Review* 36 [1995]: 665, 678, 680). He also says that judges who held the Jim Crow laws unconstitutional were "assuming that [this strong form of] assimilation and cultural degradation were the only two courses available" (678). I have no basis for assessing the judges' states of mind, but I am certain that neither black Americans nor the larger national community must make such an either/or choice.

81. For a discussion contrasting the "status goals" and "welfare goals" of black political leaders in an earlier time, see James Q. Wilson, *Negro Politics: The Search for Leadership* (Glencoe, Ill.: The Free Press, 1960), 185–213.

82. Achieving this goal would benefit individuals, but the goal is also group oriented; historically, denials of equal citizenship typically have been based on group membership.

idea of citizenship as vapid symbolism. I have only a dim hope of enlisting these citizens in our search for common ground. But others who are drawn to identity politics may want to consider joining the quest. When I refer to equal citizenship, I refer not to some hollow formal status[83] but to a substantive constitutional guarantee, centered in the Fourteenth Amendment but also resonating in other parts of the Constitution. To be an equal citizen is to be a respected, responsible participant in the public life of the community.[84] Undoubtedly, the element of respect is bound up with the symbols of group status, but these symbols are far from empty. If you are tempted to disagree, ask anyone who lived under Jim Crow.

Here we can see one common ground on which the staunch assimilationist can meet the practitioner of identity politics. For those who would pursue nationhood through integration, nothing is more important than making good on the Constitution's promise of responsible participation. And, for those who turn to identity politics, a major purpose of the turn inward to the racially defined community is captured in the idea of dignity.[85] The dignity in question is not just self-regard. It also includes the respect of others outside the racially defined community, and that respect is most likely to be earned in the public settings where our subcultures come together. Participation in the polity, we have seen, is a form of integration.

The equal citizenship value of participation most obviously demands effectuation of the Fifteenth Amendment's guarantee against abridgment of the right to vote on account of race. In this regard the Voting Rights Act of 1965 has been a considerable, if still incomplete, success.[86] But, if citizen participation begins in voting and public ser-

---

83. Cf. Peter Westen, "The Empty Idea of Equality," *Harvard Law Review* 95 (1992): 537.

84. I have explored these themes in "The Supreme Court, 1976 Term—Foreword: Equal Citizenship under the Fourteenth Amendment," *Harvard Law Review* 91 (1977): 1; and at book length, in *Belonging to America: Equal Citizenship and the Constitution* (New Haven and London: Yale University Press, 1989).

85. See Derrick A. Bell Jr., *Faces at the Bottom of the Well: The Persistance of Racism* (New York: Basic Books, 1992), 197–98.

86. For a vigorous critique of some restrictive interpretations of the act, see Lani Guinier, *The Tyranny of the Majority: Fundamental Fairness in Representative Democracy* (New York: Free Press, 1994). For additional views, see Bernard Grofman, Lisa Handley, and Richard C. Niemi, *Minority Representation and the Quest for Voting Equality* (Cambridge and New York: Cambridge University Press, 1992); and Bernard Grofman and Chandler Davidson, eds., *Controversies in Minority Voting: The Voting Rights Act in Perspective* (Washington, D.C.: Brookings Institution, 1992).

vice, it does not end there. Effective participation in our public life implies equal access to various arenas that are, for some legal purposes, characterized as "private," such as housing and employment. Here the distinction between status and material goals begins to blur. The improvement of a disadvantaged social group's status, we have seen, is critically dependent on the advancement of a large proportion of the group's members into the middle class.

It takes no economic sophistication to recognize that this advancement of a group will be hindered when employers discriminate against the group's members in hiring or in the terms of work.[87] But the harmful influence of employment discrimination on equal citizenship is not limited to these immediate material consequences. In today's America, perhaps as much as in any human society ever known, work itself is a crucial index of individual status. At one extreme of this axiom we all understand that being unemployed means the loss of a great deal more than income.[88] Work is more than participation; it is also our most typical way of enacting a citizen's sense of responsibility.[89] Just as the public world of work is a venue for demonstrating to others our worth as individuals, so the systematic denial of employment opportunities on the basis of race or ethnicity has serious effects on the perception—and thus the status—of social groups. Considering that unemployment continues to be far more severe among black Americans than among their white co-citizens, a determined national economic policy to maintain full employ-

---

87. See generally Melvin L. Oliver and Thomas M. Shapiro, *Black Wealth/White Wealth: A New Perspective on Racial Inequality* (New York: Routledge, 1995); Hochschild, *Facing Up*.

88. See Elliot Liebow, *Tally's Corner: A Study of Negro Streetcorner Men* (Boston: Little, Brown, 1967); Carol Stack, *All Our Kin: Strategies for Survival in a Black Community* (New York: Harper and Row, 1974); Elijah Anderson, *A Place on the Corner* (Chicago: University of Chicago Press, 1976).

89. The basic modern text here is Judith Shklar, *American Citizenship: The Quest for Inclusion* (Cambridge, Mass.: Harvard University Press, 1991), 1–3, 13–23, 63–101. William Forbath has thoughtfully elaborated this theme, arguing persuasively for public policies to provide decent work for all, together with efforts to organize work in ways that maximize opportunities for employees to exercise judgment and responsibility ("Why Is This Rights Talk Different from All Other Rights Talk? Demoting the Court and Reimagining the Constitution" [reviewing Cass R. Sunstein, *The Partial Constitution*], *Stanford Law Review* 46 [1994]: 1771, 1790–93). For an elaboration of my own views, see Kenneth L. Karst, "The Coming Crisis of Work in Constitutional Perspective," *Cornell Law Review* 82 (1996): 523, 530–38.

ment would be a great boost for the integration process.[90] Under current policies, however, full employment is anything but a major national priority. To the contrary, every time the employment figures rise, that gain is taken to signal an "overheated" inflation-prone economy that must be cooled off by an increase in interest rates. On this subject the national priority is to maintain *unemployment* at an appropriately high level,[91] with the consistent result that disproportionate harms are visited on Americans who are both poor and black.

Citizenship, as a social status, needs material support. So, as we seek common ground for cultural nationalists and assimilationists, an indispensable element is the material advancement of the members of historically disadvantaged racial and ethnic minorities. In his monumental essay *Plural but Equal* Harold Cruse argues the case for separate political and economic development of the black community, and he places great emphasis on the need for cooperative black-managed economic organization.[92] A black political party would be his first step, but he looks ultimately toward a "systematic reorganization" of "black life" into "whatever internal economic organizations are possible within a capitalistic, free-market system."[93]

Assimilationists, take heart. Despite its strongly separatist theme, Cruse's prescription for political and economic organization is a recipe for integration. Let no one think that the operations of a market will rid us of racial discrimination, absent the enforcement of antidiscrimination laws.[94] But one highly predictable result of effective participation in the economy—participation that produces a black middle class in proportions that match the white middle class—will be the racial inte-

---

90. For dramatic figures showing strong decreases in black male unemployment from times of recession to times of recovery—decreases far greater than for all young men—see E. Douglas Williams and Richard H. Sander, "The Prospects for 'Putting America to Work' in the Inner City," *Georgetown Law Journal* 81 (1993): 2003, 2026 (quoting from a study by Richard B. Freeman).

91. See, e.g., Rebecca M. Blank and Alan S. Blinder, "Macroeconomics, Income Distribution, and Poverty," in *Fighting Poverty: What Works and What Doesn't*, ed. Sheldon H. Danziger and Daniel H. Weinberg (Cambridge, Mass.: Harvard University Press, 1986), 180–97; Karst, note 89 supra, at 523–24.

92. Harold Cruse, *Plural but Equal: A Critical Study of Blacks and Minorities in America's Plural Society* (New York: Quill, 1987), esp. 269–342.

93. Ibid., 378.

94. See, e.g., Cass R. Sunstein, "Why Markets Don't Stop Discrimination," *Social Philosophy and Policy* 8, no. 2 (1991): 22.

gration of a great many American institutions, including neighborhoods[95] and interracial marriages.[96] In the nineteenth century an opening national market provided our diverse peoples with a common lexicon, a "language of how much, how many, how far."[97] In a market that is open to all, because the law is effectively enforced against racial and ethnic discrimination, the color that matters most will be green.

I have objected to laws that directly coerce individuals to abandon their cultural inheritance in favor of the dominant cultural forms, and I have also objected to laws that directly forbid people to cross racial or ethnic boundaries. But I do understand that antidiscrimination laws are themselves directly coercive, penalizing employers, landlords, and operators of public accommodations when they deny access to markets on the basis of race or ethnicity. To speak of law is, inevitably, to speak of coercion.[98]

As the intermittent debate over multicultural education illustrates, direct coercion by law is by no means the most important way in which government seeks to influence acculturation; more typically, such efforts take the form of the deployment of public resources. Consider the case of *Bob Jones University v. United States*,[99] decided by the Supreme Court in 1983. The Internal Revenue Service had denied tax-exempt status to a fundamentalist Christian university on the ground that it engaged in racial discrimination. On religious grounds the university prohibited students from interracial dating or marriage, but the Supreme Court held that the national policy against racial discrimination was sufficiently compelling to outweigh the university's claim of religious freedom. In the era of the welfare state it is no good saying that the denial of tax exemption is not coercive. True, the university was free to act on its religious belief in racial separation, but to do so it

---

95. See n. 46.
96. See Kalmijn, "Trends." Cf. M. Belinda Tucker and Claudia Mitchell-Kernan, "Social Structural and Psychological Correlates of Interethnic Dating," *Journal of Sociology and Personal Relationships* 12 (1995): 341, 343.
97. Robert H. Wiebe, *The Opening of American Society: From the Adoption of the Constitution to the Eve of Disunion* (New York: Vintage, Random House, 1984), 375.
98. See generally Robert M. Cover, "The Supreme Court, 1982 Term—Foreword: Nomos and Narrative," *Harvard Law Review* 97 (1983): 1; Robert M. Cover, "Violence and the Word," *Yale Law Journal* 95 (1986): 1601; *Law's Violence*, ed. Austin Sarat and Thomas R. Kearns (Ann Arbor: University of Michigan Press, 1991).
99. 461 U.S. 574 (1983).

had to relinquish a tax subsidy that was routinely available to other universities.

There was little common ground in the *Bob Jones University* case, and most commentary on the decision has been polarized. Elsewhere I have suggested that, although the Court should have taken the claim of religious freedom more seriously, it reached the right result.[100] But no one can claim that the decision rested on a constitutional principle of neutrality. Indeed, the case seems an invention of the devil, designed to torment judges and scholars who are wedded to a neutrality principle. Bob Jones University finds nothing neutral in the outcome, nor would a contrary outcome be seen as neutral by anyone who agrees with me that the government has no business funding a policy of racial segregation. Here, as with the laws forbidding racial discrimination in employment or housing, I am willing to come down foursquare on the side of opening the institutions of our public life to all. If this be integrationism, make the most of it.

A more recent Supreme Court case seemed to some observers to present an equally polarized choice. I refer to *United States v. Fordice*,[101] decided in 1992. For many years prior to *Brown v. Board of Education* Mississippi had maintained three universities for black students but had not funded these schools at levels commensurate with the funding of the other state universities. Even after *Brown,* and after the previously all-white universities began to accept black applicants, the historically black universities retained their racial makeup, largely because they accepted applicants with lower test scores than those required by the predominantly white universities.[102] Eventually, this pattern was challenged in court. After protracted litigation the Supreme Court held that the state had a duty to dismantle its separate and unequal university system. Some plaintiffs urged the Court to order increased funding for the historically black colleges. They preferred this remedy, despite its faint overtones of "separate but equal" education, over a desegregation order that would end a system that would leave no schools that were racially identifiable as "white" or "black." The Court declined at

---

100. Kenneth L. Karst, "Religious Freedom and Equal Citizenship: Reflections on Lukumi," *Tulane Law Review* 69 (1994): 335, 365–71.

101. 505 U.S. 717 (1992).

102. A significant proportion of black applicants could not meet the "white" universities' test score requirements.

this stage to hold that the Constitution required equalized funding and remanded the case for the lower courts to reconsider questions of remedy. In a separate opinion Justice Clarence Thomas emphasized that the Court was not denying that there might be "sound educational justification" for continuing state support for historically black colleges even though the student bodies remained largely black.[103]

Upon remand the district court ordered equal admission requirements for all the state's four-year colleges to be equalized at a level between the two test score levels previously used.[104] The court also left room for the state to do some desegregating by consolidating some of the colleges. These integrating results are broadly consistent with the *Bob Jones University* decision. But for two of the historically black schools, Jackson State University and Alcorn State University, the district court ordered upgrading of their offerings, with concomitant increases in state funding.

The Jackson/Alcorn result, which is consistent with Justice Thomas's admonition, may seem in one perspective to stand in contrast with the integrationism of the *Bob Jones University* decision. But an important difference is that Mississippi, unlike Bob Jones University, has not imposed a race-based condition on access to any university. If Jackson State and Alcorn State should remain identifiably black, then— if the proper constitutional test were identical to the test governing the dismantling of dual systems of elementary and secondary schools—the "upgrading" remedy might be constitutionally insufficient. But Justice Thomas was right in arguing that the state colleges need not be subjected to such a test.[105] All of Mississippi's state colleges will be open to applicants of any race who can meet the newly equalized standards of

---

103. 505 U.S. at 748.

104. *Ayers v. Fordice*, 879 F. Supp. 1419 (N.D. Miss. 1995). The court also ordered that the new admissions criteria use high school grades in combination with test scores and summer remedial courses for "at risk" students. The United States and the private plaintiffs have appealed, arguing that the court's admissions standards will cause a 35 percent reduction in enrollments at the three historically black colleges ("Justice Department Appeals Miss. Desegregation Ruling," *Baton Rouge Advocate*, 21 June 1995). It remains to be seen whether (or how much) the addition of a high school grades component will offset the heightening of minimum test scores for entry to those three colleges.

105. In the public school context it is entirely appropriate to view the whole school district as a system; after all, the school board assigns individual children to particular schools. It is justifiable to insist on a measure of actual integration as a token of the school board's good faith in dismantling the dual system (see, e.g., *Swann v. Charlotte-Mecklenburg Board of Education*, 402 U.S. 1 [1971]). The students who apply to a particular Mississippi state college, of course, select themselves as candidates for admission.

admission.[106] When a historically black college continues to be identifiably black as a result of truly voluntary choices by individual applicants, there should be no finding of a constitutional violation.

This kind of freedom of choice is central to the constitutional principles that govern the uses of law to mediate interactions between ethnic identity and identity as an American. In matters cultural our law has achieved its best results when it has removed barriers to those individual choices that—in the aggregate and after the fact—we label as cultural change, or the growth and decline of groups. The law has been least legitimate, and least successful, when it has been used to restrict choices like these. One type of illegitimate coercion is the deployment of law directly to force individuals to conform to some official definition of "American" culture—in the manner of today's English-only laws. An egregious historical example is the official campaign to eradicate Native American cultural and religious ceremonies (notably the ghost dance and the peyote ceremony) on the insolent assumption that Native Americans needed to be Americanized. A second type of illegitimate coercion is the deployment of law to police some supposed cultural boundary in the interest of cultural preservation or racial purity. The Jim Crow era offers many examples; among these none is more poignant than the ban on interracial marriage.

We are not headed toward genocide, and we are not headed toward balkanization either. Today's children of intercultural unions are walking metaphors for the intertwining and intermixture of cultural forms that are inevitable in any complex society. A few years ago a thought-provoking book announced the arrival of something called "Asian American panethnicity."[107] The idea expressed in the book's title is attacked and defended in a number of recent writings by legal academics—and some of the writings are high in emotional content.[108]

---

106. This statement will need qualification if the new admissions standards really do turn out to slash black enrollments, as the plaintiffs are arguing (see n. 104). Even in this eventuality it is at least possible that the courts will conclude that it is constitutionally sufficient for the state to direct students with lower grades and test scores to community colleges, with the option of transfer to the state university system after two successful years.

107. Yen Le Espiritu, *Asian American Panethnicity: Bridging Institutions and Identities* (Philadelphia: Temple University Press, 1992).

108. E.g., Robert S. Chang, "Toward an Asian American Legal Scholarship: Critical Race Theory, Post-Structuralism, and Narrative Space," *California Law Review* 81 (1993): 1241; Jim Chen, "Unloving," *Iowa Law Review* 80 (1994): 145 (responding to Chang); colloquy, *Iowa Law Review* 81 (1996): 1467 (nine authors commenting on Chen, and Chen's response).

In the world outside the academy the panethnicity idea will rise or fall in response to the beliefs and actions of individuals who self-identify as Asian Americans or as members of diverse cultural groups—or, perhaps most commonly, as both.[109] Whatever else may be said of these contests over the meanings of behavior, their pedigree is impeccably American. The pattern of ethnic and racial groups in this country has always been to diverge and to coalesce, to separate and to assimilate. Does integration have a future? Yes and no—and yes.

---

109. See, e.g., Michael J. Balaoing, "The Challenge of Asian Pacific American Diversity and Unity: A Study of Individual Ethnic Bar Associations within the Asian Pacific Community of Los Angeles," *UCLA Asian Pacific American Law Journal* 2 (1994): 1; Eric K. Yamamoto, "Rethinking Alliances: Agency, Responsibility and Interracial Justice," *UCLA Asian Pacific American Law Journal* 33 (1995): 3.

Contributors

Lauren Berlant is Professor of English at the University of Chicago.

Elizabeth B. Clark was Associate Professor of Law at Boston University School of Law before her death.

Kenneth L. Karst is David G. Price and Dallas P. Price Professor of Law at UCLA.

Thomas R. Kearns is William Hastie Professor of Philosophy and Professor of Law, Jurisprudence and Social Thought at Amherst College.

George Lipsitz is Professor of Ethnic Studies at University of California, San Diego.

Dorothy E. Roberts is Professor at Northwestern University School of Law.

Austin Sarat is William Nelson Cromwell Professor of Jurisprudence and Political Science and Professor of Law, Jurisprudence and Social Thought at Amherst College. He is President of the Law and Society Association.

Index

Abolitionism, 17, 27–47. *See also* Slavery
Abortion, 18–19, 55–56, 79; and *Planned Parenthood of Southeastern Pennsylvania v. Casey*, 19, 61–62, 65–67, 70; and *Roe v. Wade*, 65, 67, 68, 70
Accommodation, 13–14
Addis, Adeno, 1n. 2
Affirmative action, 6–7, 87, 92; and hiring practices, 129; and integration, 158–59; Karst on, 158–59; Lipsitz on, 21, 112, 129, 133–34
AFL-CIO, 125, 127. *See also* Trade unions
African Americans, 6–7, 18–22, 31, 95–105, 108–10; and apartheid, 62; and cultural defenses in criminal trials, 95–98; and employment discrimination, 90, 126–32; extension of citizenship to, 16; and identity politics and civil rights, 112–20, 126–38; and integration, 145–47, 149, 151, 156–57; and state cruelty, 75; studies, 4. *See also* Integration; Racism; Segregation
Afro-Brazilian social protest, 104–5
Alcott, Bronson, 36
Allen, Robert, 104
Alterity, 58. *See also* Other
American identity, unified, 91–92, 105–10
Americanism, 7, 135, 136
Americanization movement, 142, 155–56, 159

American Medical Association, 69
Amish, 12
Anthropology, 86, 99
Antilegalism, 35–36
Apartheid, 62. *See also* African Americans; Racism
Appiah, Anthony, 108, 109
Apprenticeship, 29, 128–29
Asian Americans, 4, 90, 94–95, 98–99; and the Chinese Exclusion Act, 136, 154; and integration, 136, 144, 151, 154, 167–68; in the military, 135–36
Assimilation, 2, 7–8, 15; Karst on, 24, 139–40, 142, 148–53, 157–60, 163–64; Roberts on, 98
Authenticity, 102

Bakke, Allan, 123, 125
Balibar, Etienne, 4–5, 111
Balkanization, 92, 158, 167
Banality, occasions of, 60, 62–63
Bell, Derrick, 132
Bell Curve, The (Murray and Hernstein), 137
Berlant, Lauren, 17–20, 49–84
Bible, 35–37, 47
Bilingual education, 6. *See also* English language
Bill of Rights, 64–65, 109
Birth control, 18, 61–70, 77–78
Black Awakening in Capitalist America (Allen), 104
Blackmun, Harry, 65

171

Black nationalism, 22, 101, 102–4, 107, 110
Black Panthers, 104
Blacks. *See* African Americans
Black separatism, 132–38, 152
Black Soul movement, 104–5
Blackstone, William, 29
Bob Jones University v. United States, 164–66
Body, 31–32, 38, 42, 46, 55–56
Bowers v. Hardwick, 68, 75, 96
Bradley v. Milliken, 121–22, 131
Brown, Pat, 114–15
Brown, Wendy, 76–77
Brown v. Board of Education, 22, 120–22, 125, 128, 155, 160n. 80, 165
Buchanan, Pat, 91
Bundy, McGeorge, 98
Burger, Warren, 12

Cambridge Nonviolence Action Committee, 126
Capitalism, 51–52, 75, 79, 83, 138
Catholicism, 43, 152. *See also* Christianity
Channing, William E., 34, 36, 38
Chauvanism, cultural, 157
Chen, Dong-Lu, 95, 98, 99
Chicago Housing Authority, 116
Children: and consciousness of pain, 72, 74; exploitation of, in the workplace, 52, 54–55, 57–58. *See also* Education
Chin, Victor, 95
Chinese Exclusion Act, 136, 154
Christianity, 21–22, 33–39, 100, 112, 164; Catholicism, 43, 152; Protestantism, 33–34, 36, 43, 46. *See also* Bible; God
Citizenship, 2, 15–17; Berlant on, 53, 55–56, 61, 66, 68–69, 78; and black nationalism, 102–4; Clark on, 27–46; equal, 93, 161–62; Karst on, 93, 161–62, 163; Mouffe on, 4; and multiculturalism, 21, 109; and national sentimentality, 53; Roberts on, 21, 108–9; Scalia on, 7; and the subject of true feeling, 53, 55–56, 61, 66, 68–69, 78; universalist notions of, 53; and the zone of privacy, 68–69
City of Richmond v. J. A. Croson Co., 130–31
Civil rights, 22–23, 111–38, 142, 155. *See also* Civil Rights Act
Civil Rights Act, 7, 107, 111, 114, 122, 135; and the AFL-CIO, 127–28; "grandfather" clause in, 128; Title VII, 21–22, 128–29. *See also* Civil rights
Civil War, 42
Clark, Elizabeth B., 16–18, 27–48
Clark, Ramsey, 128
Clarke, James Freeman, 35
Class, 30, 79, 162, 163–64
Coleridge, Samuel Taylor, 32–33
Collective bargaining agreements, 130
Color-blind standards, 11, 130, 133, 137, 139–40
Coltrane, John, 100
Commentaries on the Laws of England (Blackstone), 29
Commission on Civil Rights (United States), 127, 129
Commodity, the fetus as, 55
Community, 9, 105, 146, 153, 159, 163
Community Investment Act, 118
Conformity, 9, 10, 155
Connolly, William, 13
Conquest of America, The (Todorov), 1
Conscience, 34–35, 37–38, 55–56. *See also* Morality
Consent, informed, 67
Constitution (United States): Bill of Rights, 64–65, 109; and cultural preservation, 93; Eighth Amendment, 75; Emerson on, 33; Fifteenth Amendment, 161; Fifth Amendment, 62–63; First Amendment,

62–63, 97–98; Fourteenth Amendment, 61–62, 62–63, 85; Fourth Amendment, 62–63; Ninth Amendment, 62–63; and the protection of rights-bearing individuals, 32, 39; references to race in, lack of, 136
Consumer price index, 119–20
Coser, Lewis, 158
Cosmopolitanism, 86, 108
Covenants, restricted, 114, 118
Criminal trials, 20, 94–95, 97–99, 101
Critical Legal Studies, 71n. 42
Critical Race Theory, 13, 18–19
Cruel and unusual punishment clause (Eighth Amendment), 74, 75
Cruse, Harold, 101, 103, 163
Cultural defenses, 20, 94–95, 97–99, 101
Cultural genocide, 88–89, 156–57, 167
Culture, 85–110; changes in, Karst on, 154–68; heterogeneous, 144–47; neutrality of, fallacy of, 88–90; preservation of, 92–99, 154–68; streams of, and time, 147–54; unified American, 91–92, 105–10. *See also* Cultural defenses; Cultural genocide
Custody rights, 44

Dances with Wolves (film), 104
Defenses, cultural, 20, 94–95, 97–99, 101
Declaration of Independence, 44
Deed restrictions, 114
De jure segregation, 120–21. *See also* Segregation
Delgado, Richard, 89
Democracy, 10, 39–40, 104, 110; and the civil rights movement, 134; Mouffe on, 4; and social change, 101
Democracy of Christianity, The (Goodell), 39–40
Democratic Party, 134
Department of Housing and Urban Development (HUD), 113–19
Department of Justice, 118
Depth, of experience, 17, 28
Derrida, Jacques, 83
Desegregation, 120–25, 165–66. See also *Brown v. Board of Education*; Segregation
Difference, 7–10, 13–14. *See also* Diversity; Pluralism
Disavowal, of racism, 132–38
Diversity, 9, 20, 28, 32, 85–110. *See also* Difference; Pluralism
Divorce, 44, 45
Domestic violence, 98–99
Domination, and social change, 101–2
Douglas, William O., 62–64
Du Bois, W. E. B., 103
Duden, Barbara, 79
Due Process clause (Fourteenth Amendment), 61–62
Dunne, Peter Finley, 153

Education, 6–7, 133; and *Brown v. Board of Education*, 22, 120–22, 125, 128, 155, 165; and integration, 149, 157; and Kwanzaa, 107–8; Lipsitz on, 21–23, 111; and natural persons, rights of, 31, 46–47; and *Regents of the University of California v. Bakke*, 123–25; and *Wisconsin v. Yoder*, 12, 20; and women's rights, 46
Egalitarianism, 30
Eighth Amendment, 75
Eisenstadt v. Baird, 65
Emerson, Ralph Waldo, 33
Empathy, 33, 72, 106–7, 108
English language, 6, 148, 149, 167
Enlightenment, 32, 33
Epistemology, 33
Equal Credit Opportunity Act, 118
Equality, 13–14, 23, 81; Clark on, 44; and cultural pluralism, 92, 109. *See also* Affirmative action
Essentialism, 103, 104

Ethics, 72. *See also* Morality
Ethnocentrism, 157
Evangelicals, 33, 34. *See also* Christianity
Executive orders, 89, 114, 126, 136
"External" law, 35

Fair Housing Amendments Act, 119, 128
Fantasy, 57, 60, 98, 108
FCC v. Metro Broadcasting, 106
Federal Communications Commission (FCC), 106
Federal Deposit Insurance Corporation (FDIC), 118
Federal Home Loan Bank Board, 117
Federal Housing Administration (FHA), 21–22, 113, 114
"Feeling" culture, 17, 49–84
Femininity, 68–69, 80
Feminism, 44–47, 97
Fetus, 55, 56, 79–81. *See also* Pregnancy
Fifteenth Amendment, 161
Fifth Amendment, 62–63
First Amendment, 62–63, 97–98
Forster, E. M., 108
Fourteenth Amendment, 61–62, 62–63, 85
Fourth Amendment, 62–63
Franklin, Benjamin, 91
Freedom, 9, 34, 45; and the subject of true feeling, 53–54, 61, 65–66, 81; and the zone of privacy, 65–66
Freud, Sigmund, 56
Fugitive Slave Law, 37
Fujitani, Takashi, 136

Garrison, William Lloyd, 37
Garrisonian abolitionists, 32, 34, 39, 47. *See also* Abolitionism
Garvey, Marcus, 152
Gates, Henry Louis, Jr., 97
Gays/lesbians, 7, 55, 75; and cultural defenses in criminal trials, 95–96; and cultural pluralism, 95–96, 102
Geertz, Clifford, 140
Gender, 11, 16–18, 98; and natural persons, rights of, 27, 30, 42, 44–45; and the subject of true feeling, 79, 82
General Services Administration, 113
Genocide, cultural, 88–89, 156–57, 167
George, Lisa Steele, 59, 80–82
German romanticism, 32
Gilded Age, 45
Giroux, Henry A., 101–2
Globalization, 5, 49–50
God, 33–41, 100
Goetz, Bernhard, 95
Goldberg, Arthur, 61–62, 64
Goodell, William, 37, 39–40
Green, Percy, 126, 128
Green v. County School Board of New Kent County, Virginia, 121
Griswold v. Connecticut, 18, 61–69, 70, 77–78

Hanchard, Michael, 104, 105
Hand, Learned, 64
Harlan, John Marshall, 61–62, 64
Harris, Cheryl I., 121, 123, 125, 128, 130
Harris, Patricia Robert, 116
Hawkins, Yusef, 95
Hegemony, 54, 76, 77, 78, 141–42
Hernstein, Richard, 137
Heterosexuality, 56, 60, 69–70, 77
Higginson, Thomas Wentworth, 34–36
Hill, Herbert, 128
Hiring practices, 21–23, 125–33, 162, 165
Hispanics, 4, 75
Holocaust, 78
Home Loan Bank Board, 118
Home Mortgage Disclosure Act, 118
Home Owners Loan Corporation, 21, 112

Index

Homophobia, 96. *See also* Gays/lesbians
Homosexuality. *See* Gays/lesbians
hooks, bell, 108
Hosmer, William, 38
Housing discrimination, 21–22, 112–20, 122, 133; and hiring practices, 127, 130; and the Housing and Community Development Act, 119; Housing and Urban Development Act, 113; Karst on, 162
Housing Market Practices Surveys, 117
Houston, Charles Hamilton, 152
HUD (Department of Housing and Urban Development), 113–19
Humanitarianism, 30
Hurlbut, Elisha, 41

Identity: and aversive identifications, 55–56; political model of, 70–77; unified American, problem of, 91–93, 105–10. *See also* Identity politics; Self
Identity politics, 1–8, 11, 13, 15–18, 52; and civil rights rhetoric, 111–38; Karst on, 23–25, 139–68; Roberts on, 21, 93, 104–5; and the subject of true feeling, 53, 59, 76–77. *See also* Identity
Ideology, 82, 100–101, 104; and cultural pluralism, 87, 101; and the subject of true feeling, 53–54, 58, 59, 77; and white privilege, 23
Immigration, 9, 75, 94–95, 98–99; efforts to limit, 91–92; illegal, 91; Karst on, 141; and racism, 136–37
Immigration and Naturalization Act, 136
Incest, 68
Indian Child Welfare Act, 20, 94, 98
Individualism, 89, 101. *See also* Identity
Individuation strategy, 16
Inflation, 113, 163

Integration, 88, 91–92, 139–68
Intelligence, 137
Intermarriage, 130, 149–50, 151, 164
Internal Revenue Service (IRS), 164
Intimacy, 67–68, 82
Intuition, 32, 33, 34, 35, 38
Irish Americans, 148–49, 153
Italian Americans, 148–49

Jackson State University, 166
Japanese-Americans, 135–36, 151, 154–55. *See also* Asian-Americans
Jazz music, 100
Jefferson, Thomas, 30
Jews, 4, 7, 102, 154
Jim Crow laws, 154, 156, 159, 161, 167. *See also* Segregation
Johnson, Lyndon B., 115, 122
Justice, 77–84, 89
Justice Department, 118
Justicia, statue of, 13

Kammen, Michael, 9–10, 15
Kant, Immanuel, 32
Karabel, Jerome, 124–25
Karen, David, 124–25
Karst, Kenneth, 10, 23–25, 93, 102, 139–68
Kearns, Thomas R., 1–25
Kennedy, Anthony, 65
Kennedy, Duncan, 87
Kennedy, John F., 114
Kennedy, Randall, 106
King, Martin Luther, Jr., 128, 133, 138, 152
Kiss, Elizabeth, 102

Latinos, 90, 96
Legal cases: *Bob Jones University v. United States*, 164–66; *Bowers v. Hardwick*, 68, 75, 96; *Bradley v. Milliken*, 121–22, 131; *Brown v. Board of Education*, 22, 120–22, 125, 128, 155, 160n. 80, 165; *Eisenstadt v. Baird*, 65; *FCC v. Metro Broadcasting*, 106;

Legal cases (*continued*)
  Green v. County School Board of New Kent County, Virginia, 121; *Griswold v. Connecticut*, 18, 61–69, 70, 77–78; *Lorance v. ATT Technologies, Inc.*, 131; *Martin v. Wilks*, 131; *People v. Odinga*, 96–97; *Planned Parenthood of Southeastern Pennsylvania v. Casey*, 19, 61–62, 65–67, 70; *Plessy v. Ferguson*, 85; *Regents of the University of California v. Bakke*, 123–25; *Roe v. Wade*, 65, 67, 68, 70; *Rogers v. American Airlines*, 90; *San Antonio Independent School District v. Rodriguez*, 121–22; *Swan v. Charlotte Mecklenberg Board of Education*, 121; *United States v. Carolene Products Co.*, 131; *United States v. Fordice*, 165; *Wisconsin v. Yoder*, 12, 20; *Wygant v. Jackson Board of Education*, 130
Liberalism, Lockean, 33–34
Liberty Bell, 109
Lind, Michael, 145n. 21
Lipsitz, George, 21–23, 25, 111–38
Locke, John, 33–34
Lorance v. ATT Technologies, Inc., 131

MacKinnon, Catherine, 13–14, 18, 69, 73n. 44
McKnight, Reginald, 146
Madison, James, 158
Malcolm X, 6–7, 104, 134, 146, 152
Marginality, 20, 101
Marriage, 64, 79, 81, 82, 156; and birth control, 61–62; inter-, 130, 149–50, 151, 164; and natural persons, rights of, 29, 30–32, 39, 44–45
Marshall, Thurgood, 130
Martin v. Wilks, 131
Martin, Emily, 79
Materialism, 101
Matsuda, Mari, 70, 100–101
McClure, Kirstie, 9n. 42
Melting pot, metaphor of, 8, 92

Merit, concept of, 89
Misogyny, 74, 83, 97
Mitchell, John, 116
Mohanty, Chandra, 19n. 67
Morality, 32–36, 54–55, 101, 135. *See also* Conscience; Ethics
Mormons, 156
Mortgage insurance programs, 114–15
Mouffe, Chantal, 3
"Mulatto," cultural, 146–47
Multiculturalism, 24, 139–42, 146–47, 157–60; and citizenship, 21, 109; and cultural pluralism, 87, 92, 95, 106, 108
Murder trials, 95, 98, 99
Murray, Charles, 137
Music, 97, 100, 104–5, 107
Muslims, 96–97, 108
Myers, David N., 109

NAACP (National Association for the Advancement of Colored People), 125–26, 128
NARAL (National Abortion Rights Action League), 55
Narrative, Authority, and Law (West), 73
National identity, 24, 53, 91–93, 105–10. *See also* Nationalism; Nationhood
Nationalism, 102, 139, 146, 160–61, 163. *See also* Black nationalism; National identity
National Labor Relations Act, 125–26
National Women's Suffrage Association, 46
Nationhood: and integration, 144–47, 161; and national identity, 24, 53, 91–93, 105–10. *See also* Nationalism
Native Americans, 101, 144, 155; culture of, preservation of, 88–89, 94; and the Indian Child Welfare Act, 20, 94, 98
Natural persons, 16, 27–46

Neutrality: of cultural, fallacy of, 88–90; of law, 13, 28; race, 22
New Deal, 126, 137
Newton, Huey, 104
NHA (National Housing Act), 21, 112–20
Nichols, Mike, 141
Nietzche, Friedrich, 68, 76
Ninth Amendment, 62–63
Nixon, Richard, 116–17, 122, 131
Nussbaum, Martha, 107

Objectivity, of painful feeling, 13, 17, 52, 57
Obscenity, 97. *See also* Pornography
O'Connor, Sandra Day, 65–66, 69, 131
Oliver, Melvin L., 120
Orfield, Gary, 122–23
Other, 1, 108. *See also* Alterity

Pain, 16–17, 28, 49–59, 66, 72–84
Paperwork Reduction Act, 119
Paranoia, 59, 77–84, 96–97
Parker, Theodore, 35, 38
Patriarchy, 69, 70, 98
Peaceful Pregnancy Meditations (George), 59, 79–80
Peller, Gary, 4
Pennsylvania Abortion Control Act of 1982, 66–67
People v. Odinga, 96–97
Pershing Redevelopment Company, 117–18
Philadelphia Plumbers Union, 128
Piazza, Thomas, 111–12, 132, 134–35, 137
Pitkin, Hannah, 10n. 42
Planned Parenthood of Southeastern Pennsylvania v. Casey, 19, 61–62, 65–67, 70
Plessy v. Ferguson, 85
Plural but Equal (Cruse), 163
Pluralism, 2–8, 11–13, 15, 18–21; Karst on, 23–25, 139–68; legal, 105; liberal, 92; Roberts on, 19–21, 85–110

Police, 98, 99
Pornography, 56, 74
Postmodernism, 102
Poverty, 98, 110
Powell, Lewis, 123–24, 130
Prayer, 47, 81
Pregnancy, 77–84. *See also* Abortion
Preservation, cultural, 92–99, 154–68
Privacy, 18–19, 59–70, 77–78
Property rights, 29, 31, 44–45, 89, 114–20
Protestantism, 33–34, 36, 43, 46
Protestant Reformation, 33

Quakers, 43

Racism, 16–19, 21, 74, 83; disavowal of, 132–38; Lipsitz on, 23, 132–38; and natural persons, rights of, 27, 30; and the separate but equal doctrine, 85. *See also* Desegregation; Segregation
Rape, 69, 96
Rap music, 97, 107
Rapp, Rayna, 79
Rationalism, 32
Reagan, Ronald, 118, 119, 135, 137
Regents of the University of California v. Bakke, 123–25
Ressentiment, 76–77
Restricted covenants, 114, 118
Rights: Christian notion of, 35, 38–39; of natural persons, 16, 27–48; property, 29, 31, 44–45, 89, 114–20
Riley, Denise, 79
Roberts, Dorothy, 19–21, 85–110
Roe v. Wade, 65, 67, 68, 70
Rogers v. American Airlines, 90
Romanticism, 17, 32–33
Rooney, Ellen, 92
Roosevelt, Franklin Delano, 126, 135–37

Said, Edward, 105
San Antonio Independent School District v. Rodriguez, 121–22

Sarat, Austin, 1–25
Scalia, Antonin, 6–7, 9, 67–68
Scar of Race, The (Piazza and Sniderman), 111, 134–35
Scarry, Elaine, 54n. 9, 75
Scott, Joan, 4n. 20
Scottish Common Sense scholars, 33
Segregation, 23, 85–86, 135–36, 139–68. *See also* Desegregation; Jim Crow laws
Self, 18, 56. *See also* Identity
Self-evidence, 17, 52, 57
Sentimentalism, 17–18, 33, 53, 54, 81–84
Separate but equal doctrine, 85
Separatism, 6, 15, 21, 24; black, 132–38, 152; and integration, 152; Lipsitz on, 112, 132–38
Sexism, 97
Sexual harassment law, 74
Sexuality, 28, 44–45, 59–70, 97. *See also* Sexual orientation
Sexual orientation, 11, 144. *See also* Gays/lesbians; Heterosexuality
Shakespeare, William, 158
Shapiro, Tom, 120
Shelley v. Kraemer, 114
Shepp, Archie, 100
Sierra Club, 151–52
Simmel, Georg, 158
Slavery, 29, 30, 36, 100, 144. *See also* Abolitionism
Smith, Gerrit, 39, 43
Sniderman, Paul M., 111–12, 132, 134–35, 137
Social Security Act, 137
Soul, 31, 32, 37, 38, 42
Souter, William, 65
Sovereignty, 70, 110
Spivak, Gayatri, 62
Stanton, Elizabeth Cady, 44, 45
Stare decisis, 63, 65, 68
Stefancic, Jean, 89
Stewart, Potter, 122, 131
Stolzenberg, Nomi Maya, 109

Subjectivity, 59, 71–72, 75, 77, 79; and morality, 34; national, 59; and natural persons, rights of, 32, 34. *See also* Identity
Suffering, 17–18, 68–69, 78, 79
Suffrage, 17, 44, 46–47
Swan v. Charlotte Mecklenberg Board of Education, 121

Taxation, 164–65
Taylor, Charles, 1–2, 93
Thomas, Clarence, 6–7, 166
Thomas, Kendall, 74–75
Thurmond, Strom, 122
Time, 62, 147–54
Tocqueville, Alexis de, 8
Todorov, Tzvetan, 1
Trade unions, 125, 126, 127–29, 130
Transcendentalism, 32–34
Trauma, 18, 57–59, 69–72, 74, 76, 82–84
Truth, 32, 33, 35, 38, 58
2 Live Crew rap group, 97. *See also* Rap music

"Undue burden" rule, 67
Unemployment, 98, 107, 126, 162–63
Uniform Relocation Assistance and Real Property Acquisition Act, 117
Unions, 125, 126, 127–29, 130
Unitarianism, 32–34, 35, 43
United States v. Carolene Products Co., 131
United States v. Fordice, 165
Universalism, 16–17, 32–33, 38, 83, 105–6
U.S. Commission on Civil Rights, 127, 129
Utopianism, 50, 52–53, 57, 60, 71; Roberts on, 110; and the zone of privacy, 66, 68

Veterans Administration, 113
Voting rights, 44, 154, 161–62
Voting Rights Act, 161

Wagner Act, 125, 137
Waldron, Jeremy, 5
Wallernstein, Immanuel, 4–5
Walzer, Michael, 93
WCTU (Woman's Christian Temperance Union), 46, 47
West, Robin, 73
White Citizens' Councils, 143
White supremacism, 136–38, 143
Wilkinson, Harvey, 106, 107
Willard, Frances, 47
Williams, Patricia, 65, 74n. 45, 101

Williamson, Joel, 147
Wisconsin v. Yoder, 12, 20
Wizard of Oz, The (film), 60
Wolin, Sheldon, 34
Wollstonecraft, Mary, 27
World War I, 155
World War II, 154–55
Wright, Henry Clark, 36
Wu, Helen, 95, 98
Wygant v. Jackson Board of Education, 130

Young, Iris, 4n. 22